Sultan in Arabia

SULTAN IN ARABIA
A Private Life

John Beasant and Christopher Ling

MAINSTREAM
PUBLISHING
EDINBURGH AND LONDON

First published in Great Britain in 2004 by
MAINSTREAM PUBLISHING COMPANY (EDINBURGH) LTD
7 Albany Street
Edinburgh EH1 3UG

ISBN 1 84018 815 4

A catalogue record for this book is available from the British Library

Typeset in Apollo and Bodoni

Printed in Great Britain by
Antony Rowe, Chippenham, Wiltshire

CONTENTS

ACKNOWLEDGEMENTS

The writing of *Sultan in Arabia: A Private Life* has been an extraordinary experience, as extraordinary, in fact, as the life and times of the monarch it chronicles. Perhaps, as he is the absolute ruler of an Arab Islamic state at a time when the condition of the Middle East is the topic of international debate as never before, it was inevitable that knowledge of the fact that it was being written would attract the interest and commitment of such a comprehensive, and internationally representative, group of people who, in their very own respective ways, were of the considered opinion that, when the personal history of Arabia's very last Sultan was being recorded, it was an account to which they had a contribution to make. Such an aspect of the work is even more extraordinary given the fact that many, whilst making a most valuable contribution to painting as full a picture as, in the event, proved possible, were obliged by circumstance of their own positions to require anonymity. Such requests have, to the letter, been both respected and honoured, and in such a spirit an express gratitude is recorded here for their candour and their provocatively brave commitment to a story that has for so long been promised but remained until now unfulfilled.

Those who are able to be identified and whose contribution has been of equal significance include Dr Eugene Rogan, Director of the Middle East Centre at St Antony's College, Oxford; Dr Peter Thwaites and Andrew Orgill of the Royal Military Academy at Sandhurst; Mark Hollingsworth; John Wright; Ian Cummins; Mary Jones; Oliver Donachie; and staff at the School of Oriental and African Studies, London. Personal debts of gratitude are recorded to the Lady Hermione Grimston, Kate Thomas, Nina Johns, Michael and Barbara Williams, Geoffrey Bellamy, Mary Morgan and Raghuveer Shettigar. Similarly, express appreciation is registered to the Mainstream team – Bill Campbell, Sharon Atherton, Ailsa Bathgate, Claire Rose and Graeme Blaikie – whose patience, professionalism and good humour has been pivotal.

Permission to carry extracts from Judith Miller's interview with Sultan Qaboos, as published in the journal *Foreign Affairs*, May/June 1997, Vol. 76, No. 3, was kindly granted by the US Council on Foreign Relations. Grateful acknowledgement is made to America's Middle East Institute for permission to carry Professor Dale Eickelman's essay 'Kings and People: Oman's State Consultative Council', published in the Institute's *Middle East Journal*, Vol. 38, No. 1, Winter 1984. Professor Eickelman's essay 'From Theocracy to Monarchy: Authority and Legitimacy in Inner Oman, 1935–1957', published in the *International Journal of Middle East Studies*, Vol. 17, 1985, appears by permission of the Cambridge University Press, New York, and such sanction is most gratefully acknowledged.

John Beasant and Christopher Ling
March, 2004

Chapter 1

DYNASTY

In a world obsessed with trivia, the inconsequential, the cheap and the tawdry, a downward spiral of human expectation inevitably ensues. At a time when, increasingly, history is regarded by many as no more than a branch of tourism and presented as soap opera, the term 'Dynasty' retains still the power to inspire, to conjure pictures in the mind with colour and flair and to celebrate the value of continuity, tradition and stability.

Add 'Arab' and, better still, 'Sultan' to the term, and an age-old tapestry is unveiled, a rich and colourful excitement of the senses is promised: tales of derring-do conducted in the shadow of a desert fort; courtly scenes of human splendour; riches way beyond the dreams of avarice; frankincense-perfumed air; gardens bedecked with strutting peacocks; an olive-skinned, bejewelled hand, decorated with ringed rubies as large as pigeon eggs, dismissing with a discreet wave liveried servants proudly black as the deepest desert night; assignations with bewhiskered, robed envoys whispering urgent commands; dhows ploughing through clear blue water, powered by white, wind-whipped lateen sails; the black tents of the Bedouin, anchored in the lee of billowing sand-dunes; the haunting, melancholy beauty of the muezzin's call to prayer from the towering minaret; members of the Sultan's Court, daggers at their waists, departing backwards from the presence of their Sovereign with customary dignity; the falcon on the sleeve, the cheetah at the chair. The picture fades, the crescent moon waxes and wanes, the scene is all but gone.

But not quite. For two Sultans remain, the world's very last absolute rulers, both of whom preside over affairs of state that the Ottomans of Constantinople would immediately recognise and, what is more, embrace with undisguised enthusiasm. One is, of course, that one-time 'Playboy of the Eastern World' and, indeed, the world beyond, the Sultan of Brunei, whose very flamboyance has, on so many occasions, propelled him into the world's headlines. The other remaining Sultan is, however, an arch-exponent of the very British practice of discretion and reticence, which is far from surprising given that he owes his throne to the intrigues and machinations of a very British coup. Indeed, Sultan Qaboos of Oman exercises such secretive aloofness about his past, his own personal affairs and those of his country, that the society he has straddled for the past three decades and more with such unfettered dominance has been described, with some justification, as the 'North Korea of the Arab World' and the 'Sultanate of Secrets'.

His authority is immediate, his exercise of personal power absolute. Many have attempted, unsuccessfully, a social and political analysis of this enigmatic ruler, his early years, spent behind the walls of his father's antique palace by the Arabian Sea, in the southern Oman province of Dhofar, his first cautious, controlled view of the world beyond those very same palace walls, his bizarre experience of being placed with arch-representatives of 'Middle England' in a damp claustrophobic Suffolk village and his subsequent endurance of the bully-boy, intolerant regime of the Royal Military Academy, Sandhurst. In terms both clear and unambiguous, Qaboos bin Said Al Said is a man about whom the world knows precious little. The secrecy which protects the man who usurped his father's throne continues to be the subject of gossip and conjecture, which can only intensify as the world's obsession with all things Arab and Islamic continues to hold sway.

Thirty years ago the political writer Professor Fred Halliday, now of the London School of Economics, wrote *Arabia Without Sultans*. Yet the future that Halliday so confidently predicted and of which he so earnestly wrote has, in the case of Sultan Qaboos of Oman, defied such an academic prediction. From the very moment he seized the throne by the hazardous expedient of armed insurrection against his own father, Qaboos was assailed by the slings and arrows of outrageous fortune. He assumed power at a time when his country became embroiled with a particularly cruel foe, the armed apostles of Marx, Engels and Lenin, messengers of 'Scientific Socialism', an ungodly creed that had reduced the land from which they came, the neighbouring People's Democratic Republic of Yemen, from one of prosperity and progress to one of desperate poverty. In the event, with a little help from his friends – Jordanians, Iranians, a legion of brave Britons, soldiers from what was then Rhodesia and South Africa, allied to the quiet determination, skill and bravery of his own Armed Forces – Qaboos prevailed against the enemy, becoming in the process the first Arab monarch, as well as the first leader in the Islamic world, to roundly defeat the internationally arrayed forces of Communism. Not that all of his difficulties were imported or, indeed, came from the barrel of an alien gun. For, as had been the case with his ancestors, much of the mischief that confronted him was home-grown, inspired by the nature of Omani society, aspects of which proved, and continue to prove, as complex and as difficult to combat as an armed enemy from beyond the borders of the land he sought, with courage and conviction, to transform from a state of medieval character and atmosphere to one, in appearances at least, of the contemporary world. In fact, alongside the nobility of Qaboos bin Said Al Said's instincts designed to alleviate his people from conditions of poverty and despair, he was obliged to wage a constant and sometimes dispiriting war against deceit, intrigue, betrayal and violent greed. It is, then, small wonder that the story of Qaboos of Oman, for all its majesty and achievement, is one, too, at which despair and, on occasions, corrosion of the spirit are in equal attendance. So who, exactly, is Sultan Qaboos bin Said Al Said? What of his journey without maps which led him to be complicit in the armed overthrow of his father? What 'country' does he inhabit when alone, when the day's governance is done and liveried servants have withdrawn to their own quarters?

What are his thoughts, over three decades after the event, of Britain's role in the forced removal of his father, who had been for nearly 40 years a staunch friend of Britain in times of both peace and war? And, crucial to his own personal story, what of the long-exercised debate, so often the source of ribald conjecture, about his emotional condition? The marriage that never was and the all-too-often scandalous rumour and speculation which has for so long besieged him? And as the winds of change reach hurricane force throughout the Arab Islamic world, what are his thoughts for the future?

The Arab Islamic world has never failed to capture the imagination of the wider world beyond its borders, with its tales born of the austere dignity and human nobility demanded of those whose home is so often a harsh, starkly beautiful but unforgiving desert terrain. The Arab ethos speaks, too, of an exercise of human discipline, befitting a race whose spiritual foundation, Islam, requires a self-determining limitation on human appetites based on humanity's selfish instincts, a form of discipline which has as much to do with the protection of the soul from base temptations as it does with ultimate survival in an all-too-often arid land. It is an ethos that many, particularly in the West, have attempted to capture in poetry and prose, by artistic skill in oils and watercolours, by academic dissertation and in such legendary works as the internationally celebrated *The Arabian Nights' Entertainments*. It is in one of Arabia's most evocative, most dramatic areas, one of heart-stirring landscape, the land of 'Aladdin' and home to some of Arabia's most accomplished navigators, where the mountains fall to the sea, that the Al Said dynasty began its long and distinguished record of service and statecraft and to where Sultan Qaboos can trace his roots. If indeed an individual, a family, community or tribe is shaped by environment, then the northern region of Oman, best characterised by the towering heights of the Musandam, fashioned the independent spirit, the instinct for survival allied to an aptitude and an appetite for political strategy of the Al Busaid tribe (of which the Al Saids were an important branch), marking them out as natural leaders of men. The social chemistry which set the Al Said tribal leaders apart and on the road to power and the subsequent consolidation of a nation state is, alas, now difficult to analyse but what is abundantly clear is that they, as a group, not only survived but prevailed in the hostile climate of constant bickering, duplicity, envy, intrigues and communal disagreements that was such a characteristic feature of life on the Arabian peninsula throughout the eighteenth century and, indeed, well beyond.

The 'birth' of Oman's ruling Royal Family can, however, be regarded as having started, in terms of an exercise of far-reaching authority, via a sustained ability to forge a sense of unity among the quarrelling, fractious tribes and with it a sense of national purpose, in 1744 when Ahmad bin Said bin Mohammed Al Busaid, a particularly vigorous tribal leader, inspired and personally led an armed attack on the Persians who had invaded the northern region of the country seven years earlier. Those who had been inspired to rally to Ahmad's banner fought under his leadership with skill and bravery and when their united effort resulted in the expulsion of the occupying Persians they elected him, by democratic public acclamation, as their Imam, the Islamic term for a national leader – 'He who is Just'. He was to be the first of what has proved to be a long line of Al Saids who, against all the vicissitudes of power and with the title of the leadership changing from Imam to Sultan, Sultan to Imam, and in the face of a multitude of family divisions and tribal insurrections, have provided Oman with a quality and continuity of governance without parallel in the Arab world.

A pivotal aspect of Al Said rule has been the stability, via a continuity of rule, that the family, through the hereditary system, has bequeathed the country, a remarkable achievement, unique within the context of the Arab Islamic world, given the highly volatile nature and chronic instability of Middle Eastern politics. A particularly good example is the fact that the twentieth century saw but four Omani Sultans which, on this fact alone, sets the country and indeed its people well apart from others in the region.

Ruling Oman has, however, never been an easy or straightforward task with the tribal divisions between the people of the coast and the country's vast hinterland, where the Islamic principle of Imamate rule by election – as opposed to the hereditary principle epitomised by Sultanic, Al Said rule – was so frequently challenged, often violently. This led to that long and troubled period during which the country was divided into two separate entities, Muscat and Oman, a political arrangement designed by Britain's pro-consuls of Empire based on a separation of powers between the Sultan and the powerful tribal leaders of the interior. Known as the Treaty of Seeb, it was signed in 1921 by Sultan Qaboos's grandfather, Sultan Taimour, and remained in force until Qaboos's seizure of his father's throne on 23 July 1970, which led to the birth of the Sultanate of Oman. It was the exhausting and all-too-often dispiriting nature of ruling, in effect, a dual nation, one at odds with itself, that reduced Sultan Taimour to a state of melancholy and hopelessness and, again with British influence playing a significant role, he abdicated his throne on 11 February 1932. His instrument of abdication named not his first-born son as heir to the throne but Said bin Taimour, a young man who had received part of his education at Mayo College in British India, where successive generations of the sons of India's maharajas had been educated. He was, his father decreed, of Sultanic material and as such an ideal candidate for the throne of Muscat and Oman and with it the challenge of high governance. In such a sad style and manner Sultan Taimour stood down, devoting the rest of his life to exercising one of his passions, foreign travel, particularly in the Far East, making a home, and marrying, in Japan and living incognito for many years in India, for which he entertained a particular affection. He gave himself the pseudonym 'T.F.T. Al Said', with the name appearing for many years on a brass plate outside his apartment in a Bombay tenement building. The life of this one-time most reluctant Sultan drew to a quiet and unremarked-upon end with his death in 1965.

Sultan Said bin Taimour Al Said inherited not only a divided people but also a country whose coffers were empty. The country was in the most appalling debt, with the State being in considerable hock to many in its merchant class. Clearly there was work to be done and Oman and Muscat's new ruler set to the task with a refreshing determination and sense of purpose.

The pragmatism inherent in a hereditary system which had allowed his father to name not his first-born son as heir to the throne but a subsequent one – in tune and sympathy with the Arab principle that high office will be allocated only to those whose character, sense of service and probity indicate it – was very soon proved to have been well founded for, by a comprehensive range of cost-cutting measures and innovations in State revenue enhancement, the new Sultan had, by the close of 1933, broken the country's chain of debt and consequent dependence on others. It was an astonishing achievement even if, particularly after the Second World War, the spectre of debt arose once more. It was, however, a regime of national austerity practised at eventual high cost to Sultan Said, for it bred within him an equally austere brand of conservatism, one which gave birth to not only a prosecution throughout his reign of State economies but a programme of social prohibitions way beyond those decreed by the Islamic faith, from the imposition of night-time curfew to the wearing of dark glasses, which, over time, gave others the justification they needed to overthrow him. His reluctance to establish State institutions, such as schools and hospitals, was, of course, prompted by his abiding fear of national debt, from which he had so adroitly rescued the country, having done so with sparse resources. The export of dates, fishing and minimal State levies were achieved in the face of his administration's inability to meet the costs of such development without recourse to borrowing – a factor so conveniently overlooked by those who should have known better at the time of his armed overthrow.

However, the fact cannot be denied that Sultan Said's prolonged attachment to frugality did, indeed, generate a wholly understandable resentment among Omani society and particularly so when, with the advent of the oil age in neighbouring states, from the late 1960s onwards, programmes of national development took place on a scale that astonished not just those Arab states without the new black gold – oil – beneath their own sands, but the world. And by this time the winds of change had begun their unstoppable passage across the national landscape of Muscat and Oman. Attempts to prevent the social and, therefore, political change they were inevitably to bring were too late.

In keeping with his fellow Islamic leaders, Sultan Said regarded personal security as an essential priority, with consequent expenditure. But to this burden was added his need to be in a position to repel frequent armed attempts at insurrection from the rebellious tribes in the interior, where his writ most decidedly did not run. The overall consequence of maintaining what can only be described as a minimal standing army resulted nonetheless in expenditure which strained severely his most limited financial resources. Then, in the mid-1960s, was added the very considerable burden of countering armed rebellion being waged against him from beyond the borders of his own desert realm. It was a serious turn of events which the Sultan's administration was ill prepared to counter. Throughout the preceding decade he had been obliged to continue to accept subsidies from the British in order to bring some semblance of financial stability to Oman. But, true to his character, Sultan Said did not rely solely upon a campaign of State austerity and accepting subventions from the British. Indeed, in the late 1950s, and with what must have been for him a most painful strategy to implement, he sold an Omani overseas territory – the enclave and port of Gwadur situated on Pakistan's southern shore – to the Government in Karachi for the very considerable sum at the time of £3 million. The money was sorely needed, with Oman's entry into the oil age remaining uncertain and, in the event, a decade away.

Sultan's Said's endeavours were not confined, however, to achieving financial stability alone. One of his principal ambitions was to forge a unity of the land that the Treaty of Seeb had officially divided and with it bring an orderly end to the efforts of the tribal leaders in the interior to reinstate Imamate government by popular acclaim and drive out the practice of hereditary, Sultanic rule as personified by the Al Said dynasty. But his attempts to forge a union of his realm were bedevilled by distractions of a most unwelcome kind. The Buraimi Oasis, to the north of Muscat, was a disputed area, with an uneasy truce having long been maintained by a

British-sponsored arrangement whereby it was regarded as being under the jurisdiction of Muscat and Oman and Abu Dhabi. But mischief was now afoot, with the Saudis casting covetous eyes upon the Oasis, which they had long claimed and which was so temptingly located on their border. Then, as now, oil was, quite literally, at the bottom of Sultan Said's new crisis, with it being widely believed that significant deposits of oil lay beneath the sands of the Oasis. The rulers of both Muscat and Oman and the then Sheikhdom of Abu Dhabi had both agreed to a further round of British arbitration, to decide once and for all under whose authority the Oasis should rest. The avaricious Saudis, however, with the encouragement and pivotal assistance of Aramco (the Arabian–American Oil Company which was playing an ever greater role in the governance of the Saudi Kingdom), and fearful that the British would rule in Sultan Said's favour, occupied Buraimi by force on 31 August 1952. Sultan Said was not slow to act and unilaterally took action to expel the invaders. Mounting a force of 8,000 armed tribesmen, he prepared to expel the Saudis.

Interestingly, they had offered cash inducements to leaders of the Imamate movement in Oman's interior to back their occupation of Buraimi but such blandishments were, much to Saudi angst and Sultan Said's delight, promptly rejected. In the event, however, Sultan Said was persuaded by the British to back down, on a promise that London would make further attempts to persuade the Saudis to depart the Oasis and return to arbitration, even though, eventually, the crisis of Saudi claims and occupation was resolved only by their expulsion by the British-led Trucial Oman Scouts. Nonetheless, it had, for Sultan Said, been a costly exercise, not just in terms of him losing face with his own people but also with regard to financial costs, placing yet further strain upon his severely limited financial resources. But there was worse to come.

By May 1954, moderation had fled the Imamate scene. The death of Imam Khalili, who had worked in cooperation with Sultan Said on many occasions, had ushered in a far more bellicose climate. He had been replaced by Ghalib Al Hinai, a man of very different intent and temperament who was in an unseemly hurry not only to extend his role as Imam but also to bring an end to Oman's rule by Sultans.

He knew of the explorations for oil in Oman's interior and was most anxious that in the event of discoveries of a financially viable kind he would be in control of the very considerable revenues that would then accrue, as opposed to a Sultan whose rule he vigorously disputed. Imam Ghalib was still financed by the Saudis, so when, in October 1954, Sultan Said's troops marched into the interior town of Ibri, an area where oil was expected to be found, and with it now being in the control of the Sultan his lines of communication with his Saudi backers were cut, he reacted with ill-restrained fury. He petulantly declared that Oman's Imamate was, henceforth, independent of Muscat and the Sultan's rule. But when the liberation of Buraimi from Saudi occupation was achieved, the Imamate was effectively cut in two. Its final dismemberment was not long in coming.

Acting with growing force and confidence, Sultan Said ordered his troops to take Nizwa, Oman's ancient capital in the interior, from where Imam Ghalib had exercised his rule. With the arrival of the Sultan's troops, and with little or no resistance being offered by his own men, Ghalib fled to Saudi Arabia. The Imamate was, for the time being at least, both routed and frustrated and Sultan Said was now master of all he surveyed. It proved to be a historic moment for both Oman and the Al Said dynasty, an end to the divisions of the past, given an equally historic significance when, on 24 December 1954, the Sultan arrived at Nizwa, addressing an assembly of thousands at the town's Great Fort.

Yet the arch-exponents of Imamate rule, whilst routed in Oman, were not yet done. In their exile in neighbouring Saudi Arabia, Ghalib and his brother Talib began to plot their return and, again with Saudi funds, began, in April 1957, a campaign of secret infiltrations across the border into their native land. Initially, when given reports of such guerrilla activity, Sultan Said dismissed them as fanciful but in mid-June 1957 he was obliged to abandon his scepticism when Imamate rebels, led by Talib, attacked Nizwa, expelled the Sultan's forces and reoccupied the Great Fort. The white flag of Imamate rule flew once more over Oman's interior. Faced with such a grim turn of events, Sultan Said took a course of action which he knew would disenchant many with Al Said rule and be used against him in Talib's Imamate propaganda. Having come to the inescapable conclusion that he had little choice in the matter, he turned to the British and appealed for prompt military assistance.

London was quick to respond, dispatching a detachment of the Cameronians who, supported by the Sultan's own troops and the British-led Trucial Oman Scouts (who had ejected the Saudis from the Buraimi Oasis), took Nizwa in the Sultan's name, driving Talib and his rebels into the towering heights of Jebel Akhdar, Oman's famous Green Mountain, from where a series of guerrilla-style hit-and-run skirmishes against Omani and British troops were conducted. But, despite sustained attempts to dislodge the rebels from their positions on the Green Mountain – attempts in which the Royal Air Force was now involved – the rebels remained very much a force to be reckoned with. In the autumn of 1957, the British, fearful of becoming bogged down in a long drawn-out guerrilla campaign, withdrew, leaving the Sultan's troops to do what best they could to defend Nizwa and prevent rebel supply lines, as ever funded by the Saudis, from reaching their intended destination on the Green Mountain.

But London kept an ever-watchful eye on the situation in Muscat and Oman and, for his part, Sultan Said kept the British well briefed on what was turning out to be just what they had feared: a costly, protracted and debilitating campaign, with the distinct possibility that Talib and his Imamate rebels, still able to draw on Saudi funds for support, could cause the Green Mountain War to escalate into something much more serious. In January 1958, London dispatched its Under-Secretary of State for War, Julian Amery, a highly skilled and polished politician, to Muscat for talks on the situation with the Sultan. His visit was followed in the summer of that year by the Sultan making one of his rare trips abroad, on this occasion to London. In the event it was agreed that Britain would make one final effort to dislodge Talib and his men, not just to dislodge the rebels from their positions on the Green Mountain but to make a concerted effort that would drive them out of Oman and effectively eradicate the Imamate movement, driving it once and for all into the history books.

19

Within weeks of such an agreement, the Royal Air Force, supported on the ground by men of Britain's elite Special Air Service, the celebrated SAS, was pounding rebel positions on the Green Mountain. The end was not long in coming. Significantly aided by Sultan Said's troops, who had been reorganised by Colonel David Smiley, a British professional soldier of considerable skill and courage, into a highly credible fighting force, a final assault, in January 1959, was made on Talib's positions on the Mountain. Yet again Talib and his lieutenants managed to evade capture, slipping over the border into Saudi Arabia. While, for the next four years, Imamate rebels mounted isolated, sporadic cross-border attacks, such as sniping on Omani military patrols and the mining of roads, the rebellion eventually petered out. The Imamate was, finally, at an end and Said became the first Omani Sultan for 200 years to preside with confidence over a united nation.

More auspicious financial conditions were also emerging. The age of oil was clearly on the horizon. But, with riches beyond the dreams of avarice come danger, greed, intrigue, uncertainty and treachery. Indeed, this high-octane mixture of human weakness was on parade in such strength that Sultan Said proved not to be immune to such a dubious 'rule'. Of course, the Sultan, being intelligent as distinct from being clever, knew full well that easy money was on its swaggering way and that in its viscous wake would come to Oman's shores that ever-present international tribe, ever on the prowl: those motivated by the creed of enlightened self-interest. He knew, also, and with equal conviction, that after years of penny-pinching, during which austerity had been an essential State virtue, many of the country's customs and traditions would come under extreme pressure, possibly to be swept aside for ever. The Sultan had given much thought as to how such unprecedented riches were to be spent by his Government and within three months of the first oil revenues being received had published, on 1 January 1968, a statement ('The Word of Sultan Said bin Taimour'), made available for all to see, that set out in considerable detail the entire financial circumstance of his then 36-year reign, his inheritance of State debt, his many and varied efforts to redeem this situation and, most crucially of all, detailed proposals for Oman's development in health, education and communications, to be paid for with the revenues from the country's black gold.

The Sultan set in motion plans that would, with a scale of finance denied to his predecessors, take the country and its people into the twentieth century. In the same month that he set out his intentions and gave an account of Oman's difficult financial past, he established a Development Board, appointed a Development Secretary and a Director of Public Works, and announced a series of modernising projects that would in time, given the cautious nature of Oman's monarch, bring dramatic change and consequent benefit to the Omani nation.

The country's first exports of oil had commenced in August of the previous year, 1967, so the Sultan wasted no time in seeing to it that the revenues now flowing into the coffers of the State were used for the social advancement of all Omanis. However, it has to be recorded that, ever anxious on the matter of security, Sultan Said directed some 50 per cent of the new revenues to the expansion and modernisation of his Armed Forces. And, as events were quickly to prove, there was indeed work for them to do.

There is a cruel irony that, at such a fortuitous time in the fortunes of Arabia's oldest Royal dynasty, the dark shadow of armed conflict designed to bring Al Said rule to a violent, permanent end should fall across the national landscape.

To the many social and political complexities that gave rise to the Dhofar War, which took its name from Oman's southern province where most of the guerrilla-style conflict was waged between mid-1967 and late 1975, was laid the charge, by those who sought justification for Sultan Said's overthrow in 1970, that the conservative nature of his rule had made armed revolution an inevitability.

However, if the Dhofar War is to be put into any accurate context, and quite aside from the role so dubiously played by those who plotted against the Sultan for their own selfish ends, the fervour of Pan-Arabism then sweeping throughout the Arab world has to be taken into account. The international humiliation of Britain, France and Israel at the hands of that contemporary father of Pan-Arabism,

Egypt's President Nasser, caused by the Suez Canal crisis of 1956, was, by the time the first shots in the Dhofar War were fired, but eight years distant. It was a crisis that had considerably fuelled the fires of resentment already burning bright against the West, and particularly Britain, for its abdication, in the face of Jewish terrorism, of responsibility for Palestine and its people. It was a resentment that the Pan-Arabists channelled with unstinting deliberation towards Oman's Sultan, who had for so long been portrayed throughout an increasingly nationalist Arab world as a willing tool of the British. Nationalist rhetoric was, of course, an intoxicating brew and particularly to those all too ready in any event to sup at the bitter chalice of violent revolution, one made all the more enticing by the promise of a Marxist earthly paradise. Oman had a neighbour, across its Dhofar border, only too prepared to export onto its soil not just its own exponents of 'Scientific Socialism', an ill-assorted band whose own leaders had knocked their once prosperous and progressive land back into the Stone Age, but to whose tattered and bloodstained banner they had rallied Omani malcontents. The People's Democratic Republic of Yemen had emerged from Britain's Crown Colony and Protectorate of Aden in 1967, at the end of a long and bloody guerrilla war, and began an almost immediate descent into the political contortions of a pariah state, home to just about any revolutionary movement that sought sanctuary from its pursuers.

It was not long, of course, before it began attempts to export its Marxist message of spite, and Oman was a target as easy as it was obvious. The Dhofar War was, without doubt, the single biggest threat to the continuity of the Al Said dynasty and while Sultan Said did devote, as has been mentioned, up to 50 per cent of his oil revenues on an expansion of his Armed Forces, it was judged by his many detractors as 'too little, too late'. He did little for his reputation, both at home and abroad, by retreating, in the wake of his triumph over the Imamate rebels on the Green Mountain, to his palace on the shores of the Arabian Sea in his beloved Dhofar, thus removing himself from his capital, over 1,000 kilometres to the north, and putting himself way beyond the reach of his own people. Some years later, in forced exile in London, in passing comment on his habitual addiction to Dhofar, he said that one of the reasons for such a strategy, particularly when the oil had begun to flow, was to put himself beyond the many supplicants who would, without end, have approached him with hands outstretched for cash!

But as 1970 dawned, with the war far from being won and daily reports from his small team of British military advisers bringing him ever more dire reports from the field of battle, Sultan Said was to face an unseen, unspoken foe: men who were plotting against him in the dark halls of a capital, London, to which, throughout his reign, in war and peace, he had shown a constant quality of loyalty virtually without parallel in the Arab Islamic world. On 23 July 1970, on a hot, humid Dhofar afternoon, the plotters struck, removing Sultan Said from his throne and bundling him without ceremony into an exile from which he was never to return. The country, quickly renamed the Sultanate of Oman, now had a new ruler, the 14th Sultan in the Al Said dynastic line, Sultan Said's only son, Qaboos bin Said Al Said. Oman now had a new man on its national watch, one quite unknown to the world beyond the shores of his own native land. But not for long. Indeed, Sultan Qaboos was destined to preside over dramatic social change and Oman would never, could never, be quite the same again.

Chapter 2

A DHOFAR CHILDHOOD

Life at the Court of Sultan Said had a set pattern, a daily rhythm that was very much in sympathy with an Arab ruler's household of the sixteenth century. Haste and the unseemly self-importance which inevitably accompanied it was an expression of vulgarity not to be practised within this particular Sultan's halls. The pace was that of the camel, slow, sure and conducted with a dignity now long vanished from the currency of our daily routines. So, however much the world beyond the walls of Al Hisn Palace on the shores of the Arabian Sea at Salalah, capital of the southern province of Dhofar, to where the Queen of Sheba had sent emissaries to collect consignments of the precious frankincense to give to King Solomon as a form of tribute, accelerated, the courtly manner so well associated in both fact and fiction with the life of an Arab Islamic ruler continued in its time-honoured tradition.

Dignified sheikhs from the interior arrived at Al Hisn, often having travelled for days by camel, with petitions craving Royal sanction of a particular community initiative, or, in the case of a tribal dispute, arbitration. Others came for financial assistance and, in an age before Oman had its own national currency, were, on occasions, afforded such by being handed a bag of the large, round silver coins bearing the matronly image of Maria Theresa, Empress of the Austro-Hungarian Empire. Known as thalers, from which the term 'dollars' derives, the coins had been introduced into the country in the mid-nineteenth century as a means of annual payment to Muscat by its former colony of Zanzibar, following the separation of the island from the direct rule of Muscat. Coffee, scented with cardamom, would be served by the Sultan's personal servants, the Khadeem, descendants of African slaves, who padded around the palace in bare feet, bowing low as and when etiquette required, men who exercised the grace and dignity which was so in sympathy with the abiding atmosphere of this particular ruler's Court, men indeed who considered themselves fortunate to be in Royal service and who entertained a proud and fierce loyalty to their monarch and master. They would also serve the plump, rich brown dates for which Oman is so justly renowned and on other occasions would bring forth from the Royal kitchen small dishes bearing halwa, the sweetmeat so beloved by those who associate it with the perfumed wonder of Arabia Felix. As dusk fell, servants would wander along the corridors of the palace and through the Royal apartments, carrying incense-burners from which wafted the delicate, delicious scent of that legendary gift of nature, the aromatic frankincense. In short, life within Al Hisn's walls was a living example of all that was so admirable, so evocative, of the Arabia of old.

It was a picture that Sultan Said saw little reason to re-draw. Indeed, Oman's absolute ruler had, in the very best sense that the term can be employed, simple tastes. Not for him extravagant cuisine, gold jewellery dripping from his hands, an expensive stable of luxury cars or, for that matter, a string of racehorses, even given that he knew a good thoroughbred when he saw one. It has been said that such simple tastes had become a habit born of the years of austerity which assailed him from the moment he came to the throne, but this ignores the fact that when oil revenues began to flow, the very notion that he should bedeck himself, or his palaces in Muscat and Salalah, with jewelled baubles quite appalled him. In an age when vulgarity and ostentation were increasingly regarded as a virtue, Sultan Said remained solidly unimpressed. He knew who he was, did not require material adornments to prove any point or to impress, and remained to the end of his days very much his own man. One of his domestic pleasures was a parrot, which quickly obtained celebrity status at the palace, being shown off and, by all accounts, showing off to visitors to the Sultan's Court. Indeed, many a pro-consul of the British Empire would not consider an audience of Sultan Said complete without paying their respects to the object of so much Royal affection!

In 1940 the Sultan took as his third wife a young lady of grace and beauty from the Al Mashaani tribe, Mizoon bin Ahmed, who came from the fishing village of Taqa, east of the Dhofari capital of Salalah. He had two daughters, born of previous wives, but his abiding affection for his new consort marked her out as a very special person indeed, so much so that once married to Mizoon he never again embarked upon matrimony. It is evident, too, from contemporary reports, that for her part Mizoon knew her husband well, his strengths and weaknesses, and grew to be his guide, philosopher and, indeed, his friend. And she gave him his only son, an heir to the throne of Oman, which, for so long, Sultan Said had craved.

It was into this scene of settled domesticity, albeit a Royal palace and home to the ruler of a nation, that, on 18 November 1940, Qaboos bin Said Al Said was born, a date now celebrated in the Sultanate of Oman as the country's national day. While the dark clouds of war rolled across the skies of Europe, in distant Dhofar, distant indeed from so much of the rest of Oman, life continued its slow and steady pace. Tribal leaders continued to call on their Sultan, the occasional high-ranking servant of the State or an officer of senior rank in the Sultan's Armed Forces would be summoned to Al Hisn Palace, and when Britain required landing rights for its aircraft or docking rights for a British ship at one of Oman's ports, then a visit from the British Political Agent, who was stationed at the British Residency in Muscat, would take place.

Given the virtual non-existence of a road between Muscat and Salalah, many of the official visitors travelled from Muscat to Salalah by sea and, as a young boy, Qaboos often used to watch their arrival on Dhofar's shores, with his mother or one of the devoted Khadeem, from the latticed windows of the palace or from its walls, gaining an early insight into the daily trappings and occasions of an Arab ruler's court. Having no brothers, the young Qaboos's early companions in the palace were restricted to members of the Khadeem, and he became fond of several of them. They were kind and gentle with their charge, the boy born to rule, and held the responsibility given to them as very much a trust that bordered on the sacred. Qaboos was a gentle, unassuming child, bereft of either airs or graces, who responded to those charged with his daily welfare with courtesy and good humour. According to one contemporary report, the Khadeem, 'those gentle giants', liaised closely with Qaboos's mother about their duties to her son, discharging well her instructions, including arrangements for his early initial visits beyond the palace walls. Without brothers he most certainly was, but his personal servants, who watched over his every waking hour and saw to his every need, fulfilled the role of surrogates and rendered a significantly superior quality of sibling protection, guidance and camaraderie than a brother born of the Blood Royal would have provided, given that it was free of rivalry, which can so often assume a corrosive force.

Like both his parents, Qaboos quickly developed an interest in and affection for the natural world, of which rural Dhofar, both in the mountains and on the seashore below, was something of an exotic showcase. Dhofar, while defying the use of the much-abused noun 'paradise', was very much an Arabian arcadia, a unique aspect of the Arabia of pitiless, sun-scorched sands and billowing dunes. Butterflies of glorious, technicolour hues danced on the air, alighting on tropical flowers of equal vibrancy, the sweetly perfumed frangipani, the trumpet-shaped hibiscus and the pink and purple spreading bougainvillea. Such kaleidoscopic displays of natural wonder rarely fail to fascinate the very young and Qaboos proved no exception to such a reliable rule.

On visits to the rolling beach, accompanied by his mother, to whom he was devoted, being so much more accessible than his stern father, or a member of the Khadeem, Qaboos would chase the army of russet-backed sand-crabs, whose double-quick-time ballet across the wet sands to their burrows was a constant source of amusement.

On visits to Dhofar's version of the interior's Green Mountain, the glorious rolling downland of the Jebel, which commands the horizon from Salalah town, Oman's Crown Prince would see a landscape redolent of more temperate climes, where the downland itself and the pastures that bordered it were dressed in thick, rich green grass. Here, every summer, the monsoon-borne Khareef would sweep in from the Arabian Sea, cloaking the Jebel with impenetrable white mist, an annual wonder of nature that would revitalise the land with life-giving moisture. When the mist cleared, revealing a land refreshed and revitalised, there were picnics to be enjoyed on the rolling downs, events in the life of Qaboos which added considerably to his keen interest in natural history. Indeed, the flocks of migratory and resident birds were also of keen interest to the boy and developed in him an early commitment to conservation of the natural world, a concern for the environment that exists to the present day.

Another oasis of natural wonder to which the young Prince would often go, and which had been patiently and painstakingly created over a period believed to have commenced in the nineteenth century by his ancestors as a place of private Sultanic retreat from the cares of high office, was the Mamoura Palace Gardens, an exquisite escape, a botanical celebration presided over by a small, white palace that captured completely the spirit of classical arabesque architecture. Inland from the coast, not far from the crenellated walls of the formal grandeur of Al Hisn, Mamoura's tapestry of flowers, shrubs and trees were nourished by an aqueduct which channelled water into the gardens from the verdant, brooding Jebel. The Mamoura aqueduct is a particularly fine example of the falaj system of irrigation, which had been introduced into Oman by the Persians in the early eighteenth century.

The long periods he chose to spend at Mamoura during his youth, often alone, were an early indication of the nature of the man and ruler he would, in time, become: a man given to quiet contemplation, an individual who knows the true value of being able to live with oneself, one who appreciates that it is only those aspects of life born of human intellect and a respect for, and understanding of, the nature of creation which are of any lasting value. Small wonder, therefore, that generations of the Al Said dynasty had come to regard Dhofar as a very special place indeed, one that was held in high esteem and affection like no other part of their realm, a land which, whilst not producing that mainstay of the Arab diet, dates, did produce just about everything else which man desired, and needed, for his daily sustenance.

Dhofar province, while being dwarfed in size by intimidating deserts, was very much Oman's 'garden', its 'granary', and given that it is one's early years which form us for the rest of our days on earth, then the impact life in the province had on the young Qaboos defies, for all practical purposes, over-estimation.

But, away from Mamoura, that place of dreams, Al Hisn Palace had its very own story to tell the young Qaboos, its walls speaking of not just his country's past but the relentless burden of high command that would, one day, be his lot. The palace faced the Arabian Sea, with its extensive crenellated ramparts constituting an imposing arabesque facade. Within its walls a warren of alleyways and concoction of courtyards often resulted in those who were new to the building becoming temporarily lost, a device of design which, given the Byzantine nature of Arab politics, could well have been the intention.

On many an occasion, Qaboos would have seen the 'Good and the Great' of the time sweep through Al Hisn's double-gated tower, escorted down the gracious avenue of palms which led to the palace itself and, inside, along highly polished halls scented with delicate frankincense, with the robed Khadeem strategically placed bowing low, to an audience with his dignified and remote Royal father, the 13th Sultan of Muscat and Oman. Those luminaries of his time, who in name and appearance owed much to Colonel T.E. Lawrence (Lawrence of Arabia), Gertrude Bell and Bertram Thomas, were latter-day pro-consuls of Empire such as Neil Innes, the Sultan's British-born Foreign Minister, Major St John Armitage of the Dhofar Force, Lieutenant-Colonel Cheeseman of the Sultan's Armed Forces known as the Muscat and Oman Field Force and, pro-consuls to a man, senior members of the British Political Residency from the island of Bahrain, who kept slightly more than an avuncular eye on events in Muscat and Oman. Others calling on the Sultan would have been officers of the Royal Air Force, such as Group Captain Jasper Coates. The Royal Air Force had long held landing rights at Bait Al Falaj, an airstrip on the outskirts of Muscat; on the offshore island of Masirah; and, not far from Al Hisn, had a small camp and aerodrome, an important stepping-stone on the way to Britain's Imperial possessions east of Suez. Such a cast-list of British visitors to the palace is known to have impressed upon the Sultan's son and heir at a very early age the serious nature of the British connection and the practical impact it had had for so long on the Al Busaid dynasty.

Al Hisn dominated the town of Salalah which, up to Oman's entry proper into the age of high revenues from its export of oil, was no more than a collection of village communities housed, more often than not, in dilapidated buildings of traditional material: tawny-hued mud, timber beams, wooden doors, though often intricately carved and, occasionally, windows with brightly coloured glass. The centre of the life of these communities was the souq, or market, where a cornucopia of Dhofar's bounty, the produce from its gardens, was piled high. Fruit and vegetables were in colourful abundance though the air was dominated by the pungency rising from that other natural bounty, fish, fresh from the waters of the Arabian Sea.

Among the stallholders wandered near-naked men of the Jebeli tribe, from their homes on the Jebel, a unique breed of men whose ancestry is obscure, speaking their own language which is quite divorced from Arabic, classical or otherwise; women cloaked in the black shroud of the burkha; excited, animated children exclaiming in wonder at the piles of brightly coloured fish; courtly Bedouin, with Lee-Enfield rifles slung casually over their shoulders; and men with silver daggers, the celebrated Omani khunjars, at their waists.

It was with such subjects of his father that Qaboos had early contact. Remote as his father was from the commonweal of those he ruled, it was not to be so with his heir. A good example of such social intercourse came about from his father's equestrian instincts. Sultan Said knew that one of the very best ways to be seen by one's subjects was the dignity afforded a man by exercising, in the best traditions of the Arab ethos, a skilful command of a thoroughbred horse of good, dependable Arab stock. Consequently, Qaboos was given, at an early age, riding lessons – much to the initial concern of his ever-attentive mother. He could ride – and ride well – almost before he could walk. Indeed, Sultan Qaboos is, today, a horseman of considerable skill and style. It was on his many youthful canters up and down the wide, all but deserted lengths of beach which stretched out in front of his father's palace that Qaboos would often pause, dismount and speak with the fishermen of Dhofar as they hauled in their nets from their wooden boats. It was an early example of the ease and confidence with which he could, and does, engage in conversation with not just his own people but, indeed, with all sorts and conditions of men. He has a natural talent for putting people completely at their ease. Had such a manner been exercised by his autocratic father, then history may not have visited upon him the ultimate humiliation of being forcibly removed from the throne.

And so the days went by in this rural idyll, one with horses to ride, a beach at one's door, a mountain of such greenery that it was a wonder to behold, in effect a 'secret garden' where boyhood dreams could unfold amid peace and beauty, a veritable showcase of fauna and flora, adoring servants to cater to every youthful whim and, above all other considerations, a mother whose love was all-enveloping. But as with every idyllic circumstance there was a serpent in the garden of the young Qaboos and the poison it generated was to change the history not just of the country the world then knew as Muscat and Oman but also the chart of the Al Busaid dynasty, the ultimate consequences of which the world continues to remain unsure.

In 1949, Qaboos commenced scholastic study, his father having decided, with egalitarian deftness, that he should attend a local Salalah institution, the Al Saidiyah School. He was, however, given his own tutor, the Headmaster at Al Saidiyah, Hafeedh Salim Al Ghassani, who tutored his Royal charge in history, Arabic and mathematics. Qaboos's tuition in the English language, upon which his father, who practised an excellent, grammatical command of the tongue, placed particular importance, was to take place by private tuition within the palace walls. Sultan Said knew the value and latent power of having a command of languages and spoke several.

The schoolboy Qaboos is well remembered as an active, industrious pupil, serious by nature and, as recalled by a contemporary, with a somewhat more mature aspect than that usually expected of one so young, almost as if the very prospect of his destiny demanded such a demeanour of him. It was an attitude which his tutor did much to encourage, being justly proud of the fact that the Sultan had entrusted to his academic care his son and heir. There are many in the Dhofari capital today who remember the young Prince walking back to Al Hisn, with his satchel on his back, at the end of the school day. It was a time in his life which shaped the man he was to become, a time which, for all the remoteness of his father, is now recalled as very much a 'golden age', one during which the nature and consistency of human kindness shown by those around him generated a quality and consistency of conviction in the rightness of the role bequeathed him by birth and history.

His schooldays passed in a climate of personal self-confidence and a growing anticipation of the promise which the world beyond Dhofar represented. But, as ever with Qaboos, it was the relationship he enjoyed with his mother that was his anchor, it was her love and guidance upon which he could always rely. And it was the Sultana who nurtured her son's abiding affection for Dhofar, for its seas, meadows and mountains, and ignited what has proved to be a lifelong interest in and respect for Dhofari culture, its songs and dances, its artistic merit, its music and its poetry. And Salalah, too, came to hold a special place in the affection of Qaboos. During the years of his boyhood, it had all the air of a market town, with its traders' gossip and the arguments of primary politics from which one can learn not only of the principal concerns and priorities of the community but also of those exercising the minds of the country at large. It was his close and personal experience of life as it was lived in Salalah and Dhofar generally, Sultan Qaboos has observed, which, far more than his youthful observance of the traffic of people through his father's palace, gave him not only an instinct for rule but also an awareness of the major political concerns of the people who would, one day, become his subjects.

In any event, and quite apart from the importance that the town and the region served for Oman's 14th Sultan as a training ground, the affection which he came to hold for the province and its people has endured, an affection that was not diluted by his rise to absolute rule. Indeed, during the early years of his reign he could be seen walking the streets of Salalah and engaging in animated conservation with those he had met during his days at the local school. Of course, his mother was a Dhofari, which gave Qaboos a very special blood-link with the locals, a fact that the Sultana never forgot and, on occasions and particularly after her son's accession to the throne, used with political deftness, more often than not with considerable success. But the umbilical cord with the land of his birth, the period of the young Prince's 'golden age' Dhofar days, was, all too soon, to be cut. Indeed, as adolescence beckoned, Sultan Said had become ever more preoccupied with what form the next stage of his heir's education should take.

Sultan Said had, as he once observed, 'been thrown out of the nest' at an early age, when his father, Sultan Taimour, had packed him off to India. There he had studied alongside the sons of maharajas at Mayo College, a celebrated institution established during the days of the British Raj and often described as the 'Eton of India'. It was a decision that Sultan Said's father had taken in close consultation with the Muscat-based British Political Agent of the day and, like father like son, he too sought the counsel of the British on the future academic and vocational tutoring of Qaboos. The Sultan had long decided that his son's days at senior school and college should take place in a British environment, which would well equip him with a practical experience and knowledge of the people with whom Qaboos, as Sultan, would have to deal. It was counsel of which Sultan Said felt sorely in need. While it had been his ultimate decision for Qaboos to attend the local Salalah school, a decision strongly urged upon him by his wife, the Sultana, he later came to doubt the wisdom of such a step, believing that it had made his son too accessible at an early, vulnerable, impressionable age to the wiles and public appetites exercised by schoolboys who had not had the restraints of life within the walls of a Royal palace. Indeed, at one point in the decision-making process, when the nature and style of Qaboos's years of education had been under discussion, it had been suggested by the British that he should attend Victoria College in the Egyptian port city of Alexandria, another academic institution founded by the British. However, and partly in deference to the anxieties of the Sultana, vexed at the prospect of her only son being dispatched to another country at such a tender age, the idea was quietly dropped. Nonetheless, there exists no doubt whatsoever that the social climate at Victoria College, quite apart from the benefit that its record of academic excellence would have bestowed on Qaboos, would most certainly have been in greater social sympathy with the young Omani Prince's somewhat cloistered early years spent within the walls of his father's palace, an observation given particular weight when it is recorded that a fellow pupil at this educational jewel in the British Middle Eastern Crown would have been the future King Hussein, heir to the Hashemite throne of Jordan. But, with Qaboos approaching his 18th birthday, a decision could no longer be postponed.

A man with whom Sultan Said had worked particularly well was the British Consul-General at the time, Major Frank Chauncey. Chauncey had played a somewhat more than effective role, at London's behest, during the crisis caused by the Saudi occupation, with Washington's covert blessing, of the Buraimi Oasis. Making a theatrical sprint from Muscat to Sohar, where the Sultan had assembled his men in preparation for their planned march on Buraimi, Chauncey arrived in the nick of time and succeeded in persuading the Omani ruler to hold his fire and stand down his men.

And now Major Chauncey, in a less public role, came to the Sultan's side to advise him in the all-important matter of the future education of the heir to the throne of Oman. The Major (in a demonstration of perception with which he had, in Oman at least, not previously been associated and while agreeing with the Sultan that in keeping with so many Crown Princes in the Arab world Qaboos should study and be trained at the Royal Military Academy, Sandhurst) advised the Omani ruler that prior to his entrance to the Academy his son should spend some time in England, where not only could he be coached in various academic subjects, and particularly the English language, but could broaden in general terms his experience of the British way of life and, indeed, the wider world. Chauncey would have been well aware of the strict regime at Sandhurst and that a young man of the sensitivity of Qaboos would not have an easy time there. Qaboos was, by now, an extraordinarily handsome young man, with one diplomatic dispatch to London commenting on his 'princely bearing, dignity and charm', human qualities which came pretty low down the scale at the training ground for Britain's military establishment.

In September 1958, the young Qaboos travelled, courtesy, in part, of the Royal Air Force, to the land which for so long had had, for both good and ill, such a pivotal influence on his own country and that of the dynasty of which he was the latest scion. He was just two months short of his 18th birthday and for one so young the prospect of such a departure from a regime which he had, since adolescence, found somewhat claustrophobic could only be regarded as high adventure. His father, in choosing a course of army training for his son, had chosen well for then, as now, Qaboos was fascinated with all things to do with the military. Indeed, shortly into his reign he commented that had he not been born to rule, then a career in his country's Armed Services would have been the life for him.

A greater cultural shock for the young Arab Prince than his introduction to what Major Chauncey had described as 'the British way of life' would be difficult to imagine. 'Refreshing' it may well have been, as described in one secret Foreign Office minute of the time, but if so then it was, without doubt, of the nature of a particularly cold shower. Indeed, a greater contrast from the sunlit world of Dhofar with its wide rolling beaches, washed by the azure waters of the fabled Arabian Sea, its towering mountains of green grandeur, its perpetual harvest of tropical fruit, trees from which sang birds of many colours, including the chattering weaver birds which nested in such profusion in the grounds of his father's palace, and the austere beauty of its billowing sand dunes would be difficult to imagine. 'Austerity' was most certainly a prominent factor in his new life. In short, this latest representative of the Al Busaid line had entered a completely different world – which, for two years, was to be his home. It was, however, one to which he became accustomed and for which he was to develop an affection which remains with him to the present day.

Philip and Lorna Romans were in so many respects arch-representatives of the middle-class values and virtues of 'Middle England'. Philip, a retired schoolmaster and future cleric of the Anglican Church, was now serving as a 'crammer', those legendary tutors of boys who were 'behind' in their preparatory school studies but whose parental anxieties centred on their offspring passing the Common Entrance exams for their chosen public school. When Major Chauncey, back in Muscat and Oman, had suggested to the Sultan that his son should, in effect, be 'crammed' prior to entering the Academy, he had advised that he knew of just the man for the job. It would have been of greater accuracy for the Major to have told Oman's ruler that it was the Foreign Office in London who knew 'just the man for the job' but in any event it was to the Romans household that the heir to the throne of Oman arrived.

While the Romans practised and preached the values and virtues of middle-class England, the village of Felsham, near Bury St Edmunds in rural Suffolk, was without doubt one of the best places to do it. The Romans were, in practising a scale of social mores so soon to be challenged and placed under unrelenting pressure by the standard-bearers of self-styled 'progressives', in sympathy with the social fabric of Felsham and it with them. The Romans ran not so much a tight ship as one which, by its very organisation and atmosphere, represented a rebuke to what they regarded, with no small justification, as the collapsing world of British morality. Philip and his tall, dignified wife, with her cornflower-blue eyes, were, in short, conservatives, attempting to hold at bay what they regarded as a hostile world, one which, while sweeping away the values and virtues of the past, was replacing them with nothing of real and enduring value. In this sense, the 'back-room boys' at the Foreign Office had chosen well and wisely for the young, traditional Arab Prince now so far from home.

One of the aspects of modern living to which the Romans had taken particular exception were the dubious 'benefits' of the cathode-ray tube. In short, television was regarded, especially by the lady of the house, as being very much an instrument of the devil, an opinion not shared by their young princely guest, albeit one from the Islamic world which practised its own code of moral conduct. For young Qaboos, to watch television was to enter a whole new world, from which he would learn much about the culture of the people with whom he was destined to spend some years. So the Calvinistic regime imposed by Lorna Romans had to be circumnavigated by a strategy which led to the Arab Prince, once he had stood at the kitchen sink and helped with washing the dishes, being welcomed into the home of neighbours where a black-and-white television set held pride of place. It was a kindness Qaboos never forgot, indeed it is in his nature not to, and shortly into his reign the kindly English village couple who had always been so pleased to see him at their home received, unannounced, a colour television set of splendid proportions.

His cramming sessions with Philip Romans were a pleasant affair and Qaboos proved a willing and able pupil. Against all the odds, he soon settled into a domestic situation from which he derived considerable contentment and, indeed, happiness, which, in itself, says much about the adaptability of the youthful Prince. To place him in an English village, with a depressingly cold, damp atmosphere outside and a Calvinistic one within, was, by any measure, a truly bizarre arrangement, but the speed with which he adapted to such alien climes speaks volumes about his strength of character and his quiet innate ability to survive. He recognised, it is now known, that the strict domestic regime imposed by Laura Romans, while having its distinct disadvantages for a young man eager to learn more than life within a Royal palace had previously allowed him, was intended to be for his benefit, and that in her concern for his welfare she came to regard him very much as if he were her own. While, however, it has been long believed – and, indeed, peddled by many a senior figure in Muscat's febrile British community – that Lorna Romans was regarded by Qaboos as a 'mother figure' and that he was far closer to her than to her tutoring husband, Philip, the opposite is now known to have been the case. As one former expatriate member of Oman's establishment who saw the two men together and later witnessed the Sultan's dismay at the death of Philip Romans comments: 'There is no doubt that while His

Majesty regarded Lorna with affection, and did much for her in her old age, it was Philip whom he really liked and admired and with whom he was more at ease. While he respected Lorna, for the care she had shown him and for the disciplines she had insisted upon, his affection was reserved for her husband. He had, after all, been the man who had prepared him academically for entry to Sandhurst and had done so with never-failing patience, good humour and male camaraderie, even, on occasions, making gentle fun of the rigours of his wife's domestic regime.' And just as Qaboos had so enjoyed escaping the stern disciplines of his father's palace on the streets of Salalah, so was every opportunity taken to have respite from Lorna Romans' strict domestic compliances by walking the streets of Felsham village.

Today, the young Arab Prince is remembered by villagers as 'a serious, polite young man, with a lovely smile and such striking good looks', demonstrating an ability, even then, to walk with kings but still retain the common touch, an ability which has become such a pleasing, and successful, feature of his reign and one which his patrician father found so difficult to achieve.

And as the good, solid citizenry of Felsham village found their exotic guest a delight, although many were quite unaware of his Royal status, Qaboos, too, found his first contact with Britons of a very different social background from those he had experienced in Salalah a revelation. Indeed, how could it have been otherwise, when it is recorded that until his arrival in England his experience of the British had been confined to those foot-soldiers of Empire who frequently trooped through the halls of his father's palace, men who knew that Britain has neither permanent friends nor permanent enemies, only permanent interests. The very nature of this Suffolk villageconjuring up a bucolic scene now virtually wiped clean from the English landscape, where life centred on the village school, shop, public house and the church, where men spoke of the importance of 'getting the harvest in' and their women came each and every Monday morning and draped the family's weekly wash on the line to dry, where gossip centred on 'ructions up at the big house', from where the Squire's writ ran the length and breadth of the village, and what, exactly, should be taken to the vicar's 'bring-and-buy' stall at the jumble sale to be held to raise funds either in aid of the gently collapsing church tower or yet further efforts to combat the voracious appetite of the death-watch beetle as it munched its way through the timbers of the church roof. It was a human portrait of English life which the Sultan found not just a revelation, so very different from the clipped vowels and, on so many occasions, the affected manners and mannerisms of those he had met at home − 'men of honour and integrity sent abroad to lie for their country' − but one which, curiously and most tellingly, he found much in sympathy with that to be experienced in the village atmosphere of his native Salalah. It was this experience of English village life that did much to open his eyes to the existence, and inherent distinctions, between 'two Englands.' He had, prior to his Suffolk days, been quite unaware of this second one, which is now regarded as having been the genesis of his abiding affection for the land which had for long been so closely associated with his own and that of the dynasty.

And, as the two years he was to spend as a member of the Romans household approached its end and the less comfortable life of Sandhurst beckoned, Qaboos was only too ready to acknowledge that, in so many crucial respects, even given Lorna Romans' somewhat unbending rules of domestic routine, he could not have had a better introduction to a way of life so alien to all he had previously experienced. He was also ready to recognise that without Philip Romans' 'cramming' sessions, those long hours of tutorial study which had made such a significant contribution to his academic abilities, his entry into Sandhurst would, as Major Chauncey had anticipated, have been more problematical than, in the event, it proved to be. Qaboos never forgot the value of his time with the Romans, not only going to stay with them during leave from the Royal Military Academy, but, after his succession to the throne, inviting them to Oman for long holidays, usually for the five months when winter was upon England.

It was a generosity which was maintained after Philip's death, when his wife was granted a 'grace and favour' home at Kalbuh, a suburb of Muscat City, situated at the end of the crescent-shaped waterfront corniche, with the mountains behind and facing the

Arabian Sea, where servants tended to her every need and with a chauffeur-driven car at her disposal from the Royal Court. On occasions, a car would discreetly arrive at Lorna's door and the Sultan would call to say 'Hello' and check that she had everything she needed.

Those who sought to question her about the Sultan, or sought to have access to him via her, got a very short, sharp response indeed. She was a familiar figure, tall, her back still straight and eyes of cornflower blue but now with snow-white hair, at palace garden parties, State receptions and as a member of the congregation at the small Anglican church in Muscat's old town. Until her death in 1997 at her home in England, which Oman's ruler had acquired for her, Lorna Romans remained what she had always been to Sultan Qaboos: a particularly evocative reminder of his time, as a young man, in England and a representative of a society which made an impression upon him which has proved indelible and, as such, remains with him still.

Chapter 3

SERVE TO LEAD

Many Middle Eastern monarchs, that breed of men who, throughout the turbulent twentieth century and into the twenty-first, have held back the hands of the clock by continuing to exercise their absolute rule, owe, in good measure, the hold they have over their respective thrones to the training they received at the Royal Military Academy at Sandhurst. Many, of course, found the place most difficult to bear, with one member of Oman's ruling family having cut and run within six weeks of entry, so difficult did he find the regime, particularly the rigours of the assault course and the consequent humiliations heaped upon him. Another, the Emir of Qatar, His Highness Sheikh Ahmed bin Khalifa Al Thani, speaks still of the Academy's 'bully boy' childish antics, which so many officer cadets at Sandhurst are obliged to endure. But the indelible fact remains that the harsh nature of its discipline bred in these men born to rule, as opposed to reign, a resilience and an instinct for survival which has as its foundation a kind of human boldness so necessary to endure at the top in an area of the world notoriously difficult to govern. Sandhurst was once described by the Headmaster of nearby Wellington College as, 'the Hell over the Hill'. But as hellish as it may have been for so many of Arabia's aristocratic cadets, few, including the Emir of Qatar, deny the role it played in shaping their characters. One of the most notable and distinguished of its alumni was the late and much-respected Hashemite monarch, King Hussein of Jordan, whose personal courage, political adroitness and ability to survive against the most formidable odds is the stuff of which international legends are made. And Sultan Qaboos has acknowledged, in public, on more than one occasion, the sense of personal gratitude he continues to feel for his Sandhurst days which, as will be seen, were, on occasions, far from easy. Indeed, as he left behind him in September 1960, after two years, the reserved atmosphere of the Romans' home and the respectful friendliness shown him by so many in the village of Felsham, and made his way to Sandhurst, the heir to the Omani throne, still only 19 years of age, was, as he was later to recall, full of trepidation. He knew full well of Sandhurst's reputation, that while it is regarded as the pre-eminent military training establishment in the world, the course its officer cadets are put through is never, even for the toughest, an experience of ease.

He knew, too, that while 'the RMA', as it is internationally known among the world's military elite, was designed along classic lines and that its external appearance, whilst not beautiful, was most impressive, it was a facade that concealed a daily routine that was not just tough and intimidating but for many proved to be quite overwhelming. Consequently, it was a daunting proposition for the young Prince, but he knew that both his personal honour and that of his father's realm rested squarely upon his shoulders.

Contemporary records show that 'Officer Cadet Qabus Ibn Said' (*sic*) joined the Academy along with 257 other young men, one of whom was James Timothy Whittington Landon, he of the 'Landon factor' in the reign of Sultan Qaboos (which will be addressed later on) about which there has been considerable comment and speculation, much of which is now known to have been inaccurate, so tightly drawn is the veil over the relationship between the two men. However, it can now be recorded that the future Sultan of Oman and Landon, his future confidant and adviser, were in different colleges and companies within the Academy. This being so, the paths of the two cadets would not, in the normal course of events, have crossed and they would not, therefore, have been aware of each other. Qaboos was allocated a place at the Academy's New College, described by a contemporary of his as 'an ugly Edwardian redbrick building . . . inside were long, green- and brown-tiled corridors that gave the impression of a monstrously large public lavatory'.

While, today, the Academy's training regime has a degree of sophistication that would, almost certainly, be derided by those of generations long since gone, forty years ago the first term of the two-year course was designed, deliberately and painstakingly, to deliver a somewhat more than severe physical and cultural shock to the system of a cadet. The Academy was a hard place for youths who would, at the successful completion of the course, have been transformed into particularly tough fighting men, with, as a quite separate but complementary dimension, a keen academic and practical concept of the strategies of waging war. Small wonder, then, that, against such a background, some fell by the wayside, of both the home-grown variety and those from overseas. In Qaboos's year there were thirty-four other cadets from foreign lands, among whom were three other Arab nationals, all from Iraq. Given the style and nature of his early, formative years in his father's palace and the leisurely, indolent manner that the climate of Dhofar encouraged, it will come as no real surprise to learn that the Sandhurst regime for Qaboos, particularly during the first term, came as a real shock, a very nasty and discomforting surprise. And it showed. A Sandhurst contemporary of the young Arab clearly recalls Qaboos as 'presenting a somewhat soft and unimpressive' face to the world of the RMA and that, all too soon, he began to experience the bullying with which Sandhurst's reputation was so deservedly associated.

Officer Cadet Qaboos, however, was to prove to be a man of quiet mettle, of an undemonstrative determination, whose reticent, gentle, sensitive air was no reason whatsoever to underestimate his instincts for survival. Indeed, there were many who, in the event, were obliged to reconsider, particularly as the two-year course drew to a close, their earlier estimations of the young Arab. In short, Qaboos survived the rigours of Britain's premier military training establishment, a considerable achievement in itself, with the Academy making its very own mark on him, one he was not to forget or cease to be grateful for.

During Qaboos's time at Sandhurst, the Drill Square, upon which it has long been said 'would-be soldiers are either made or broken', was presided over by the intimidating figure of Regimental Sergeant Major J.C. Lord, whose formidable reputation was spoken of in somewhat hushed tones throughout the British Army and further afield. As befits a professional soldier whose task was to turn boys into men, Lord was no respecter of persons, with the Prince suffering the lash of his stentorian tones every bit as much as fellow cadets. It was a crash course in the raw democracy of the Drill Square that 'Officer Cadet Qabus Ibn Said' was never to forget. Once the embryo army officers had acclimatised to the 'temperature' of Sandhurst – had, in other words, found their boot-clad feet – they were expected to arrange what can best be described as 'escapades', designed to show that they did have that essential quality of those who seek to be the leaders of men: initiative. Such diversions from the academic and physical demands being made on cadets were, in the tradition of the place, every bit as bizarre as they were outrageous and carried out with degrees of deftness which did not in any way result in those taking part being caught or identified after the deed was done. Such rites of passage came as something of a further jolt to Officer Cadet Qaboos, challenging, as they did, ordained authority and appearing, depending on the degree of outrageousness involved, somewhat distasteful to an aesthetic, as he had now undeniably become, preferring to spend his evenings listening to classical music, to which Philip Romans had introduced him, as opposed to joining in the vacuous, beer-fuelled roistering enjoyed by so many of his fellow officer cadets. But, in yet further testimony to his survival instincts, his involvement in such 'japes', jolly or otherwise, never led to him being apprehended by his instructors.

It is a most fitting tribute to the impression made by the Academy that those of so many different races and social backgrounds, across the generations, who have progressed through its halls of learning have rarely ceased to remember their time there with warmth and gratitude. And Qaboos of Muscat and Oman has proved to be no exception. While as a boy in Al Hisn Palace, he had watched his father's troops parade, which had given him a youthful interest in matters military, an interest to which his Sandhurst days added greatly. Indeed, one of his first tasks as Sultan, when Oman's Armed Services were reorganised and became better equipped than they had ever previously been, was to give as much attention, often in very great detail, to the uniforms of his men as he did the choice of a tank, a fighter aircraft or a frigate for his new navy. Indeed, many hours of intense discussion always precede the final decision as to the design and colour of a particular cap-badge or epaulette, as a direct result of which the Sultanate of Oman's Armed Forces are among the smartest not just in the Arab world but to be found anywhere. In practical terms, too, his keen, express interest in military affairs, and particularly in military strategies, much of which he learnt at Sandhurst, made a pivotal contribution to the successful waging of the Dhofar War, when his throne and country were assailed by a particularly determined and vicious foe. Principal to such an unprecedented victory in the Arab Islamic world was the strategic decision to attack the insurgents' lines of supply, as opposed to attacking their actual bases, and, as a consequence of such attrition, starve them of the means to prosecute the conflict.

Qaboos's sense of personal debt to Sandhurst has, over the years, taken two practical, and most generous, dimensions. In 1978, he personally presented the Royal Military Academy with funds to construct and equip a new gymnasium, a gift quite unsolicited and one that will serve as a lasting reminder of his days there. And then, in April 1983, came a most tangible tribute by Britain and Sandhurst to the Sultan of Oman's links with the Academy and his generosity towards it. He was invited to take the salute at the Sovereign's Parade, when senior cadets pass out as newly commissioned officers. It was a rare and privileged invitation, given the long-standing tradition that it is usually reserved for members of the British Royal Family.

It is instructive to place on record the text of the Sultan's speech because it demonstrates, in terms both clear and unequivocal, his own personal interpretation of the important role of a military establishment in the national life of a state, an interpretation which, in a turbulent part of the globe, is of particular significance. The address is interesting, too, because it upholds, again in the most straightforward terms, his own personal belief in impeccable conduct, particularly when wearing the uniform of one's own country. It is, in effect, a call for a sense of duty and personal honour – for so long admirable objectives with which the Arab was closely associated, but which, in the greater majority of instances have, alas, long fled the scene – to be upheld:

> Gentlemen, it is an honour and a great privilege for me to take the Sovereign's Parade today on behalf of Her Majesty the Queen. It is also a great pleasure to be able to share with you what I know will be one of the most profoundly memorable moments of your life. As one who has stood on parade on a similar occasion where you stand now, I think I know something of the emotion you are experiencing: elation at having successfully completed many months of hard and demanding effort and a feeling of excitement at the prospect of the future that now lies ahead, mingled, perhaps, with a faint shadow of sadness that the time has come to leave this famous Academy, which has come to be such a part of your lives, and the friends whom you have made here.
>
> The privilege of having been an officer cadet at the Royal Military Academy is something that can only be fully appreciated by those of us who have had the good fortune to be numbered among that brotherhood. And I know that one becomes increasingly conscious of the privilege, and more deeply grateful for it, as the years go by and one has to shoulder the responsibilities that life brings. For myself, I know that the values that I absorbed here have remained with me for ever afterwards. It was here that I learned that discipline is not just something that one imposes on others; it is something that one has, above all, to apply to oneself if one is to be worthy to be a leader of men. I learned also the true meaning of service: that it is to give and not to expect

to receive; that it is the team and not oneself that matters. I learned that with responsibility come obligations.

When, like you, the time came for me to leave, I felt that I had matured and could face the future with confidence. I was also deeply conscious of the debt I owed to my instructors for the patience, dedication and friendship with which they had given so much to a young man who had had so much to learn. I am sure that you feel today as I did then. You are about to set out on your separate ways, to follow your destinies through the years that lie ahead and you will carry with you the pride and hopes of all of us who are here with you today. It is certain that the path will not be easy. There will be times when the demands upon your courage and fortitude will be great, when your morale and physical endurance will be tested to the utmost. For these are times when the standards for which man has striven are under constant attack, when there are those who would surrender those standards rather than defend them. These are times which call for unceasing effort in every one of us, if those standards are to be maintained. I am confident that you will not be found wanting. May God bless you.

Chapter 4

A YEAR WITH THE SCOTS

On Saturday, 25 October 2003, *The Times* ran a report by staff journalist Alan Hamilton, himself a Scot, with a curious headline, one designed to amuse and, in so doing, attract the reader's eye: 'The Oil Pipes a' Calling as Sultan Orders Own Tartan'. What this newspaper, or for that matter the journalist who had written the report, did not know, however, was that behind the headline was a story which has for so long endured: that of the abiding respect and affection for the Scots held by one of only two remaining Sultans in the world. The report, in part, ran:

> The Sultan of Oman, who has no known Scottish blood but is a long-standing admirer of Britain, has ordered his own tartan. Sultan Qaboos does not himself intend to stride about his arid Gulf state in a kilt. The design is intended for his army, which has associations with British forces going back to the nineteenth century, and which boasts its own pipe band.
>
> The Strathmore Woollen Company, a Forfar-based mill, designed the tartan incorporating the red, green and white of the Omani flag, and rushed out a bolt in time for a

contingent of the Royal Omani Army to perform in their new uniforms at this year's Edinburgh Military Tattoo.

David Cowley, a director of the mill, said yesterday, 'We won the order because our former mill manager is a friend of John Bruce, the Omani Army's pipe-major and the only Scot in the band. All the other pipers are Omani.'

The design has been sent for approval to the Scottish Tartan Authority, based in Crieff, Perthshire, which checks new designs to ensure that they do not duplicate any of the 4,000 tartans it already holds on its files. Apart from that one proviso, there is no law to prevent any citizen of any country from wearing any tartan.

The report concluded:

The Royal Omani Army will not be taking to the kilt, a warm garment for a desert kingdom. Instead, they will stick to trousers and tunics, with a tartan plaid over the shoulder. Oman boasts one of the world's more exotic military musical ensembles, the Royal Oman Police Mounted Camel Pipe Band.

In fact, it was the Sultan's father, Said bin Taimour, who was the first member of the Al Busaid dynasty to have thrilled to the skirl of the pipes and to have had good cause to be grateful for the presence in Muscat and Oman of Scottish men of arms, who, in 1957, so effectively put down the Imamate rebellion against Sultanic rule. It was an episode in the life of the country which was pivotal to the survival of the dynasty and, indeed, the emergence of Muscat and Oman as a State united. This being so, the respect and affection with which the Cameronians, of 'Scottish Rifle' distinction, who saw off Imam Talib, were held by Sultan Said and, today, by his son, Qaboos, is very easy to understand. So when, in July 1962, Prince Qaboos passed out from Sandhurst and the matter of his secondment arose, there was no real surprise at all amongst those who had a good grasp on the history of his country when he requested to join the ranks of those who, five years earlier, had been, in very real effect, the saviours of his father's throne.

The Cameronians were, on the face of it, an unlikely choice for the heir apparent to an Islamic throne. Indeed, of all the infantry regiments in the British Army the Cameronians would appear to be the least likely for such a secondment. But, true to his family's sense of the past, its respect and appreciation of past service to its national fabric, allied to the abiding affection that attended it, Qaboos made his choice for the year-long secondment. The Cameronians it was to be.

The regiment's origins are unique. It was raised in Lanarkshire in 1689 and, most curiously of all, was done so within the context of religion. Indeed, the regiment's 'founding fathers' constituted a sect, and a highly militant one at that, of the Presbyterian Church, which saw its duty, both spiritual and temporal, to defend and uphold the Scottish National Covenant of 1638. The Covenanters, as Richard Cameron and his supporters became known and, indeed, styled themselves, were regarded, from the very outset of their foundation, by the State and the established Church as virtual outlaws and were obliged to resort to holding their meetings in secret locations deep in the Scottish countryside. Given their firm convictions and abiding commitment to the harsh and unbending strictures of their very own brand of Presbyterianism, they did in actual fact assume the proportions of a congregation, more than a military force, a description given particular emphasis when it is recorded that each company had an appointed 'Elder', with one of his most important daily duties being to make sure that each and every man was carrying a Bible – a somewhat radical departure from the age-old army epithet that, metaphorically at least, every soldier should carry a (potential) Field-Marshal's baton in his knapsack! Throughout the early years of their existence, the matter of the Covenanters' personal security was one of constant anxiety and unease. Consequently, at every parade outlying sentries stood guard, 'look-outs' were mounted and plans made for their defence should, in the event, their religious enemies stage an attack. Such necessary defensive measures bred in the early Cameronians an instinctive tenacity of spirit, allied to the design of various militarily inspired strategies with which to defeat any well-armed foe, an attitude of mind and range of practices that has not only remained with them throughout their long and distinguished military history, but, as their contribution to the successful prosecution of the conflict on Oman's Green Mountain proved some 46 years ago, has stood them in very good stead indeed.

But it was the prospect of the arrival on Britain's shores of William of Orange, in a bid to assume the throne, which galvanised the Covenanters to make plans to consolidate their ranks by raising a banner and an invitation to the men of Lanarkshire to rally to it and, in the process, form a regiment. It was an initiative which met with ample success, as a result of which the Covenanters passed into military history to be replaced by the name the regiment has borne ever since, the Cameronians. From the time it achieved regimental status, the Cameronians took a heroic and distinguished place in the annals of British military history, with a record of disciplined valour which marked its men out as soldiers of special distinction. Indeed, military historians have long reserved a very special place for these outstanding representatives of Scottish skill and tenacity.

The Cameronians' traditional area of recruitment remained Lanarkshire and the conurbation of Glasgow, with the result that the type of soldier recruited to its ranks came from some of the most socially disadvantaged, economically deprived areas of Scotland, those who, in brutal terms, had resided at the very bottom of Lowland society. The nature of human conduct born of such desperate environments gave rise to a not always enlightening experience in the barracks of the Cameronians, but the insolence which was so often a feature of such conduct was, of course, a far from inconsiderable bonus when practised on the field of battle. In short, they were fighting men of the most marvellous kind, tempered by a harsh discipline meted out by their officers, harsh by even the old-fashioned standards of the British Army which, for centuries, had been used to hold in check unruly behaviour in the ranks.

There are many examples where the rigours of such harsh discipline came, however, a decidedly poor second to the initiatives of men of the regiment who had decided upon a certain course of action. During the Second World War the regiment served in the Burmese jungle and, having taken offence at a certain officer's attitude towards them, which they deemed to be of a disobliging nature, took measures to detonate his tent. This was, indeed, duly blown up, though the officer in question was not in residence at the time of the explosion.

Although their role was not as crucial, or as involved, as that in the Green Mountain campaign, the very first experience the regiment had of Muscat and Oman occurred in the mid-1950s, when it was, temporarily, serving in the Middle East and was called upon to support the Trucial Oman Scouts, a local force raised in 1951, initially styled the Trucial Oman Levies, who were based in the then Emirate of Abu Dhabi, now, of course, a constituent part of the United Arab Emirates. As referred to earlier, the Buraimi Oasis had become a bone of contention between Saudi Arabia, Abu Dhabi and Oman, the point of contention residing in disputed ownership of the Oasis, where the borders of the three territories met, or, to be more precise, the ownership of what might have lain beneath the sands of the Oasis: oil. The 'boiling point' of the crisis came when the Saudi Arabians, with American support, dispatched an armed convoy into the Oasis, indeed some 600 miles beyond what had been up to that time the accepted frontier. The Saudi occupiers were, in the event, expelled from Buraimi by the Scouts but with the Cameronians playing a crucially important supporting role.

The successful conclusion of the exercise – successful, that is, for Sultan Said, the Trucial Oman Scouts and the Cameronians – was, however, something of a sideshow when compared to the fires of potential revolution that the spark of Pan-Arabism, ignited by Egypt's Gamel Abdul Nasser, had kindled. It was a fire that threatened an inferno for the conservative, autocratic rulers of the Gulf and was thus viewed by them with mounting alarm. Britain, as ever mindful of its strategic interests in the region, took prompt measures to boost the security of the traditional Arab rulers. In the face of frequent disturbances in the sheikhdoms by a growing band of radical malcontents who were responding to Colonel Nasser's revolutionary call, Britain took the decision, in 1957, just one year after the Suez Canal fiasco, which had seen the humiliation of Britain, France and Israel at the hands of the fiery Colonel, a brilliant political strategist whose influence in the Arab world they greatly feared, to base a resident unit of the Cameronians in the

Gulf. All too soon, it was proved to have been a most timely decision.

While Muscat and Oman had not been at all affected by public demonstrations in support of Nasser's brand of Pan-Arabist rhetoric, this did not mean that it was without its own troubles. Indeed, those apostles of the Imamate, with their direct challenge to the rule of Sultan Said and the integrity of his State, continued to prove that for the Al Busaid dynasty they still had the appetite and the initiative to cause trouble – so much so that by 1957 the Sultan's Armed Forces, in the face of a series of tactical defeats, as a result of which much of the interior of the country had been surrendered to Imamate rebel forces, were in a rout. It was a situation which could not be allowed to deteriorate further. Something most decidedly had to be done and, in the event, Muscat and Oman's decisive battle arrived and to its most timely aid came the Cameronians. By the beginning of August that year, the initial detachment of Cameronians had been flown from their base on the island of Bahrain and had set up camp at Ibri, in Muscat and Oman's interior, alongside the Trucial Oman Scouts, the Sultan's own troops and a number of armoured cars under British command. The advance on Nizwa, the 'capital' of the Imamates, began within days of the arrival at Ibri of the Cameronians, but their main foe was the heat. The Arabian summer was intense, with temperatures of 50 degrees Celcius not being uncommon but, nonetheless, the enemy was quickly engaged, with the result that within the week Nizwa was taken for the Sultan. The rump of the rebels fled to the fastness of the nearby mountains, which proved to be their last redoubt and from where the Imamate movement was finally expunged. This conflict, the Green Mountain War, was a success to which the Cameronians had made a pivotal contribution and in so doing had written yet another chapter of valour in the pages of British military history. As for Sultan Said bin Taimour, he could, finally, lay claim to a realm in its entirety.

Throughout the early days of the campaign, men of the Cameronians had proudly worn their regimental balmoral headdress; until, that is, supplies of bush-hats were flown in, which afforded greater protection from the furnace of the Arabian summer sun. The only casualties suffered by the Cameronians had been caused by the heat. At the end of the Nizwa campaign the Cameronians were flown back to their base on Bahrain but, although they had gone, the memory of these courageous Scots – not only their valour but the brightness of the tartan colours on their balmoral headdress – was never forgotten in Oman; indeed, has never been forgotten, with the Muscat Regiment having adopted the balmoral as their very own headdress, which they wear with pride to this day.

In addition to exercising, as his father had done, a sense of gratitude for the pivotal role played by the Cameronians in the resolution of two of his country's conflicts – the expulsion of the Saudi invaders from the Buraimi Oasis and the recapture of Nizwa from Imamate forces – Qaboos also embraced much of the cultural ethos of the regiment, reflected today in his Armed Services, such as the wearing by its men of the Cameronian tartan and, when on parade, the playing of bagpipes. What, however, he was to make of the Cameronians once off the field of battle is quite another matter. At the time Qaboos joined the regiment for a year's secondment it was a part of the British Army of the Rhine (BAOR), Britain's army of occupation, together with those of the United States, the USSR and France, which came about in the wake of the defeat of Nazi Germany in 1945. The Cameronians were based at Minden, long a byword among many, including not a few Germans themselves, for boredom, being an enclave of middle-class, unimaginative dullness. It was not a social atmosphere that the Lowland Scots took kindly to at all and it was not long before the tedium of it all began to extract its inevitable toll. In short, the time had come, in their estimation at least, for many in the regiment's number to kick over the traces of garrison life, to bring a little excitement, as they regarded it, to a tedium without apparent end. The time had arrived to have a 'little fun', in the best tradition of the backstreets of Glasgow from which so many of them had come.

And in keeping with Scottish Lowland Saturday night and, indeed, Cameronian 'tradition', it was an excess of alcohol which fuelled a catalogue of misconduct that came as something of a most unpleasant surprise, not only to the young Arab Prince, from a land where the state religion forbade the consumption of alcohol, but also to the prim and proper, staid and stolid men and women of Minden itself. The real serpent in Minden's garden was a plentiful supply of cheap alcohol, the immodest consumption of which prompted so many in the ranks of the Cameronians to abdicate the disciplines inculcated into them by their officers and which had been of such value when on the field of battle. It is sad to record that on more than one occasion these Scottish lions lost control on the streets of Minden, ran riot and by such disgraceful conduct laid temporarily low the name of the regiment to which, so recently, they had brought so much honour. While the local inhabitants were well accustomed to seeing British troops on their streets, they had never before seen such riotous, frightening behaviour. It was not long before the Cameronians were labelled by the locals as the 'Poisoned Dwarfs', with their truly appalling behaviour inflicting serious damage, both at home and abroad, on the British Army's reputation. Many in the regiment felt a palpable sense of shame, not least the young Arab Prince who had chosen to spend his postgraduate year from Sandhurst as one of their number.

What those who rampaged through the streets of Minden could not have known, however, was that the long and proud history of their regiment was about to pass for ever into history – proof that, on some occasions, old soldiers do not simply fade away but die with the stroke of a mandarin's pen. For within five years of the 'Minden experience', the Ministry of Defence, in yet a further round of cost-cutting measures, disbanded the Cameronians, incorporating the men within its ranks into other regiments. Although official confirmation was never forthcoming, it cannot have been a coincidence that the regiment met its demise and disappeared completely from the Army List after 279 years of distinguished service to Crown and country, save that of the violent revels of a few in a small town in Germany, so soon after the collapse of a quality of discipline with which it had in the past been so well associated.

But what the Whitehall cost-cutting crusaders could not expunge from the pages of history was the remarkable, and enduring, link that this Scottish regiment had forged, both in the furnace of battle and the days of peace, with a Middle Eastern country. Sultan

Qaboos of Oman retains to this day an appreciation of the achievements of this band of brave Lowland Scots in the land of his birth and over which he now rules, an appreciation which can be seen and heard on the parade grounds of his Armed Forces and his Royal Oman Police. It is a remarkable compliment, which both marks and celebrates a Royal Arab connection to the Scots, one which will endure for as long as mankind continues to respect the past.

Chapter 5

SHADOWS AND SUBSTANCE

Just as a country is the whole of its many parts, so too an executive head of government or a head of state, irrespective of the route they took to the top – election, patronage, birth or by force of arms – can be regarded with equal truth as reflecting aspects of the society over which they preside. Many, of course, may rage at the way in which they are perceived by so many, both at home and abroad, but such vapouring rarely evades the simple truth that all they are doing, just like Caliban, is to rage at their own reflection in the mirror. Human nature being what it is, and universally so, it has always to be taken into full account that much adverse comment levelled against those who thrive within a country's corridors of power is often motivated by personal dislike of the incumbent, raw jealousy at the position they hold or, most corrosive of all, an abiding, fiery resentment at the riches the position of power has given them. This latter consideration is, alas, particularly true in those Arab states which have been 'blessed' with the benefit of 'easy money' – and lots of it – which, daily, gushes from the ground.

The life-changing effect, the handmaiden of the coming of oil exports to a country, is more often than not (and with some considerable degree of justification) presented as being the harbinger of all that is good, progressive and modern. Multi-storey office blocks, smart hotels and opulent homes have risen from the sands of the Gulf States in wondrous profusion and its people have had, as a direct result of high oil revenues, vastly improved services in health, education and communications, contradicting the age-old epithet that all that glistens is not gold, for in Kuwait, Saudi Arabia, Qatar, the United Arab Emirates and the Sultanate of Oman, all that shines so very bright in the searchlight of the sun is, indeed, 'golden' to behold, even if it is born of the earth's black gold: oil. But with such abundant riches has come a corrosive air, a reshaping of appetites which has meant the decay and despoliation of so much that was good in the Arab ethos and celebrated since the time of the ancients. Indeed, the Sultanate of Oman is a living witness to the sad fact that the effects that the vast riches of a tide of oil can bring to the shores of a state are far from being limited to a dramatic change to its city skyline. The physical changes such easy wealth prompts are but a veneer, and an exceedingly thin one at that, but one which all too often conceals a far more distasteful state of affairs. For while Oman is not the only state in the Arab world to bear testimony to the cultural carnage wrought by what has appeared on occasions to be an unstoppable flow of cash, there has been in the Sultanate a particularly shameful coarsening of manners, a warping of the national psyche, proving the quite terrible capacity easy money has to fundamentally effect a nation's conduct. Nowadays, a plethora of commission agents haunt the country, from both within the Government and without, offering a variety of 'deals', many of which are obscure in origin and which the naturally cautious would be well advised to decline. It can be seen in the vulgar, hideous and pretentious 'palaces' constructed by those who have supped heavily at the oil-laced chalice of opportunism, and on the streets, down which proceed a raucous, horn-blasting convoy of cars demanding that they be made way for against allcomers, strutting bucks full of greedy, boastful conversation. Gone are the courtly manners, the understated airs of gentlemen naturally born, to be replaced by avarice and amorality, the austere disciplines of former times having been usurped by material appetites of a particularly offensive kind and a keen awareness of the power that money can bring.

It can be of small consolation to record that Colonel T.E. Lawrence, a man who loved the Arabs with all the emotion and conviction at his command, saw, some 80 years ago, such a sad state of affairs descending on Arabia with all the destructive force of a plague. He wrote: 'If forced into the "civilised life" they will succumb like any savage race to its diseases, meanness, luxury, cruelty, crooked dealing, artifice and, like savages, they will suffer them exaggeratedly for lack of inoculation.' Much earlier, that great Englishman of letters, Dr Samuel Johnson, wrote in his novel *The History of Rasselas, Prince of Abyssinia* (1759), that 'the Arab race was conducting an hereditary war against all mankind but coveted nor envied the possessions of others'. Today, alas, the second part of that statement has been stood upon its head. Gone are the naturally quiet tones, the intellectual traditions of moving towards a mutually successful end to a business transaction, the gentleness born of an inner strength, the endless cups of coffee laced with cardamom.

Now such occasions have a sense of impatience, a hint of menace, if it is believed that an advantage has been secured or, if an advantage has been lost, the introduction of a grotesque ingratiating air. And it has permeated all levels of society. Indeed, the age-old Arab principles of honesty, honour and reputation have been forfeited in favour of a rapid accumulation of riches – proof, if such was needed, of the wholesale corrosive impact that the oil-based economy has had on so many Omanis, those Aristocrats of the Arab World, those Gentlemen of the Gulf. Aristocrats, those born to such a role and those who by their courtly and courageous manner epitomised all that was noble have, alas willingly, become some of the most despicable in their unbridled abdication of all that made them great, in their equally unbridled gallop towards the bank.

It is a national state of affairs that is known to trouble Sultan Qaboos greatly, particularly as it tarnishes not only the face his regime presents to the world but also continues to distort to an alarming degree his people's appetites and expectations and damages the national fabric in a particularly grievous manner. Yet, as a fish does indeed rot from the head, most of this corruption of the Arab spirit originated from within the ranks of those to whom he entrusted high office and the power which attends it. As the scale of the problem assumed the proportions of a national disgrace, particularly from the late 1970s to mid-1980s, Royal decrees were issued, designed to either bring the outrageous nature of the problem to an end or, at the very least, to limit such looting. There were occasions when, with an abruptness that shocked those most involved but delighted many, top members of his team were summarily dismissed, others put behind bars, but still the problem persisted. Indeed, it was the very scale of the problem that is known to have acted as a brake on the Sultan's various efforts to outlaw such practices which, on one occasion at least, he has described in despairing tones as 'theft'.

Qaboos is cautious in such matters, fearful of creating a cadre of sacked Ministers who, by the nature of their departure from high office, have the will to form a potential threat to his rule. His inhibitions are well founded for, as the history of his country demonstrates, the relationship between the Sultan and the merchant class, from which so many of his Ministers were for so long drawn, is not altogether a happy one. Indeed, his own father, when ascending the throne in 1932, took immediate steps to wipe out the debt his administration was in with so many of Muscat's merchants. It was an aspect of Oman's past which does not sit lightly on his son's shoulders and has led him to be 'outrageously tolerant', according to one former Minister who was appalled at the scale of the problem during his time in Muscat's corridors of power, and thus infirm of purpose in instituting measures that would prevent further malpractice by so many at the top which continues to threaten public unrest. The problem of such conduct by a disgruntled minority has become ever more apparent to the majority, particularly among Oman's rapidly increasing educated constituency, young men and women who are exercising a greater political awareness and thereby gaining an appetite for political change. The situation constitutes a 'time bomb' and Oman's 14th Sultan must know that it is one with an ever-shortening fuse. It is an object lesson for any state about to enter the easy-money stakes and is, indeed, a present danger of which the world's latest entrant into the oil age is well aware.

Sao Tome is an island state, formerly a Portuguese colony, in the

Gulf of Guinea, off the shores of West Africa. Today, it is, in social terms, much where Oman was before its entry into the age of oil revenues. Poor, with a population principally made up of fishermen and small-scale farmers, it is a land about to endure the type of rapid, dramatic change experienced 30 years ago by Oman. The average annual income of those in work is about £167. The country has just forty-seven doctors and only one in seven of its children progresses to a secondary school education. It is one of the most indebted countries in the world, but not for much longer. The oilmen have found an estimated 12 billion barrels off its island shores and the times are about to change, for ever. Indeed, the Government of Sao Tome is set to receive, early in 2004, a down-payment of $100 million from the men from Exxon, which precedes a convoy of American oil companies all set to take control of the country's new-found oil reserves. The $100 million represents twice the state's annual income and more is most definitely on the way. Indeed, it is reliably anticipated that within the next decade Sao Tome will become one of the world's major exporters of oil, with the possibility that it will, or could, become, on a per capita basis, the richest country in Africa. But, even before that enticing $100 million down-payment has arrived safely in Sao Tome's State Bank, the dark clouds of corruption have appeared overhead.

The prospect of such previously undreamt-of riches has already spawned a coup which, just like that which befell Sultan Said at the start of Oman's oil age, is being described as 'bloodless'. In short, Sao Tome is in political turmoil, with people jostling for positions of power before the trickle of oil turns into a national geyser. Already, corruption has reached unprecedented heights. In an interview with John Vidal, the *Guardian* newspaper's Environmental Editor, the former President, Manuel Pinto da Costa, made remarks which that newspaper published on 1 November 2003: 'When there is a smell of oil, minds get stirred up. It creates a mirage in people's heads. If we do not know how to manage it, it will be hell here.' It is of no small interest, and highly instructive, that Sao Tome's former executive head of state used 'mirage' to describe one of the principal dangers which easy riches bring to a country where poverty has, hitherto, so characterised the nation's condition and how, with sickening speed, it generates a quite frightening national climate in which greed and menace rule the roost. The use of the term 'mirage' – an optical illusion caused by atmospheric conditions – is particularly appropriate to describe the prevailing climate in Oman, one which caused, and to some degree continues to cause, conduct which has been so very detrimental to the State itself. One aspect of this is that so many individuals have conducted themselves in a manner suggesting that they are beyond the law. It is a situation which Sultan Qaboos has, manifestly, been quite unable to prevent, commenting to an insider of his Court, 'It seems that the best that can be done is to tell Ministers to limit their "commissions" and "kickbacks", because excessive arrangements can lead only to eventual trouble.' Of course, the mirage aspect of easy wealth is far from being confined to illicit financial gain. It breeds a climate of indolence and casual greed, which all too soon has an adverse effect on public morals, usually starting from the top.

In *Sultan in Oman* (1957), the incisive writer Jan Morris, in a lament to the damage that high oil revenues would inflict on the Omani character, commented, 'Often in this coarsening process the old Arab principles of honesty and candour found themselves swamped. Nobody begrudged some splendid Arab princeling his moments of salacious pleasure or roaring eroticism, but hypocrisy in such gorgeous libertines was hard to stomach.'

Yet again, it is a commentary which, with its skilful use of words, such as the one-time President of Sao Tome exercised in his own lament at what is about to engulf his small island state, uses the terms 'salacious' and 'eroticism' to highlight an atmosphere, so prevalent in Oman, in which an aspect of the Arab character has been both distorted and, on so many occasions, wilfully misrepresented. Sadly, it is a corrosive circumstance which Sultan Qaboos, even given all the tools of social engineering at his national command, has not been able to dispel. There are many who believe that far from taking measures to inhibit the salacious stories that have so assailed his throne, he has, by his own conduct, encouraged them.

However, before examining in any detail the nature of the unhealthy climate of rumour and speculation (all too often of the most salacious and sensational kind) which for so long has swirled about the Court of Sultan Qaboos, pervading its atmosphere and polluting its environment, it is interesting to return to the methods used by Muscat's manipulators of public opinion, the Ministry of Information, to describe the method by which Oman's 14th Sultan ascended the throne of his father, before, of course, it had actually been vacated. There are many observers of the Omani scene who are of the opinion that it was as a result of the attempts at public deceit over the sudden and dramatic change of ruler that the Omani national pastime of rumour-mongering and ill-informed, wild speculation, became virtually inevitable. A former senior figure who spent many years prowling Muscat's corridors of power recalls a piece of rhetoric of his time, one beloved of Omanis and expatriates alike and which had as its origins the climate of illusion so prevalent in Oman's capital, where the official line on any matter was rarely believed, or for that matter believable, all of which did much to generate an almost permanent climate of rumour and speculation. It ran as follows: 'Why should Muscat be twinned with Moscow? Because, say veteran Kremlinologists and Qaboos-watchers, Oman and the former Workers' Paradise both suffer from highly unpredictable histories.' The fact, of course, that Josef Stalin routinely resorted to lying on a breathtaking scale is universally known, for example using lies to 'explain' or deny catastrophes such as the mass starvation following the collectivisation of agriculture. Less well known, however, is the fact that according to the Government's 'spin doctors' in Muscat, Qaboos arrived on the throne by a process peculiarly akin to immaculate conception. The former Muscat insider takes up the story:

> The reality, of course, was that on 23 July 1970, a gang of plotters, including the throne's current incumbent, rushed the Salalah Palace of Sultan Said bin Taimour, Qaboos's father, and, in a blizzard of noise and small-arms fire, ousted the old boy. Although there was an undeniable Gilbert and Sullivan air to the whole affair, there is not even a scintilla of doubt that what was planned and executed was a classic coup. And it was, almost, bloodless! The old Sultan was shot in the foot. In early Government handbooks, in English, some semblance

of the truth was maintained in descriptions which, in clear and unambiguous terms, stated that Qaboos 'seized power', a phrase heavy with cordite-in-the-air implications and quite properly so. Later, however, as each annual edition came off the presses, the handbooks began to relate an entirely different, and altogether softer, version of events. Initially, Qaboos 'took power', rather than seizing it. Later, he 'acceded' in the matter of grabbing the top job. And finally, with a disregard for the truth bordering on the sensational, the handbooks reported that Qaboos 'ascended the throne on the abdication of his father'. Listen carefully and from beyond the grave you can hear Stalin applauding! The trouble, of course, with this sort of lying, so clearly sanctioned, so clearly officially commissioned of the writer, with support from the man at the pinnacle of power, is that it set a bad and ultimately extremely dangerous example for all officials. Soon, all too soon, everybody is at it and that is precisely what happened.

This former 'Oman-watcher' from within explains the palpable nonsense that such a State-sponsored appetite for creating illusions generated, citing one particularly ludicrous example from the early 1990s:

What happened was, on occasions, superficially, farcical. Late one afternoon a helicopter belonging to the Sultan's Royal Flight plunged to the ground soon after take-off. The wretched machine was being test-flown, having just been serviced. Fortunately, the pilot was not killed, even though the impact was horrendous. Now, the key thing is that the accident happened near Seeb International Airport, close, very close, to the multi-lane motorway serving the airport and linking the capital to the interior of the country. The accident was witnessed by at least 100 people, including taxi drivers who pulled their vehicles onto the hard shoulders of the road to watch. And at least one of the witnesses telephoned the offices of the local newspaper to report the crash. Crash? What crash? There was no crash according to an official spokesman at the Ministry of Information and those who were claiming otherwise were obviously hallucinating.

As indeed they were when they reported monster clouds of smoke and violent flames when an American fuel-tanker crashed at the end of the runway during the first Iraq War in 1991. Oman's refinery, for the duration of hostilities, was switched to 24-hour production of aviation fuel for the Allied warplanes. Thousands of flights were made by tanker aircraft, one crashed – or not, according to the Qaboos Government. There was no crash, no smoke, no flames, no fire – *official*. I tried very hard to explain to a Cabinet Minister and his Under-Secretary that the consequences of lying about publicly witnessed events is that all witnesses, their families, friends, acquaintances and, indeed, anybody who will listen to them in the local coffee shop, at the fish market or the souq, know that the Government is lying and thus decline, in ever-greater numbers, to believe a word they say, about anything.

It goes without saying that both men would, of course, deny that such a conversation ever took place.

While such a strategy of denial and deception had as its principal architect an octogenerian functionary, Anthony Clayton Ashworth, formerly of the British Intelligence department MI6, whose designation at the Ministry of Information was that of Adviser, it is inconceivable, given the Sultan's grasp on the nation's affairs, that he would not have been aware that such dubious and wholly counter-productive practices were being perpetrated and, if they continued unchecked, could lead only to the widespread discrediting of his Government both at home and abroad. Such an observation leads to the persistent question, just what is it in the Sultan's sense of judgement that, on repeated occasions, has led him down a wholly inappropriate path? It is a question that many of his immediate counsellors, both Omani and expatriate alike, have had good cause to put during his 33-year-long reign. Indeed, it is a question which continues to arise and does so because such an appetite for the inexplicable, some say 'erratic', by Qaboos is an ever-present possibility.

Such conduct is, of course, far from being a recent phenomenon in those who rule, absolute or otherwise, born to rule or there by election, and it is best witnessed by Ovid's Latin lament, '*Video melliora proboque, deteriora sequor*' – 'I see the right path to follow, yet I take the wrong one.' It remains a matter of sad astonishment that alongside so much that Oman's Sultan has achieved in the field of development, a national progress born of a forensic intelligence, allied to a keen sense of value and an aesthetic intellect, there are so many instances in the conduct of his nation's affairs when he has, manifestly, abdicated the need to put into place a 'checks and balances' mechanism. Indeed, given his demonstrable intellect, intelligence and that most valuable human asset, courage, his natural epithet should be Descartes' fundamental basis of philosophy: '*Cogito, ergo sum*' – 'I think, therefore, I am.' But, inexplicably, it is not and this, alas, is a flaw in the otherwise very fine nature and character of a man and ruler which dismays his friends, who are legion in number, and delights those few enemies he has.

Of course, when such practices are allowed to run amok, it is not long before the 'trickle-down' effect comes into play. Indeed, what originated as a means of maintaining the 'broad sunlit uplands' illusion of the national condition (to which Oman's Ministry of Information is a serial addict of the severest kind, where no cloud is allowed to darken the national horizon lest it be seen as a blemish on the rule of the Sultan) led all too quickly to a wider corruption carried out by so many at the top of the Sultanate pile. Such Ministry officials were emboldened by the fact that if one kind of corruption, the putting of facts to the sword, was tolerated and, on occasions, encouraged, surely other acts of personal initiative would not be regarded as morally reprehensible. In short, in the words of a former Minister of the Omani Crown:

> His Majesty's outrageous tolerance of practices which were not compatible with good government, and the maintenance of public confidence, sent entirely the wrong message, set, in fact, the worst kind of national example. I know why he decided to overlook such blatant 'indiscretions': to maintain the peace among what has always been a very small pool of

talent at his disposal for the running of the Government. But it has proved to be a peace which has come at too high a price.

The one-time Oman-based insider again takes up the story:

And then there's the matter of corruption. This has been a major problem in Oman from the earliest years of Qaboos's rule. Given the sudden flood of money from oil production after almost a century of grinding poverty for the vast majority, corruption was always going to be a big issue unless, that is, the most rigorous of checks were put in place. Yet Qaboos always, from the very outset of his reign, seemed oddly ambivalent about the matter. To be sure, the matter surfaced publicly and official 'crackdowns' were launched. Sometimes, some particularly hapless soul was named, shamed and sacked. I remember only three paying the price of massive graft. In private, Court officials closest to Qaboos said that the Sultan appeared to lose interest in the subject soon after each 'crackdown' was announced. For myself, I think Qaboos was always too conscious of his own extraordinarily vulnerable position in relation to corruption. It is, after all, inconceivable that oil could be sold to both Salisbury [now the Zimbabwean capital, Harare] and Pretoria [the South African capital] without his knowledge and consent. Then, of course, there's the matter of arms deals, Brigadier Landon and his chums, the Ashland scandal [when that American Company invested in a chrome mine which didn't exist, which led to the forced resignation of its Chairman and ignominy being heaped upon Landon, one of Qaboos's closest advisers, by the US legal authorities] . . . the list, in actual fact, is depressingly long. Sometimes, it seemed as though everybody had their nose in the trough.

I well recall the horrified reaction of a friend who was a very senior civil servant and expert adviser/consultant to a Ministry when he was briefing a recently appointed Minister following a modest Cabinet shuffle. The new man, a member of the Al Said family, sat with growing impatience in the lecture theatre as my friend, with the aid of stills, video and bits of film, showed him the progress being made on a score or more of vitally important infrastructure projects, all of a complicated and technically demanding nature. 'Yes, yes, yes. All very interesting, Mr X, but what's in it for me? That's what I want to know!'

Even in Oman, at the height of the feeding frenzy following the collapse of oil prices, when it looked as though the golden goose had actually died, it was uncommon for bribes to be solicited quite so blatantly. I repeat, given his vast network of narks, spies, double agents and toadies, it's inconceivable that Qaboos was ignorant of this sort of thing.

Just as Qaboos's father, Sultan Said bin Taimour Al Said, who adopted for so much of his reign the manners of an earlier age, would have been better suited by far to the seventeenth century as opposed to the twentieth, with his courtly airs, his very clear understanding of the value and importance of honour, integrity, that a man's word was his bond, public reticence and that ostentation was all too often an exercise in vulgarity, so his son has the misfortune to reign at a time when it is virtually impossible for the public to be separated from the private, as the British Royal Family has learned to its cost. In short, Sultan Said was caught out, ran out of time, was overtaken and swept up by the winds of a social revolution which demanded instant change and which, with a snarl and an insolent snapping of its fingers, quite literally laughed out of court the principles and the priorities by which he had conducted his life. The warning delivered by a former American President, Woodrow Wilson, in the 1920s appears most apt and, whilst constituting too late a warning for Sultan Said, could, with a reasonable degree of justification, be well regarded as a most appropriate caution to his son: 'People will endure their tyrants for years but tear their deliverers to pieces if a millennium is not created immediately.' Change, universally, is once again on the march, an international development from which the Sultanate of Oman will not prove to be immune.

Chapter 6

SALACIOUS SCANDALS

For members of Royal Houses, wherever they may have stood, or stand, the twentieth century was not particularly kind, a circumstance from which, on early evidence, the twenty-first century is not set to offer any relief. Given that the depraved public appetite for rumour and speculation of the salacious kind is an appetite that can never be satiated, royals have found themselves the most regular and vulnerable of targets. Even that epitome of probity and sound conduct, Queen Victoria, was subject to scandal based on her trust and confidence in her Scottish gillie, John Brown. Later, her son, Edward VII, ran the gamut of a whole catalogue of salacious scandal, with his relationship with Mrs Alice Keppel and, in turn, the music-hall performer Lillie Langtry, coming under excited speculation in the press. Later still, Prince George, an uncle of Queen Elizabeth, was reported to be bisexual, taking as one of his lovers the actor, dramatist and composer, Noel Coward. George, setting an unfortunate precedent, was killed in an air-crash in 1942, the causes of which have never been satisfactorily explained, an incident which continues to haunt those who believe that Diana, Princess of Wales, was killed by agents of the State because of her intimate relationship with Dodi Al Fayed, son of Mohammed Al

Fayed, owner of the London department store Harrods. But the twentieth century's most damaging Royal scandal was undoubtedly that of the Prince of Wales' affair with the American divorcee, Mrs Wallis Simpson, which shook the British nation and its Empire to their very foundations and which led to Edward VIII's abdication. Not that the unpleasant breath of salacious gossip was reserved solely for the British Royal Family. Throughout the early 1900s, Tsar Nicholas II's consort, the Empress Alexandra, was plagued by rumours that her relationship with the monk Rasputin, who was being credited with the spiritual powers that brought relief to the haemophiliac son and heir to the Romanov throne, the Tsarevich Alexi, was somewhat more than platonic. And, in the winter of 2003, the media, both in Britain and abroad, was consumed with tales being told, and written, by former servants of the House of Windsor, most of which had a sexual connotation, of both a heterosexual and a homosexual nature.

As the spectre of sexual scandal has not been confined in Europe to members of Britain's Royal Family, so has similar speculation in the Arab Islamic world not been restricted to the perfumed indolence of the Ottomans of Constantinople or the lascivious appetites of Egypt's former monarch, King Farouk. Indeed, virtually since his accession to the throne of Oman, the assumption of homosexuality has pursued Sultan Qaboos relentlessly, with the subject arising not just at the smartest dinner tables of the land but in those greatest mines of gossip and innuendo, the souqs of the Arabian peninsula. It is gossip which his marriage in March 1976 to the daughter of Oman's first and only Prime Minister, Sayyid Tarik bin Taimour Al Said (a post which Qaboos abolished in the wake of Sayyid Tarik's resignation, Sayyid Tarik being frustrated with the many obstacles being put in his way) did little to alleviate. While his marriage to Sayyid Tarik's daughter, Nawwal, whose name was changed, at Qaboos's insistence, to Kamile, was the subject of much public rejoicing – an entire circus was flown in from Britain for the occasion, with its performances being free of charge to the general public – the rumours continued unabated. Simply put, it is a widely held public assumption which refuses to go away. The marriage was, very soon, dissolved, with his wife, the country's Sultana, living much of the time in Western Europe. There are those who believe that the marriage was never consummated, while others believe with equal conviction there was issue to the marriage. As is so often the case in Oman, however, the truth remains very much in pawn, yet another illusion, a mirage, which some claim to clearly see while others insist that it is just a trick of the light, and as such very much attributable to the country's 'atmospheric conditions'. Nevertheless, a former senior servant of the State has no doubts on the matter at all and, what is more, links what is basically an unhealthy air of speculation of a deeply personal, and, therefore, private, nature to the equally unhealthy climate in the country of financial corruption:

> Qaboos is even more vulnerable, fantastically so in truth, to the charge of moral corruption. Everyone in the country assumes him to be homosexual, in view of his far from concealed conduct, with many claiming it as fact. This, of course, sits very uncomfortably with the officially supported and espoused brand of Ibhadi Islam. But it seems to me that in a very Arab way nobody was going to take violent exception to this unless it was thrust, so to speak, under their very noses. Astonishingly for a man given to self-doubt and of a deeply private, withdrawn nature, Qaboos often seemed determined to ram the question of his assumed sexuality into the limelight. Who can forget, just to give one example, the National Day celebrations when he kept an entire stadium full of worthies, Ambassador, Minister, et al. waiting, together with the domestic television audience, for what was more than an hour and a half only then to appear with a long-haired youth of exquisite countenance? The intake of breath that their appearance occasioned, the youth never more than a foot away from Qaboos's side, must have been heard at the other end of the Gulf. And then there was the disgraceful business of the parent of a particularly pretty youth thrusting him forward for Royal approval as the Sultan's car swept by. Funniest of all, in a particularly sick sort of way, was the matter of what became known as the 'Ice

Cream Cars'. Young men who, it can be assumed, had pleased the Sultan especially well, were rewarded with convertible German cars, each hand-finished and costing the equivalent of about £100,000, finished in unique ice-cream colours. Qaboos had thus ensured, with at least ten of these outrageous vehicles, that each of the long-haired youths behind the steering wheels had not only benefited handsomely from his generosity, but that everyone else would fall to judgement as to the nature of service which had been rendered to gain such a reward.

Then there was the appalling business of what was termed locally the 'Kalbuh Capers'. One of the vessels in the Royal Yacht Squadron is the *Fulk a' Salamah*, which is a 'back-up' yacht for the principal vessel, the *Al Said*. Its standard mooring was about half a mile off its home port and thus close to the residential area and two mosques. On occasions, Qaboos used the vessel for social gatherings, parties at which some of his retinue of young men could, metaphorically, let their hair down. It was not long before Muscat's rumour mills began to roll, and by all accounts with some justification if, that is, only some of the stories that the boys themselves began to repeat were true. Actually, so bacchanalian did these parties on board become that even some of the participants themselves became concerned at the possibility of protests not just from Kalbuh but also from the fishing community next door and the two mosques. OK, so we all knew that the nearest villas and apartments at Kalbuh were 'grace-and-favour' jobs, but to shove such blatant, all-male horseplay, all most un-Islamic activities, under the very noses of the locals seems more, much more, than mindlessly careless.

The existence of the 'grace-and-favour' villas at Kalbuh, in a delightful cove overlooking the waters of the crescent-shaped waterfront of Muttrah, with its latticed windows and pastel-shaded, arabesque houses, the fairest port in all Arabia, has, itself, a contribution to make to the extraordinary story of Arabia's last

Sultan. For as we have already seen, each winter Mrs Lorna Romans, the matriarch who watched so closely over the welfare of the young Qaboos during his student days in England, would leave the damp bleak cold of her native land and take up residence for the duration at the villa at Kalbuh made available for her by Qaboos. Her migration to the sunshine of an Arabian winter had a well-defined social rhythm, one which was occasionally punctuated by the arrival at her door of the country's ruler. Whilst exercising an admirable reticence when being asked about Qaboos's visits, there were times when circumstances warranted a departure from such discretion and this distinguished old lady would speak to another senior member of the Muscat establishment, in more than the accepted sense of the term, about the latest visit of her former royal charge.

> It is more than just interesting, in terms of any assessment of the Sultan's character, that the visits to Lorna at Kalbuh began when he was at the height of his pomp and power. At such a time in his reign he was on so many occasions riven by doubt and desperately short of self-confidence. When he was unable to visit her personally, he would, for example, send a car and courtier to her from whichever palace he was staying in with various parcels and a plaintive note, to the effect, 'I don't know which of these to give my visitor. What do you think would be most suitable?' And thus would be unwrapped an astonishing selection of goodies intended for visiting princes, princesses, heads of government, ministers of state of foreign governments and so on.

One of the annual recipients of such fantastic largesse was not, however, an exalted visitor from abroad but the wife of a resident expatriate Adviser. Margaret Ashworth is the wife of a man a generation of visiting journalists came to refer to as 'Oman's Doorman', Anthony Ashworth, Adviser and, latterly, Consultant to the Omani Minister of Information, Abdul Aziz bin Mohammed Al Rowas.

So magnificent were the many items of jewellery that the exceptionally generous Sultan gave Margaret over the long years of their residence at Muscat that she took to inviting a chosen few round for tea, when poor old Anthony was not around, and showing off, as she had good cause to do, diamonds, rubies and platinum necklaces studded with sapphires and amethysts to her astonished, and one must say envious, guests. A conservative estimate of the total value of such jewellery was once put at well in excess of £1 million.

Not that the visits to Lorna Romans were the sole ones the Sultan used to make to seek expatriate advice. Indeed, until the late 1980s he was in the habit of leaving the palace very late at night and driving, incognito and unannounced, to a small house in Medinat Qaboos (a residential suburb of Muscat, formerly occupied principally by expatriates, which gloried in the appellation 'Weybridge on Sand'), where he would seek guidance on a whole range of matters, both personal and private, with one of his small circle of expatriate female friends.

Given the very considerable pressures upon him, which were unrelenting and particularly so during the early years of his reign, when an ambitious programme of national development was carried out, Qaboos did, on a basis which assumed a regular pattern, display some of his father's characteristics, a symptom of which had, on more than one occasion, Ministers and Advisers either cowering in a corner or making an undignified dash for the door. An Omani Adviser recalls such uncomfortable, and potentially life-threatening, incidents:

When His Majesty was confronted with particular acts of stupidity, unfailingly bad judgement, sickening greed or just general incompetence, of which I regret to have to say there were many, his face used to blacken with anger and we all knew that a right royal screaming rage was well and truly on its way. They could also be caused by anyone who dared to – how is it put in English? – 'nay say' the Sultan. Such incidents regularly occurred in the Council of Ministers, in his private apartments at one of the palaces, or, as happened in my own uncomfortable experience, in a Government office. During one particularly difficult week, when His Majesty was in residence at the Bait Al Barka Palace, the rages occurred on virtually a daily basis and it was at this time that I had the first personal experience of his use of one of his pearl-handled revolvers. Shots were fired in anger, all around the room, with flowers being shot to pieces and the locks on the doors smashed. With regard to the use of his firearms to show and relieve his frustrated anger, this was reminiscent of his father, except that Sultan Taimour restrained himself to moodily firing at lines of glass bottles set up on one of the walls of his Salalah Palace. And in his case no lives were put at potential risk!

While Sultan Said may well have vented any anger and pent-up frustrations with his own version of the party song 'Ten Green Bottles Sitting on the Wall', and have kept the greater majority of his subjects very much at arm's length, his son, when not exercising one of his pearl-handled revolvers in anger with one of his hapless Ministers or an Adviser who had, in his opinion, advised poorly, he did institute an annual tour to some of the more remote regions of his realm, designed to meet tribal leaders and local people generally who would then discuss any problems they wished to bring to the Sultan's attention. Such annual forays into the desert are billed as 'Meet the People' tours and are preceded by a photo-call of those Ministers who are to accompany him. They are usually assembled on the lawns of whatever palace the Sultan is to depart from and, to a man, armed to the teeth with a whole range of automatic weapons, more often than not grin sheepishly or self-consciously at the camera. It is a totem-pole occasion of the year around which Oman's rapidly increasing political class have woven endless jokes, particularly about the commonly held belief that so many of the Ministers are appalled and apprehensive at the prospect of spending up to three weeks in desert encampments in such close proximity to the ruler of the land. And, indeed, some Ministers of the Omani Crown do have good cause to be nervous, given the Sultan's practice of hauling them before a local Sheikh who has vigorous complaint to make at what he believes to be the poor performance of a particular Ministry. The sign that the tour is under way is always heralded by Qaboos's Range Rover, with him behind the wheel, making its way out of the palace gates with canvas water-bags hanging conspicuously off the front bumper. As one courtier comments: 'This is purely cosmetic, done to give the impression that the hardships and limitations of desert life will be experienced by His Majesty, which is far from the truth of the matter. And, what is more, Omanis know this to be so, with many being quite embarrassed by it.' Such a harmless affectation could well be dismissed as being without any importance whatsoever, yet it remains most instructive that a man of such undoubted intelligence and with an excellent grasp on just what is going on in the country at large, and most crucially of all, a deft understanding of the public mood, feels it necessary that such a blatant cosmetic device should continue. And, according to a former senior observer of the Sultanate scene, the swinging water-bags on the Range Rover are not the only illusion of the 'Meet the People' tours:

> At first sight, which was, for me, the 1985 tour, I thought the whole business to be truly splendid, the act of a caring, generous-spirited monarch keen to display his accessibility to the least privileged, least endowed, both socially and educationally, of his subjects. Well, such an early impression turned out to be, in itself, nothing but a particularly well-orchestrated illusion!
>
> In actual fact, what these increasingly opulent, extravagant and mostly symbolic affairs amount to is an unrivalled opportunity for Qaboos to display his incredible memory for landholding maps. Courtiers told me that His Majesty knew the name and rank of every owner of every piece of land bigger than a postage stamp in the Sultanate and used such precise knowledge for the ritual humiliation of his Ministers, Senior State Officials and just about anyone else on whom he found it agreeable to vent his spleen. Such an increasingly hapless band are men of power and wealth,

yet they went in fear of these tours in case Qaboos, to impress those who had assembled to meet him, demanded an instant 90 degree, or 180 degree, turn in policy, in order to accommodate some complainant or the other. The result has been, of course, that, and particularly so as the 1990s went by, he got to meet fewer and fewer 'ordinary' subjects, who have been replaced by more and more hand-picked 'specials' and praise-singers. And yes, he has, most definitely, come to believe his own publicity and does indeed lap up the nauseating sycophancy ladled out by the bin-load.

Such observations on an annual spectacle of the reign of Sultan Qaboos return, yet again, to the illusory nature of the State's fabric, that in a country where the media is strictly controlled, the air of unreality is but one aspect of the social climate which an ever-increasing number of Omanis regard as not just unhealthy but also as an adverse reflection on the absolute power their ruler wields. This, inevitably, can only be regarded as a particularly telling commentary on the nature of the man, as opposed to the monarch, who came to power by force which came to be presented as very much a development born of a sleight of hand, as is, by all accounts, the 'Meet the People' tours. The courtier again takes up the story:

> The tours really are, in all truth, a triumph of myth over reality, a mirage no less, a well-crafted act of illusion. Qaboos living in a tent, eating simply, austerely even, sleeping beneath the stars . . . it's all balls. The reality is that a full month before kick-off, sometimes less when Royal whim dictates it, the best hydrologist money can buy, who is seconded for the purpose from a State establishment where he works quietly throughout the rest of the year, is dispatched to a desert area to locate water, equipped with a rig and as much piping as may prove necessary. The amount of water consumed by the Sultan's camp in the desert is vast, tens of thousands of gallons, for showers, baths,

cooking, etc. Hair-shirts and the 'locusts for tea' style of desert life do not, most definitely, hold any appeal whatsoever for Qaboos and, to be fair, neither does it hold much attraction for the greater majority of his subjects. The tours came to be regarded as particularly wearing by Qaboos, given the constant demands made on him by people seeking water and electricity supplies, roads, schools, hospitals, those kind of State establishments. On one occasion that I personally know of, he was so sickened by the never-ending appeals for cash that he rammed his foot on the accelerator of the Mercedes 4x4 that he was driving and instructed his passengers to throw money out of the windows to the grovelling indigents. 'That's all they want,' he muttered, adding 'I'm sick of them.' Such an incident sparked the first of the 'Qaboos to quit' rumours. As it so happens, I think that he was very close to going at that point. Even for such a mercurial man, he was at a very low point indeed.

Such commentary on the Sultan's morale coincides with it being known that as the 1980s reached the halfway mark, and particularly as the decade drew to a close, he had become particularly disillusioned with just about everything, that he was learning painfully that in politics there is rarely, if ever, any lasting gratitude. Uneasy, indeed, rested the head which wore the Crown, with the remark being made to a visiting female friend from Britain, 'There is so much more that I would like to do with my life.'

It was a plaintive cry indeed, one that had not been helped at all by it becoming known to him that in the expatriate ranks of his beloved Armed Forces he was referred to as 'Sooty', the ultimate glove puppet, an appellation with racist overtones which was badly received, as well it might be. Such a barrack-room, officers' mess slur, with its inherent promise of attitudes of racial superiority, can, however, come as no surprise when it is recorded that for a good number of years the Sultan's Armed Forces had recruited men from what was then the Rhodesian Army and, in time, soldiers from South Africa, who served Oman's ruler on a contract basis.

Consider that, on a routine basis, His Majesty's Government condemned the racial policies of both southern African regimes yet recruited men from both armies, who could hardly be expected to be standard-bearers of liberal opinion, and the illusion factor in the Oman equation becomes ever more apparent. Or, as a former contract army officer who saw service in Oman but who now lives in Australia comments, 'In Oman what you believe you see is most certainly not what you get.' The mirage factor yet again.

Many believe that the instigator of the strategy of the recruitment of men from Rhodesia (now Zimbabwe) and South Africa was Tim Landon, who has strong links with both countries and to this day has an extensive ranch in Zimbabwe. It was, most certainly, Landon who, together with the Omani businessman Omar Zawawi, established 'paper companies' which sold Omani oil to both Rhodesia, before the collapse of the regime of Ian Smith, and, in turn, South Africa, a covert operation which was in defiance of both Britain and the United Nations and the oil sanctions they had imposed. A retired senior official, who held high office in the Sultan's establishment and has now retired in South Africa, comments:

> Omani oil was so important to South Africa's apartheid regime that shortly before the release from jail of Nelson Mandela and the coming to power of an ANC Government two of South Africa's last white rulers, State President F.W. De Klerk and Pik Botha, the country's Foreign Minister, paid visits to Muscat to thank the Qaboos Government for the help it had given South Africa. To say that the Sultan was unaware that such transactions were being made, that he was unaware that Oman was breaking international law for profit alone, is a complete nonsense, pure fiction in fact.

What, however, was far from fiction, although based on an assumption born of gossip and wholesale tittle-tattle, was speculation in the Sultan's Armed Forces as to the nature of their ultimate Commanding Officer's sexuality, with varying degrees of ribaldry and prurient discussion in attendance. A former officer recalls such speculation:

> Some of our most able young officers, especially those, for reasons that I could never fathom, from Rhodesia, known as the 'Zim faction', came to believe that you'd never get promotion beyond Major unless you were queer. Actually, some became convinced that the whole recruitment policy was a queer conspiracy, an assumption which was not surprising when you looked around and saw so many obvious homosexuals in positions of very senior rank throughout Oman's Armed Services. It was, of course, barrack-room theory but it was given an often bizarre impetus by certain events. One expatriate officer, to give but one example, was found, drunk and raving, in his official car on top of the SAF [Sultan's Armed Forces] roundabout at 1.30 in the morning and, when helped from the stricken vehicle, emerged wearing a green and gold ball-gown!

It is quite immaterial whether or not such prurient rumours are true. What, however, is of relevance is that such public speculation about an essentially private personal matter is repeated continuously and that so many, from banker to Bedu, from visiting duke to local dustman, pass them on without corroboration of any kind. Obviously, some choose to believe what they are told, however scandalous, others do not. But the 'stories' for such public titillation all too quickly take on a fearful momentum of their own, and when seen alongside widespread tales of, for example, ministerial greed and corruption, assume the proportions of a moral attrition which, if unchecked, saps the moral authority of the monarchy as an institution. There is, in such a circumstance, little room for levity but given that tales of ministerial corruption and incompetence are, almost permanently, rife in Oman and beyond, the following can be seen as a warning as to just how corrosive the situation can become. In the mid-1990s, following a request from Washington, Sultan Qaboos permitted the opening at Muscat of an Israeli Trade Office. Its staff were not given diplomatic status and were, accordingly, not necessarily invited, as of rote, to State receptions. It was a development, of course, which received a very frosty reception in many other parts of the Arab Islamic world.

In Colonel Gadaffi's Libya, however, it was turned into a joke that did the rounds of all the Arab capitals. It was a joke based not only on Qaboos's limited hospitality to the Zionist state but on Oman's increasingly difficult financial situation. Addressing a huge crowd on the outskirts of his capital, Tripoli, the Colonel refers to the Arab failure to secure a military victory over Israel:

> Let us fool ourselves no longer. Given that Israel will always have the help of America, we will never defeat them by a force of arms. We must consider other means. I hear that Sultan Qaboos of Oman has allowed the Israelis to open an office in Muscat. All that we have to do is to get him to persuade his new friends to have a few Omani Ministers in the Israeli cabinet. The Zionist Government will then be bankrupt within a year!

Laughter is a potent force but one which, all too quickly, can lead to ridicule, a climate laced with poison which, as some of the grimmest pages of history show, has led to violent, bloody revolution. Salacious gossip, which a disheartened people were all too ready to believe, however improbable, served as curtain-raiser to the French Revolution in 1789 and the Russian Revolution of 1917. In the case of the former, the gossip of the day centred on the principal characters in the monarchy and included rumours that the King ignored his Queen, was having an adulterous affair with three sisters and that Marie Antoinette was, at one and the same time, a nymphomaniac given to somewhat exotic tastes in sexual matters, a lesbian and had given birth to illegitimate children, none of which was true. In fact, historians have now established that the King's abiding passion was hunting while the Queen was reserved, prudish even, indeed far more so than the great majority of her husband's subjects. In the case of the latter, such unfounded rumour led not just to revolution but also to a fearful, despicable act of regicide, when the principal members of the Romanov dynasty were brutally murdered in a cellar.

Marx, Engels and Lenin may well have written the script for

revolution, but it was insinuation, innuendo and salacious gossip which undermined Tsar Nicholas II's moral authority. Gossip is an insidious alchemy, one with the ultimate power to destroy, for as the philosopher Bertrand Russell so wryly observed, 'No one gossips about other people's secret virtues.' And that earlier man of keen intellect and letters, Thomas Carlyle, wrote that history is 'a distillation of rumour' and that the French monarchy was drowned in a 'torrent of French speech'. An ominous warning indeed from the dark corridors of the past as to what can come to pass when gossip is taken as hard fact.

And there is a certain sad irony that, as this book is being written, HRH Prince Charles, Prince of Wales, is on an official visit to Oman while at home, rumour and speculation of a sexual nature swirl around him personally and his Royal Household, salacious gossip from the most unpromising, uninspiring origins and which is quite untrue. The danger to both Sultan and Prince is not the truth or otherwise of assumptions based on prurient speculation but in the readiness of the public to believe them and, in repeating them ad nauseam, adding to their currency. This can only lead to an undermining of the moral authority inherent in the monarchical system and which, with a sickening speed, can, in turn, have a terminal, corrosive effect upon the institution's very foundations.

What, however, is true is the Arab acceptance, and tolerance in others, of male love. While Islam does not condone homosexuality, it is a common practice throughout the Arab Islamic world and so long as one is discreet in its application public condemnation is indeed rare. It is an acceptance of the human condition which, among those who are so orientated, represents a tolerant social climate in which to live and in such a crucially important consideration Arab society has to be given the credit of its quality of humanity, on practising a civilised approach that can only come from a nature of sophistication with which, even now, the Western world, for all its much-vaunted liberalism and its freedoms, is still unable to come to terms. It only becomes a danger, a threat to the established order, when such an essentially private matter becomes the currency of gossip, of menace by stealth. Nonetheless, the prevalence of homosexuality in the Arab world has been an attraction for many a figure, some legendary, others more obscure. Among the former are, of course, Colonel T.E. Lawrence and Bertram Thomas, with a cast-list of others who, in basking in such acceptance and tolerance, have found their own, special place in the sun. Some have made their way to Arabia Felix by instinct, others spurred by reputation, a good example of which is the celebrated poem by C.P. Cavafy, with the title 'One of Their Gods':

> When one of them was passing through the market
> Of Seleukia, about the hour of evenfall,
> Like a tall, a beautiful, a perfect youth,
> With the joy of incorruptibility in his eyes,
> With his black and perfumed hair,
> The passers-by would look at him,
> And one would ask another if he knew him,
> And if he was a Greek, a Syrian, or a stranger. But a few
> Who observed with greater attention
> Would understand and draw aside;
> And while he disappeared under the arcades,
> In the shadows and in the lights of evening,
> Going towards the quarter which at night only
> Lives, with orgies and debauchery,
> And every kind of drunkenness and lust,
> They would wonder which it could be of Them,
> And for what disreputable sensuality
> He had come down to the streets of Seleukia
> From those Majestical All-holy Mansions.

So the gossip and the rumour visited upon one of the world's last Sultans has to be weighed in context. And if it is true, has it adversely affected the governance of the land over which he rules so absolutely? Hardly, for Oman today, in a notoriously difficult area of the world to govern, which is torn apart by frictions of a particularly savage and intractable kind, represents a land well ruled, and, for all that it falls prey to, such as being the subject of so much greed and self-interest, an admirable, tolerant and peaceful state. On all available evidence it would seem that the human condition once so famously described as 'the love that dare not speak its name' is, today, quite unable to keep its mouth shut. Yet, in Oman at least, a long period of silence on the subject would, indeed, be most welcome.

Chapter 7

IN EXILE AT HOME

With his year's tour of duty with the roistering Cameronians in Germany at an end, Qaboos Al Said returned to England, where those overseeing the young Arab Prince's time away from his cloistered existence in his father's far-off palace decreed that time spent observing the very English mysteries of local government – the obscurities of sanitation in the Shires, the importance of what the English Poet Laureate Sir John Betjeman termed 'proper drains', and the collecting of the dog tax – could be put to good use once he returned home, although to what use the compilation of an electoral roll could be put was somewhat less than obvious. Nonetheless, this year-long 'work experience' was to be spent with local authorities responsible for both urban and rural councils and took place in the counties of Bedfordshire and Warwickshire which, being landlocked areas, had very little in common with any matters of local administration over which Qaboos might, one day, be expected to preside. But, as he had during his Sandhurst days, and to a somewhat lesser extent whilst on secondment with the Cameronians at Minden, in what was then the German Federal Republic, he quickly demonstrated a deft ability to extract the maximum amount of knowledge from what appeared, superficially at least, to be of very limited promise in terms of expertise needed by a Middle Eastern ruler-in-waiting. However, there are those who, today, credit the successful operation of local councils in Oman to the Sultan's days studying the workings of local government in the English Midlands.

In terms both concise and direct, his father, Sultan Said, sent word to the British authorities that in his very considerable opinion his son had had a more than adequate exposure to the attractions, and the distractions, of the Western world. The time was being characterised, in Britain at least, as the 'Swinging Sixties', an alarming description to fall on the ears of a very conservative patriarchal figure, one steeped in the dignified and courtly manners of a hereditary Royal Arab ruler. It was a shrewd assessment that 'enough' is, as ever, 'enough', and plans were promptly made for the return of Qaboos to his father's desert realm with, as he now saw it, social restrictions that would weigh heavily on his young shoulders and sap his morale. While recognising, as he remarked to those around him in England, that the country had for so long controlled the destiny of his own, not always for the good, he had, by 1963, come to both understand and appreciate the liberating aspects of life in Britain, swinging or otherwise. Indeed, Qaboos is now known, even given the restrictions imposed on him during his Suffolk village days by Lorna Romans, not to have squandered the opportunity to sample at least some of the pleasures and delights available to him in Felsham village and, later, on visits to London. According to one who knew him well, both in Suffolk and London, 'He very quickly cultivated a taste for Western-inspired art and music, an appreciation which became one of his most impressive characteristics. As the time for his return to Muscat and Oman loomed ever closer he became quite despondent and it was obvious that it was going to be very much a reverse culture shock.'

But there was to be one further experience for him prior to returning home to the will of his father. The Foreign Office proposed that he should embark upon a modern-day version of the Victorian 'Grand Tour', as a sort of 'finishing off' to his years away, and which would give him a broader view of Europe than that provided by Britain and Germany. It was an inspired move, one which, to Qaboos's surprise, met with the sanction of his father who, apart from his youthful time at school in India and the occasional visit to England, had travelled very little. Qaboos's final port of call, which set his feet once more on the soil of Arabia, was the British Colony of Aden. He was flown home by the Royal Air Force and accorded special treatment in the great port city, Britain's sole colonial toe-hold on the Arabian peninsula. Upon being received at Government House by the British Governor of the day, and in reply to the question as to what he thought of the city, the young Prince replied, 'If, in ten years' time, Muscat is half as beautiful as Aden is today, I will be well pleased,' an early indication of the aesthetic sense developing with him. As an interesting aside to history, today Muscat is one of the cleanest, most attractive places on the planet, while Aden, as a consequence of some 35 years of neglect and mismanagement, has been knocked back into a city from the pre-industrial age.

The day of Qaboos's return finally dawned and, just as 1964 drew to a close, the Royal Air Force deposited him at its small base just outside Salalah town. Once back inside the walls of his father's palace, the former regime was reinstated. Isolated once more from the world he had so recently been a part of and again being taught the spiritual imperatives of the Koran by an Omani religious scholar, he quickly began to pine for the world he had left behind, the sole relief being visits from his mother bearing the latest issues of *The Times* to arrive in the country. Such limited activities did little to occupy his newly acquired social appetites and gave him few opportunities to exercise his new intellectual faculties, and his frustration began to grow. However, help was at hand, although the long-term implications of the strategy recommended to Sultan Said, designed to ease his son's mounting frustrations, were, in the event, to have the direst of consequences for this long and loyal friend of Britain. The burden of the recommendation from his British advisers was that Qaboos should be allowed to receive a small number of carefully chosen visitors, principally British, who, on the surface of things, would generally meet with the Omani ruler's approval.

So the tea and bridge parties began. One of those invited to Al Hisn to take tea with the young Prince was one Timothy Landon, who had studied at the Royal Military Academy at Sandhurst at the same time as Qaboos. Now, however, he was in Muscat and Oman as a seconded officer on the staff of the Sultan's Armed Forces, working as a Desert Intelligence Officer. Following his recall to London, and a crash-course in intelligence work, he returned to Muscat and Oman in 1967. The British then put his name forward to Sultan Said for the post of Senior Intelligence Officer in that part of his Armed Forces stationed in Dhofar. The plan and the plot had been laid, one that was, for the Sultan, a trap from which he would, in the sad and melancholy event, be quite unable to escape.

In any event, from that time onwards Timothy Landon's visits to the palace to sit with Qaboos became frequent, visits which took place with the Sultan's prior knowledge and consent. Or at least most of them. What Sultan Said most certainly did not have knowledge of was the subject of conversation which Landon eventually raised with his son – or, at the very least, did not become aware until it was much too late. In effect, the warning shots across the metaphorical bows of Arabia's last 'Grand Old Man' were well concealed and thus muted to a devious silence. But shots of a very different kind were, all too soon, to be fired, which echoed not just within the Sultan's palace walls and around Muscat and Oman but throughout the wider Middle East and, indeed, led, in the event, to the cocking of a very alert ear in far-off Whitehall, the nerve centre of Britain's governance.

The opening shots in what became known, as we have already seen, as the Dhofar War were fired in April 1963, during an armed attack on oil-exploration vehicles in the desert, although hostilities had been heralded as early as 1962 with small-scale acts of sabotage at the Royal Air Force base on Salalah's outskirts. In a curious twist of fate, the man who tentatively, and with much stealth, ignited the flame of armed insurrection had, prior to 1962, been employed within the grounds of Sultan Said's Al Hisn palace but had incurred his Royal master's displeasure and was consequently dismissed. Mussalim bin Nufl was not a man to nurse a grudge lightly and, following the attack on the oil company vehicles, he fled to neighbouring Saudi Arabia, taking about 30 other malcontents with him. Once in the Saudi Kingdom, he made contact and common cause – the overthrow of the Royal House of Al Said – with Sultan Said's former foe, that 'standard-bearer' of Imamate rule, Ghalib Al Hinai.

Backed, as ever, by substantial Saudi funds, this disparate band of revolutionaries, now joined by an assorted crew of dissident Dhofaris, travelled to the Iraqi capital, Baghdad, a city then, as now, in feverish thrall to Arab nationalism. Following military training at a secret army base outside Basra, which provided a special emphasis on sabotage and other guerrilla-style strategies, and, with assurances of yet further Saudi financial aid, the group, now under Nufl's leadership, clandestinely crossed the Saudi border into Dhofar province, bent on unleashing renewed attacks of sabotage and with them, a full-blown guerrilla-style war. The time was the summer of 1964 and, although it was far from being clear at the time, the days of Muscat and Oman were now numbered. Indeed, the early days of the Dhofar War can now be regarded not so much as the end of the beginning but the beginning of the end, the end for a unique land, the delight of the curious and those who loved the unusual and noble, who preferred the black-skinned tents of the Bedouin to the sweep of a triple-lane motorway, a Beau Geste fort in a saffron dusk to the skyscraper office-block blinking harshly in the scorching Arabian sun. And, of course, it marked the beginning of the end for Sultan Said and the courtly Arab courtesies he so epitomised, with their attendant allegiances and code of conduct with which he was so honourably, and justly, associated. The 'new dawn' for old Muscat and Oman was, indeed, well and truly on its way.

For Qaboos, of course, back within the walls of Al Hisn, but now in his own quarters, a small house within the grounds of the palace, such dramatic events reached him second-hand, if at all. His father continued to decline to discuss matters of State with his son and heir, even though, following his Sandhurst graduation, Qaboos had begun to develop his own opinions on the way ahead for the dynasty and the land they ruled so absolutely, opinions from which he increasingly felt his besieged father could benefit. But to no avail, and all the while Qaboos's sense of frustration, his quiet raging, intensified. It was all most unsatisfactory and something, indeed, had eventually to give.

Meanwhile his father, and then only when prevailed upon by his military advisers, made what can only be described as the most desultory moves for war believing that punitive measures against the communities from which some of the rebels came would serve as an ample deterrent. They didn't and, as was to be expected, served only to increase a sense of personal hostility to the Sultan. As the 1960s approached their end, it was becoming increasingly apparent that what was now assuming the proportions of a particularly bloody conflict, being conducted along that most pernicious of tactical lines, hit-and-run guerrilla raids and attacks, would only be met by the Armed Forces of Muscat and Oman being given the tools to do the job. This would involve expensive arms purchases, expenditure Sultan Said was particularly loath to incur, allied to a departure from the draconian measures taken against so many communities in Dhofar from which rebels had either come or which were believed to have given them support and sustenance. What, of course, such measures had achieved was the very opposite from that intended by the Sultan. Instead of pacifying any resentment they may have held for the Sultan and, via such a process, ceasing any support or succour they may have been giving to the rebels, it drove them, quite literally, into their welcoming arms.

In the harsh language of armed conflict, the war was being lost and those around the Sultan knew it. Still ensconced within his own quarters in the grounds of Al Hisn Palace, Qaboos's second-hand accounts of the rise and fall of the tide of war were relayed to him by a coterie of those sanctioned by his father to call on his son, none of whom did he regard as a particularly close friend. Very few Omanis were among them, a situation which, combined with his total ignorance of Muscat and Oman beyond Dhofar, only served to compound his sense of isolation and helplessness. As one senior British official who met him during the late 1960s commented:

> He seemed at one particularly low point to 'cut off' entirely, appearing quite unable to concentrate and giving an alarming picture of dejection. His large, almost luminous eyes betrayed his loneliness and his general air of ineffectuality. It was all very worrying.

And worrying in Whitehall they were indeed, with some voicing uncertainty that, despite such a promising period in Europe, Qaboos might prove to be a far from ideal candidate for the throne of Muscat and Oman. By this time, of course, oil revenues had begun to pour into the Sultan's coffers and then, as now, it was the presence in financially viable quantities of the black, viscous commodity that was concentrating minds in foreign capitals with such intensity. It was the strategic nature of the future stability of the country which was seen as Britain's principal, if not its sole, concern as the 1960s drew to a close. In short, Britain's long historical connection with Muscat and Oman was now regarded as being increasingly under threat, an ever-present danger given that the British Government had earlier confirmed that it would withdraw both politically and militarily from the Persian Gulf by 1971. This was a strategic decision which, whilst principally economic, had at its base an increasing reluctance by London to be seen to be supporting illiberal regimes, a pivotal consideration which has an especially woeful echo in the steps being taken by the United States to slowly but surely decrease its long-held links with the Royal Saudi Government, one of the last autocratic states in existence. However, Qaboos, who had told one of those who called upon him that the 1960s had been 'his time', now saw that the coming of the new decade would determine the long-term future of the country he was born to rule and that time was short if that future was to be one of progress and development. And then, quite suddenly, he began to emerge from his lethargy, began, in fact, to talk with his guests about his growing alarm at what was happening in Muscat and Oman and his sense of helplessness as he watched the military situation deteriorating with such fearful speed. Indeed, so outspoken did he suddenly become in his disquiet with the way his father was conducting the war that he had to be warned that his candour was gaining an ever-wider currency beyond the walls of his father's palace, a development which held the possibility of a parental reprimand that would mean him being kept virtually incommunicado, shut off from all outside contact. It was a far from appealing prospect and, accordingly, his comments assumed a more muted, discreet air. But such a change of tack did not stop the

Sultan's son and heir from continuing to consider the future with the greatest of care.

Not that he was alone in pondering the future. For so many years before the oil began to flow, Sultan Said had been regarded, and described by the British in London and by the captains of the oil industry, in Oman's case those on the quarterdeck at Shell, as being full to the brim of 'patriarchal wisdom' and, at worst, an 'enlightened despot'. But all of this was about to change; indeed, plans were being made for more than a changing of the guard at Al Hisn Palace. And can there be a better way to start such a metamorphosis than to switch from such praise to describing the Sultan as a 'tyrannical anachronism'? But this was only just the beginning of a long and concentrated campaign of denigration, one designed not just comprehensively to discredit Oman's former ruler of 38 years but to recruit an equally comprehensive justification for his traitorous overthrow. Of even greater ambiguity were those who had sworn oaths of allegiance to Sultan Said, and served beneath his standard, the British military officers on loan from their units in England who were under contract to the ruler of Muscat and Oman. Men such as Colonel Hugh Oldman, a man given to somewhat more than pompous airs, who loaded his conversation with such admirable terms as 'honour', 'loyalty' and 'integrity'. As a contemporary recalls:

> He was the sort of chap who, if he came to dinner, made you feel slightly queasy, so much so that you felt it necessary to count the spoons after he had gone. Dr Johnson got it just about right when he wrote, 'Ah, patriotism. The very last refuge of the scoundrel!'

Such acerbic comment cannot be considered to be far off the mark when it is recorded that Oldman swore on his 'honour' that while he was in Salalah on the day of the coup he had been in complete ignorance of 'all that was afoot', and had thus been an 'unwitting witness' of the event itself.

Also among their number was the Desert Intelligence Officer, Timothy Landon, who now, at his political masters' bidding in

London, moved closer to the dispirited and isolated heir to the Omani throne, in his small house in the grounds of his father's palace, and began the slow, patient litany of what might just be possible with the aid of a little artful skulduggery. It is even more poignant given that, in Arab eyes, for a son to become party to the overthrow of his father is, indeed, the most cardinal sin. It was, however, the Sultan's Intelligence supremo, Malcolm Dennison, who had recommended that Landon be granted access to his son, purely for visits of a social nature. Landon's real purpose, though, was not to discuss the latest editorial in *The Times* or to play a rubber of bridge, but to preach the art of high treason. Just as with Oldman, however, Dennison went to his grave telling anyone who would listen that he had had 'nothing whatsoever' to do with the armed, forced overthrow of Britain's oldest and most reliable ally in the Arab Islamic world.

The actual catalyst for the coup had two quite separate aspects. On the night of 11 June 1970, almost five years to the very day after the outbreak of serious hostilities in Dhofar, a group of guerrilla fighters mounted a grenade and machine-gun attack on a military outpost close to Izki, which was itself disturbingly close to an oil pipeline running through the nearby desert. While the attack failed, with the soldiers of the Sultan's Armed Forces capturing all of the rebels, the audacious nature of the attack sent shock waves throughout the country's establishment. There was even greater alarm when the defenders of Izki reported the capture of documents being carried by the rebels which revealed that the group had connections with the Dhofar Popular Front, which was known to have the support of the USSR. Only one conclusion could be drawn in the febrile imagination of those on the ground in Oman and in London; the writing may not have been actually on the wall, but it was most decidedly written in the sand: the Communists were coming! The second aspect of the catalyst for a move against Sultan Said was a change of government in London. On 18 June 1970, the citizens of the United Kingdom went to the polls in a General Election and, in the face of all expectations, dismissed Harold Wilson's Labour Government from office, replacing it with the Conservatives, led by Edward Heath. Heath was a man with a mission, to get his country into the European Union (or the Common Market, as it was then known). He knew little of the intricacies of Middle Eastern power blocs and had little appetite to learn or, indeed, for Britain to remain a Middle Eastern colonial, military power. Even before the General Election, he had made it clear that, should the Conservatives win, he had no intention of reversing Labour's decision to withdraw from its political and military commitments in the Gulf by 1971. In short, Edward Heath regarded Britain's continuing involvement in the Middle East as very much a legacy of Empire. As one former member of his Government recalls, 'He was bored with the very notion of our entanglement with the Arab world, with its constant round of accusations, counter-accusations and bitter recriminations all round. He just wanted out.' Consequently, Britain's new Prime Minister saw his country's long and troubled involvement with the Middle East as one which trespassed upon its ambition to become a fully participating member of the new Europe. Given such a trenchant view, when, during the first three weeks of his premiership, the plan for a palace coup in Muscat and Oman was put to him by the Foreign and Commonwealth Office, with the basics of such a strategy having been recommended by a small group within Britain's Military Intelligence establishment, Heath, having enquired as to its chances of success, for all practical purposes just 'nodded' the plan through.

But first the press was called upon to set the scene, both at home and abroad. At the end of June, Iranian newspapers began references to 'an impending *coup d'état*', and with commendable detail reported that it was being organised by a 'Colonel Hugh Oldman', Sultan Said's British military Adviser, who was both duty- and honour-bound by his oath of office to protect the ruler of Muscat and Oman. On 8 July, it was the turn of Qaboos's favourite newspaper, *The Times*, which commented that the Sultan of Muscat and Oman had to be got rid of. And then on 18 July, just five days before the actual coup, *The Economist* declared the hour for the 'eccentric' Sultan's departure had arrived. And with his son waiting in his quarters, in a high state of nervous anxiety but with Timothy Landon by his side for just a little more than to boost Qaboos's badly besieged morale, the time had indeed come. For Sultan Said bin

Taimour of Muscat and Oman the hour of his extremis was upon him. History with an indelible blemish was about to be perpetrated.

The afternoon of 23 July 1970 was hot and humid. The annual Khareef, a south-western monsoon responsible for the lushness of much of Dhofar province, ruled the atmosphere, bringing with it not only short, sharp bursts of torrential rain but mountain-hugging mist, all of which, according to at least one contemporary observer, 'gave the whole place a particularly depressing, ominous air'. Inside the walls of Al Hisn Palace, Sultan Said had been fractious all morning, 'jumpy' in fact, almost as if he had a premonition that all was not well, that there were, perhaps, forces afoot which bore him ill will.

Unexpected callers are, in fact and fiction, so often associated with the arrival of unwelcome news, and the arrival at the palace gates of a local man, delegated by British officers to demand that the Sultan step aside for his son, proved to be no exception. Sheikh Braik bin Hamid Al Ghafri was the son of the Wali of Dhofar, the provincial governor. As such, he was a man of considerable public standing. He had been well chosen, being known particularly as a man of considerable personal courage. He was personally known to the Sultan but to arrive uninvited and demanding to see his monarch immediately was regarded very much as an unwarranted intrusion. Nonetheless, he was escorted to the Sultan's private apartments in the belief that whatever matter had led him to present himself in such a manner had to be important. Once in the Sultan's presence, Braik asked for his monarch's immediate abdication. In a state of fury, Sultan Said called upon his loyal Khadeem, who attempted to eject Sheikh Braik from the Sultan's presence. The precise sequence of events is somewhat unclear but what is beyond doubt is that the Sultan drew his gun and opened fire, hitting Sheikh Braik in the stomach. The rest of the drama was carried out in the very best tradition of the cinema. Hearing gunfire, a small group of men who had accompanied the Sheikh to the palace burst into the Sultan's apartments to pursue the ruler of Muscat and Oman, still accompanied by some of his Khadeem, down secret tunnels and passageways. Two of the Khadeem were covering their master's retreat with sporadic gunfire. The chase lasted a full hour and a half and at the end of this struggle for power two lay dead: a member of the Khadeem and one of Sheikh Braik's men. The Sultan had, himself, sustained four wounds, one of which was self-inflicted when he accidentally discharged his own revolver into his right foot. Braik was by now losing blood from the wound to his stomach, and even though the Sultan was seriously in need of immediate medical attention, he still refused to surrender.

To those waiting for news, including Qaboos and Landon, still inside Qaboos's quarters within the palace grounds, it was now alarmingly clear that things were far from going to plan. When the news was relayed to British officers waiting beyond the walls of the palace, the decision was taken to send one of their number, the popular and fearless Major 'Spike' Powell, who was known and liked by the Sultan, to enter Al Hisn to plead with the Omani monarch to surrender.

Inside the palace scenes of wholesale chaos continued to reign, but it was becoming increasingly clear that the end was indeed near. Nonetheless, and as a last desperate measure, the Sultan ordered one of his loyal Khadeem to send an urgent message to Colonel Hugh Oldman, his Defence Secretary, for help but help came there none. London had insisted that the Sultan's British officers should 'do a Nelson' (turn a blind eye) to any appeals for help from the palace. As night fell, Major Powell arrived at Al Hisn. The Sultan agreed immediately to see him and, having spoken with him for a short while, saw the impossible situation he was in and bowed to what was, by now, the inevitable. In accepting Powell's entreaties to resist no further, the Sultan of Muscat and Oman realised that both he and his uninvited caller of earlier that day, Sheikh Braik, both stood in need of medical attention and the sooner they received it the better. But Oman's 13th ruler in the Al Busaid dynasty had one final order. He sent word to those waiting that he would surrender only to a British officer, a demand that demonstrated his deft sense of history and political judgement. In effect, Sultan Said was determined that responsibility would be placed where it belonged for what had come to pass that day in Salalah. As a member of Oman's ruling family has commented, 'Said surrendered to those who had turned out to be the enemy. Which is what is done, isn't it? You surrender to whoever defeated you. It was, to Said, as simple as that.' The doubtful, and dubious, 'honour' of accepting the surrender of Sultan Said fell to Lieutenant-Colonel Edward Turnhill of the Sultan's Desert Regiment, who arrived at the palace later that evening. It also fell to him to present two documents prepared by British officers, an instrument of abdication, one in Arabic, the other in English. After the melancholy business was done, the now former Sultan of Muscat and Oman, together with the wounded Sheikh Braik, were taken the short distance by car to the Royal Air Force base outside Salalah town and put aboard a Britannia aircraft. The plane was just about to depart for Bahrain, where they were to receive medical attention, when Said told his Private Secretary, the affable Jim Maclean, who had decided to join his Royal master on his long and lonely flight into exile, that he had signed only the instrument of abdication in English; the Arabic version remained without his signature. As Maclean was to comment later, 'He should have remained silent.' A scene straight out of the Keystone Cops then ensued. A frantic dash was made back to the palace, where an equally frantic search eventually uncovered the Arabic copy, which was then rushed back to the waiting aircraft and, at the last, signed by the former Sultan. Maclean, formerly Private Secretary to Lord Louis Mountbatten, an uncle of Queen Elizabeth and the last British Viceroy in India, was what is usually referred to as a member of the 'Old School', espousing virtues of a nobler age, and, true to character, could not bear the thought of his Sultan flying out of his realm alone and under cover of darkness. He never returned to Oman and, in later life, in his Edinburgh home, with his beloved Boxer dogs by his side, said that he had, indeed, been briefed at the very last moment of the coup, but was powerless to stop it. He died a sad and lonely man in the late 1980s and on receiving news of his death Qaboos asked that his diaries be destroyed – not the last time that Oman's monarch was to make such a demand when the matter of personal diaries of those who had served his father arose.

Following medical treatment, Sheikh Braik returned to Oman but the former Sultan, Said, was flown on RAF Britannia Flight 6393 to the base at Brize Norton in Oxfordshire, from where he was taken by road to the Royal Air Force Hospital at Wroughton, in Wiltshire.

Upon his arrival at Brize Norton he had been met by a Foreign Office official who conveyed a short, oral message from the Secretary of State for Foreign and Commonwealth Affairs. Following his recovery he was taken to his place of exile, the Dorchester Hotel, in London's Park Lane. Across the way, Foreign Office functionaries had been busy, letting it be known, 'off the record, of course', that Britain had no intention of 'embarrassing Qaboos' by giving him any credit whatsoever for his father's armed overthrow. In the event, father and son were never to meet again. Apart from short, carefully monitored visits with old friends in Britain, and a planned trip to the United States with a couple of 'minders' in tow (which was curtailed when, during the Atlantic crossing, an ultimately fatal heart attack took place on the staircase of the liner), Sultan Said bin Taimour remained in his suite of rooms at the Dorchester until his death on 19 October 1972. When the news of his death was relayed to Muscat, there was an embarrassed silence. It was only in the wake of an ultimatum by London stating that unless immediate and specific instructions were received as to Qaboos's wishes for his father's burial a unilateral decision would be taken, that word came that he could be buried in the very first Islamic cemetery to be established in Britain, at Brookwood, in Surrey. His resting place is, however, unmarked and while this is not uncommon in the case of the interment of Muslims, there are many who believe that this is a clear indication that, even in death, Sultan Said bin Taimour Al Said is considered too vital a witness to so much of Oman's past, particularly its long entanglement with Britain.

Muscat and Oman, for richer, for poorer, for better or worse, now had a new Sultan and the world of the Omani was set to change, for ever. Those British officers who had sworn fidelity to Sultan Said now sprang forward and put their signature to an identical oath of loyalty to his son. In Muscat, the Managing Director of Petroleum Development Oman (PDO, the State oil and gas company) issued a statement in which he applauded 'this historic event'. It was dated 1 August 1970, the third anniversary of another occasion, perhaps no less historic: the departure of the very first tanker loaded with Omani oil. Whether the irony of this was noted by Oman's new ruler is not known, but there can be little doubt that even if he had, he would have cared little. His hour had come and there was much for the world's newest, 29-year-old ruler to do. And, as the country's 14th Sultan, he set to with a will to do it.

The State was renamed the Sultanate of Oman, over which would fly a new flag displaying the red, white and green Omani tricolour and that cultural icon of Omani life, the khunjar, the curved dagger. And, abandoning the title held by his father of 'His Highness', Qaboos let it be known throughout the councils of the world that, henceforth, he would be styled as 'His Majesty Sultan Qaboos bin Said Al Said'. A new day had most certainly dawned. Oman's 'renaissance' was most decidedly on its life-changing way and for the country he now ruled so absolutely nothing would, or indeed could, be quite the same ever again.

Chapter 8

CEMENTING OF TIES

As the dawn of a new age broke over Oman, with what appeared to be limitless amounts of cash washing across the landscape from shining shore to shining shore, the country's new Sultan was the very first of his line to determine that the urgent need for development would be met, without delay. Of course, and of crucial importance, he was also Oman's first leader who had the tools – funds virtually without limit – to do the job. And Qaboos set to with a truly astonishing will. While the guerrilla war in the south of his realm continued to be an expensive distraction, consuming an inordinate amount of his Government's annual budget, the task of bringing to his subjects schools, hospitals, roads and a whole life-enhancing raft of communications, took principal pride of place in the endeavours of his Government. Indeed, the rapid development of the Sultanate of Oman, from the very opening moments of Qaboos's rule, is very much a success story without parallel and one for which he, personally, has to be given unstinting credit. It is all the more remarkable given that, from the very minute that Timothy Landon brought him the news of the surrender of his father, as he waited with mounting anxiety in his quarters within the grounds of Al Hisn Palace, he, according to at least one of the senior British personnel there at such an historic moment in the fortunes of Oman, 'lacked, to an almost frightening degree, self-confidence. Indeed, his lack of experience intimidated him greatly. He was nervous, ill prepared and, at first, unwilling to adopt a firm lead in directing the governance of the country he had been handed on a plate.' And whatever criticism may be directed at Landon for his subsequent rise to riches of a quite staggering degree, via his personal relationship with Qaboos, there can be no doubt whatsoever that, at such a critical time, he steadied the nerve of Oman's 14th Sultan and gave him confidence to assume his many and varied duties with a sustained quality of resolve which, in the not inconsiderable event, both consolidated his position on the throne and ensured his eventual grip on power, so necessary in a land that his Royal predecessors had not always found easy to govern.

But just as his father had grappled for decades with a severe shortage of cash with which to operate the Government of Muscat and Oman and whilst being, from the time oil revenues began to flow into his State Treasury, of good intent to, in his own time, develop the country, to bring it into the modern world, Qaboos quickly came to realise, just as his father had feared, that sudden wealth also brought with it the most unwelcome attention of those who, quite literally, sought to relieve the country of considerable amounts of its new-found wealth. The former Senior Adviser well remembers the concern Qaboos exercised about such an inevitability:

> To his credit those who came bearing what can, at best, be described as schemes of grandeur and, quite frankly, crackpot designs for 'new' industries, which were, at worst, designs for a quick and easy route to becoming rich, were promptly dismissed by the Sultan, with their proposers being sent packing. In such a regard he demonstrated an enviable shrewdness but what proved to be of greater difficulty was corruption within his own immediate team. One of the earliest occasions that I can recall of His Majesty going on the record about the extent of corruption in the Sultanate, and of the measures he intended to take to put

matters to rights, came in either late 1984 or early 1985 when he granted an interview to *South* magazine's Andrew Graham-Youlle, who was at the time its Editor. Graham-Youlle, an Argentinian, was a former BBC Correspondent and Editor of the *Buenos Aires Herald,* in short a journalist of consistent quality who always did his homework well before any interview. In the event, and with commendable candour, with poor old Tony Ashworth quietly wetting himself in the corner, the Sultan proved only too ready to acknowledge that he, and the country, had a problem with corruption and a significant one at that. Indeed, he went into some detail, confirming that it extended up to Cabinet Ministerial level. But he did not stop there, further confirming that he had every intention to institute a crackdown by way of a Commission of Inquiry which would have sweeping powers to demand, seize even, documents, records, bank statements and the like. It all sounded most impressive but, alas, never came to pass. Some Ministers were sacked, most memorably his Minister of Diwan of Royal Court, when the levels of 'take' became, quite simply, impossible to cover up, but in the main, things were just left to slide. It really was a quite terrible shame.

The Graham-Youlle interview was notable for quite another reason: His Majesty's response to questions on the eventual establishment in the Sultanate of a form of democratic process. By now, poor old Tony was on his knees, nibbling at the Persian rug through a mouthful of foam. Well, as for this business of democracy and voting, why, intoned His Majesty, people in some of the districts known to him barely had time to do anything else, since they were always having some bloody ballot or other, about the siting of bus stops, wadi crossings and the like. He was, by all accounts, pretty damn irritable by this stage, doubtless fingering the pearl-handled revolver in a meaningful manner, and continued by waxing angrily, but, as always, most eloquently, about the difficulties of governing a country which insisted on backing into the future and waving a red flag in the face of any kind of social or political progress. How very different things were then! But the question of corruption, of course, remained, both the home-grown variety and the imported kind. That it was not curbed, still has not been curbed, is an error for which the country continues to pay a very high price indeed. It really is the greatest pity and the greatest shame. Many who knew the Sultan in his early years of power reckoned that John F. Kennedy's description of himself as 'an idealist without illusions' also summed up Oman's youthful leader really rather well. It is, therefore, doubly sad that he should now, in the opinion of far too many of his own people, have become an illusionist without ideals.

It was a development concept that had as its inspiration an ideal, and a laudable one at that, but one which led not just to damaging allegations of nepotism and corruption at the highest levels of the British establishment but also, in the words of an observer of Anglo–Omani relations, a one-time senior diplomat, 'to light being shone in that darkest of corners, the relationship between His Majesty Sultan Qaboos and certain elements in the Conservative Party and particularly Margaret Thatcher during her time as Prime Minister'. The case became known as the 'Cementation Affair' and at one stage could so easily have led to the downfall of Mrs Thatcher, whose links with big business so disturbed and, indeed, appalled so many of the traditionalists within her own party and particularly so when such a relationship involved the many and varied dealings of her only son, Mark.

The genesis of the notorious university project began with a distinguished Omani of Zanzibari origin, Sheikh Amor Ali Al Marhubi, a graduate of Oxford University and a former Director of Education in the Government of Zanzibar. A year after the palace coup which brought Qaboos to power, the Sheikh had answered the new Omani leader's call for expatriate Omanis to return home and assist him in the task of building the nation. Appointed as an Adviser to the Sultan on the establishment of scholastic and academic institutions, the Sheikh made recommendation in early

1980 for the creation of a university. The Sultan did not immediately respond favourably to such an idea, demonstrating in such a regard the conservative instincts of his father, who had commented to a British Secretary of State, Julian Amery, when being urged to establish schools in the country, 'Look what happened to the British in India. You educated the people and then they threw you out!' Such a guarded response prompted the Sheikh to persuade Qaboos along the lines that if Omani students were sent overseas for higher education they would be exposed to 'foreign and democratic ideas'. So, in the event, sanction was given by Oman's new and modernising Sultan for such a concept to be investigated. That justifiably proud flag-bearer of British culture and academic excellence, the British Council, was promptly recruited to Sheikh Amor's banner, dispatching him to Britain to hold talks with his contacts at his old university, Oxford, and to meet with a whole range of individuals and organisations well placed to advise on the establishment of an institution of higher learning. By National Day, 18 November, Qaboos's birthday, of that very same year, 1980, the Sultan needed no further persuasion and in his address to the nation, an annual centrepiece of the celebrations, announced formally his plans for the establishment of a university.

It was, of course, a hugely ambitious project and there were, from the very outset, complications of a particularly daunting nature, not least of which was the absence of a budget or, indeed, any financial provision for the funding of such a hugely expensive project in the current five-year plan.

A further complication quickly arose with the involvement of two Arab Advisers in the Ministry of Education, both of whom had been educated in the United States, who began to override the scheme which was, in character, anglicised, just as Sheikh Amor had intended and, what is more, had recommended to the Sultan. The two Advisers, however, preferred, not unnaturally given their own experience of academia, American-orientated ideas. It was a clash of cultural and academic processes which was somewhat alleviated when the Sheikh turned for assistance once more to the British Council, which, early in 1981, dispatched yet another Ministerial Adviser, recently appointed, to Britain to undertake a trawl for academics, a visit which was to have featured a meeting with Mrs Margaret Thatcher, herself an Oxford graduate. In the event, however, the meeting did not take place but, in the words of the former diplomat, it is important in the unravelling of the Cementation Affair because it is the very first evidence of a connection between the British Prime Minister of the day and Oman's university project, news of which 'most certainly led to a pricking up of the Thatcher ears'.

In Oman, the Education Ministry was wasting no time in pressing forward with the project, undeterred by an absence of funds, appointing a locally based Canadian consultancy to draw up design and construction proposals. It was now beyond doubt, Sultan Qaboos University was most decidedly on its way and, enter stage right, so was the Cementation Company and with it a most un-Parliamentary affair which was to bear its name. This well-established British construction firm had a presence in the Sultanate in the form of its association with a local company, SICO, one of whose backers was the country's Minister of Foreign Affairs, Yousef bin Alawi bin Abdullah. However, at the time of the mooting of the university project, Cementation had not been granted any contracts of significance in Oman for some years. The company was a wholly owned subsidiary of Britain's Trafalgar House concern, the Chairman of which was Nigel Broakes, from whom Sultan Qaboos had purchased his very first country property in England, Wargrave Manor, outside Henley-on-Thames, in Oxfordshire, for the then considerable sum of £800,000. It is also of no small interest that Broakes, together with Denis and Mark Thatcher, were guests of Landon, where they participated in his shooting parties, at Faccombe Manor, his home on the Berkshire/Hampshire borders. Not that such privileged associations had done much for the company at the time construction firms' appetites were being considerably whetted at the prospect of the university contract, as a Muscat 'insider' recalls:

> Actually, at the time Cementation was most definitely 'out in the cold', which makes what subsequently happened all the more interesting. British construction firms in the Sultanate

tended to be awarded contracts on what is best described as a rotating basis, which, again, makes Cementation's lack of work really rather curious. It is also of significance, given the Sultan's entrenched conservative views, allied to his private allegiance to the Conservative Party, that the company had by that time established very close links with the party, by way of the most generous financial contributions, and through such largesse, the Government of Margaret Thatcher. Now it so happens that her son, Mark, had done his accountancy training with Touche Ross, who were the accountants for Trafalgar House, which furnishes the initial link of the Thatcher connection to the Cementation Affair.

In April 1981, the British Prime Minister paid an official visit to Oman. On 23 April, in private conversation with the Sultan, she requested in the strongest possible terms that he personally grant an audience to Cementation representatives. Such an unprecedented, unconventional intervention was noted with concern by the then British Ambassador, Ivor Lucas, and indeed was featured by *The Times* in a special report on Oman in September of that same year. The following day, 24 April, Mark Thatcher flew into Oman by Gulf Air, which listed him as a 'CIP', a Commercially Important Passenger, on a flight designed to reach his mother, who was the Sultan's guest at his Salalah Palace, via the very first available domestic departure for the Dhofari capital. What is not known is if, during their very private tête-à-tête, the Prime Minister told the Sultan of Oman that her son, Mark, was on Cementation's payroll as a 'consultant', although there is no doubt that, subsequent to the meeting, he was made aware of such a fact.

Arrangements for Mark Thatcher's internal flight were made by Air Vice-Marshal Sir Erik Bennett, Commander of the Sultan's Air Force at the time. CSOAF, as he was known, was a loan service RAF officer whose Air Force career was, in the event, greatly enhanced by his Omani days and particularly so given that he became a very close confidant to the Sultan. But, as ever within the circles of a Royal Court, particularly one operated on medieval lines, jealousies quickly arose over the Irish bachelor's closeness to Qaboos, with such a personal relationship being fiercely resented by Brigadier Timothy Landon, who saw, with some considerable degree of justification, his premier role as confidant to the Sultan being usurped by what he on one occasion described as 'this Air Force upstart'. It was a situation that the Omani insider well remembers: 'Machinations of a Machiavellian character were then played out, machinations and manoeuvres that would have done well in a medieval court which, of course, the palace of Qaboos had come to resemble more and more.' It was a personal battle of wills that, for the time being at least, saw the Brigadier triumph over the Air Vice-Marshal, with the former's position at Court becoming more firmly entrenched than ever. This background, this sideshow to the Cementation Affair, was described at the time by the newly arrived Chief of the Defence Staff, Sir Timothy Creasey, as an arrangement that was 'fixed by Landon in order to ingratiate himself with Margaret Thatcher. Sucking up to Maggie was the order of the day.'

This is an interesting observation given what was later to ensue, Qaboos appealing to the British Prime Minister for Timothy Landon to be awarded a knighthood, which she subsequently recommended to Queen Elizabeth. However, given Landon's Canadian origins, it is regarded as being an honorary award and as such he is prevented from being known as 'Sir' Timothy Landon. Nonetheless, old hostilities die hard and, even today, Sir Erik and 'Sir' Timothy, with the former now in the ascendancy in the Sultan's affections, remain what can only be described as the best of enemies.

A meeting described by a senior Omani courtier as 'quiet' did take place between the Sultan and Cementation representatives, including Mark Thatcher, a meeting from which members of the British Embassy were excluded, much to the understandable dismay of Her Majesty's Ambassador, Ivor Lucas. The senior Omani courtier comments, 'Basically, His Majesty was responding to the somewhat persistent request of his guest, a lady Prime Minister, although he was to say later that he regarded such nepotism as most un-Western. He was, to speak the truth, upset by the whole episode.'

As events were to prove, the Omani leader was far from being alone in his disquiet. But for Cementation the deal was all but done.

Indeed, the company wasted no time whatsoever in pressing forward with the project, so confident was its management, given the British Prime Minister's intervention with the Sultan, even though, officially at least, the contract had still to be actually awarded. Shortly after Mrs Thatcher's return to London, the company's bankers, Morgan Grenfell, made an application to the Export Credits Guarantee Department (ECGD) for credit facilities to the sum of £124 million, which was promptly granted.

The next move came with a visit to Muscat by Cementation's Middle East Director, the Lebanese-born Jamil Amyuni who, without precedent for a visiting businessman, was granted an immediate audience with Oman's executive head of state. The company was now in a hurry and, considering themselves very much in the driving seat, appointed the architectural practice YRM International, doing so in the absence of any tendering procedures (which, for any Government-inspired projects in Oman, had always been a necessity) or, indeed, an approved budget.

In March 1982, Sultan Qaboos made a State visit to London, a feature of which was the announcement of the construction costs of the university, £215 million, as well as a further £85 million for the incorporation of a hospital in the overall project. On 17 March, Mrs Thatcher gave a luncheon at 10 Downing Street for her Royal guest. Among those attending were David Douglas-Home, son of the former Tory Prime Minister, Sir Alec Douglas-Home, from Morgan Grenfell; Brigadier Timothy Landon who, during the visit, had been granted his honorary knighthood; and Mark Thatcher. Questions, albeit muted at that stage, were immediately raised as to the precise nature of Mark Thatcher's presence at the Downing Street luncheon. When the Sultan's visit had started, Mark Thatcher had been abroad, playing in a charity golf tournament from which he abruptly withdrew, giving as a reason a 'State visit' back in London which required his presence. This, in itself, raised disturbing questions as to why the British Prime Minister's son had any legitimate cause to be involved with a State visit to Britain of a Middle Eastern potentate.

The Downing Street luncheon was not the only occasion of State at which Mrs Thatcher's son made an appearance. He was seen at a further reception for the Sultan in the company of Nigel Broakes of Trafalgar House, which, again, prompted questions to be asked as to what, precisely, was going on. Even Buckingham Palace was, in the event, drawn into the controversy, with a spokesman for the Royal Household confirming that it was without precedent for such a State visit to require the presence of one of the Prime Minister's offspring.

By this time, alarmed traditionalists, particularly patrician members within the Conservative Party, were beginning to openly question the 'merchant' nature of the Thatcher administration, judging, correctly enough, that such conduct could only bring harm to the party. And, sure enough, with Mark Thatcher now laying himself open to the charge that his mother's official position, Her Britannic Majesty's Prime Minister and First Lord of the Treasury, was being used for his personal financial gain, the collective eyes and ears of the press were increasingly turned towards the corridors of power and just who was on the predatory prowl down them.

It was an unwelcome distraction from a whole series of Government-sponsored initiatives that were to change the face of Britain and drew equally unwelcome public attention to the links the Conservative Party has always had with what is usually described as big business. Increasingly, questions were being raised as to the essentially mercantile instincts of Margaret Thatcher and the role she was prepared to allocate to her immediate family to pursue them. As a Tory grandee of the Thatcher years recalls:

> In the wake of her first visit as Prime Minister to Saudi Arabia she appeared hypnotised by the vast wealth of the oil-rich Arabs and, in some cases, resentful of the manner in which it had all so easily been acquired. I, personally, was told by a member of her entourage that no sooner had the plane carrying her home reached its cruising speed than she summoned one of her aides and asked, 'Just how have these perfectly ghastly people accumulated such wealth?', or words very much to that effect. There has never been any doubt in my own mind that, back home, she advised Mark, not noted for business acumen, to concentrate on doing

business with the Gulf Arabs, which, of course, is exactly what he did. It is also of interest to note the respective roles played in the Oman saga by members of her family. During her 1981 visit to the Sultanate she was accompanied by her husband, Denis, and their daughter, Carol, both of whom were included in the Prime Ministerial official party. However, and this is of particular interest, although her daughter had the role of Personal Assistant to her mother throughout the trip, Margaret paid Carol's air-fare which, given her official role as a PA, and as such listed as an official member of the Prime Minister's party, would not normally have been the case. It was as if there were private, non-governmental matters to be attended to in Oman to which Margaret did not want others to be privy. You will know, of course, of the Ambassador's disquiet at his exclusion and that of members of his staff from some of the discussions she held with His Majesty the Sultan. All most unconventional and, one has to say, disturbing, not the least unsavoury aspect of the whole affair being that it placed her host, His Majesty, a generous, courteous gentleman, in a particularly invidious position. All most unfortunate.

To any student of the Thatcher years there has always been a remarkable variance in the respective roles played by the Thatcher twins, a feature of her Downing Street years clearly identified by John Campbell, the biographer of Britain's first woman Prime Minister. Carol Thatcher has always taken an independent line, keeping herself purposely out of the constant glare of publicity, pursuing with not inconsiderable skill and professionalism her chosen career as a journalist, although she qualified as a solicitor. Her brother, Mark, however, attempted a variety of occupations, ranging from accountancy (at which he was, by all accounts, somewhat less than successful) to selling jewellery, gaining on the way publicity for his forays into motorsports, including his celebrated disappearance in the wastes of the Sahara Desert. However, by the time the Oman saga arose, Mark Thatcher was well on course to building a not inconsiderable fortune, doing so in the poorly chartered waters of 'commission' business in the intoxicating, 'get rich quick' environment of Middle Eastern commerce, where fortunes can be made and lost with equal rapidity. Indeed, the British Prime Minister's son had well and truly 'landed on his feet', a firm footing to which his unfettered access to Britain's most powerful woman was not without relevance. Indeed, as a Cementation executive was later to confirm in a British Sunday newspaper report, Mark Thatcher had been retained, and paid, by the company, not for his commercial know-how or for any expertise in Oman, which was non-existent, but for the use to which his connections to the top could be put. It has, in all fairness, to be confirmed that such a practice is entirely compatible with the accepted way of doing business in the Arab world, where such considerations attending business ethics do not extend beyond 'a favour given is a favour returnable at some future date'. But in Britain, in theory at least, it is a different matter altogether and especially so when it relates to the highest political office in the land.

In the event, the university project got under way with Cementation firmly at the concrete-mixer's controls. But as the buildings began to rise from the desert floor, some 25 kilometres from the capital, Muscat, so, back in Britain, did the constant drip of leaks and innuendo grow too.

On 15 January 1984, *The Observer* brought the Thatcher/ Cementation Affair firmly out of the shadows by highlighting the fact of the involvement of the Prime Minister's son in terms both clear and unambiguous. The hunt was now on, with much of Britain's press in hot pursuit. The Cementation Affair looked very much, at one stage, as though it would bring Margaret Thatcher crashing down from her pedestal of power.

The following month, a prominent member of the Labour Opposition in the House of Commons, Peter Shore, a former Minister of the Crown, initiated a correspondence with the Prime Minister, seeking detailed information regarding her 1981 visit to Oman. In particular, Shore raised the question of her and her son's involvement in the university project, a correspondence concluding with the request that she make a statement on the matter given that

Mark had, in the wake of the *Observer* report, confirmed his association with Cementation and his visit to the Sultanate at the same time as his mother. The question of a conflict of private interests of Members of Parliament is far from being a recent issue, with previous premiers, Asquith and Churchill among them, having set out guiding principles on the matter, with the latter having termed them as follows: 'It is a principle of public life that Ministers must so order their affairs that no conflict arises, or appears to arise, between their private interests and their public duties.' It was a statement that had been quoted earlier in the House of Commons when the Prime Minister had been asked: 'Was there a conflict between her private, family interests and her public duties with regard to her visit to Oman and the subsequent contract to Cementation in that country?' Her Parliamentary reply wilfully ignored the reference in the question to 'family interests', stressing her intervention on the matter with the Sultan of Oman as a particularly good example of her role of 'batting for Britain'. This, of course, she may well have done, as have so many of her predecessors as Prime Minister, let alone lesser Ministers of the Crown too. But the essential difference, the all-important question, was had any one of them 'batted' for one particular company in which a family member had had a direct financial interest? Not surprisingly, it was a suggestion vehemently denied by Margaret Thatcher, although in so doing she continued to exercise an obdurate evasiveness on any question as to her son's involvement in the Cementation Affair and particularly on the question as to whether or not he had been present at the Cementation talks in Oman in April 1981, a most pertinent matter given that up to this time his presence in the Sultanate during his mother's official visit had not been acknowledged.

Peter Shore's correspondence on the matter ceased shortly after the 'batting for Britain' statement, without any genuine light being shed on anything worthwhile. But the interest of the media persisted, with Granada Television's award-winning, flagship documentary series *World in Action* turning its attention to Oman, a country then, as now, so little known in the wider world. Half of the programme was devoted to Margaret Thatcher's involvement in and with the Cementation Affair but, inevitably, the programme content suffered from the usual handicap where the Sultanate is concerned in not having been granted permission to enter the country. Nonetheless, the best was made of the material available to the production team: commentary from those who had worked in Oman and who knew well the standard tendering processes for Government contracts (which did not occur in the Cementation case); further comment by a British accountant formerly in Government service in Oman; and from a consultant with many years of experience of working in both official and commercial circles in the Sultanate. The film went some way towards shedding light on the country but was, of course, denied any real chance of success in shining light into one of the darkest corners of the long political career of Margaret Thatcher. She, of course, declined to appear in the programme, as did her son, with the result that, even today, questions of a fundamental nature as to exactly what came to pass in the Cementation Affair remain unanswered. But of one thing there is certainty: the indelible stain left by the affair, which marked relations between Sultan Qaboos and the Conservative Party leader and revealed an aspect of the association which was, on occasions, far from being of a satisfactory nature and for which the British Prime Minister was, without doubt, principally culpable. And there are those within the Conservative Party who, some 20 years after the event, would have preferred the 'whole sordid business' to have been done with 'once and for all' by a far more honest, candid account of the affair than proved possible while Margaret Thatcher remained in 10 Downing Street.

As the former Conservative grandee comments, 'Unlike the United Kingdom, the United States of America has an excellent piece of legislation in force, the Freedom of Information Act. Of course, at the time the US Government adopted, quite understandably, an arm's length interest in such goings-on.' But Washington's democratic instincts and traditions in such matters were, in the event, not to be suppressed, as demonstrated by a quote from a dispatch, dated 14 March 1984, from the US Embassy in London to the State Department:

Left-Wing Scottish Labourite, Willie Hamilton, last week accused the Prime Minister of running a squalid casino at Number 10. The Prime Minister is then gamely defended by Tory gallants, Labour front-benchers, especially Peter Shore, press for answers and the PM, obviously in a cold rage, demurs.

Allies we may well be, but while the dispatch gives a somewhat more than adequate flavour to the scene, it is possible to detect, amidst the diplomatic niceties, a faint trace of gloating at the obvious discomfiture of the British Prime Minister over the seemingly endless drip, drip of exposure relating to her son's unconventional business activities. However, as we shall now see, the Cementation Affair was not the last bizarre situation to come to pass between one of the world's last Sultans and the British Conservative leader which, metaphorically at least, ended in tears and tantrums well before bedtime.

The generosity of Sultans, both ancient and modern, is the stuff of which fantastic legends are born. What, however, is far from fantasy but has passed into Omani legend, is the curious case, born of envy and greed, of Mrs Margaret Thatcher and the Sultan's necklace or, to be more precise, the necklace he gave her during the time of her premiership. The actual time when the fabulous gift was handed over by Sultan Qaboos to the Prime Minister is not known, although it is believed to have been during her visit to the Sultanate in the spring of 1981. What is known, however, is that it was created by Asprey's, of which Qaboos, together with his fellow Sultan, Hassan of Brunei, was, at the time, a shareholder of some significance. The necklace was, by all accounts, truly spectacular, being described by at least one member of the Sultan's Court as 'more of a collar, actually, than a necklace'. It was made of platinum and liberally set with sapphires. Its value ran into many thousands of pounds, with one conservative estimate putting it at around the £200,000 mark.

This, of course, under Downing Street's long-established Rules of Engagement, rendered it the property of the British State, which applies to all gifts given to the Prime Minister of the day with a value in excess of £125. So, and much to ill-concealed fury and vocal dismay, into the Downing Street vault it went. Given that, when she was wearing the necklace, it gave the Prime Minister the appearance of having won 'Best of Breed' at Cruft's, it may well have been assumed that the matter would be allowed to drop, but Margaret Thatcher was not so disposed.

Shortly into the premiership of John Major, she saw his wife, Norma, wearing the necklace at an official function. The 'Iron Lady' at once suffered a case of extreme metal fatigue and, apparently seething with rage unconfined, remarked to a former colleague, 'That was given to me. It really is mine.' It was an assertion that travelled with her and, on a private visit to the Gulf in the wake of the 1991 Gulf War, at a dinner at Bait Al Falaj (the principal barracks of the Sultan's Armed Forces in Muscat), she asked Sultan Qaboos if a replacement necklace could be provided. According to an eminent Omani present at the dinner, it was a request too far even for a Sultan internationally known, and justly so, for his acts of kindness and generosity which, on occasion, border on the extreme. He was, by all accounts, 'visibly shocked' by such a request and, far from a replacement being made available, there is a persistent belief that, in later conversation with the British Ambassador of the day, the Sultan suggested that, as the necklace had become such an object of contention, the better course would be for it to be discreetly returned, although, as is always the case when the convoluted nature of Anglo–Omani relations come under the spotlight, it is quite impossible to establish whether or not such a Royal suggestion actually came to pass. But what this sad little story does establish beyond all reasonable doubt is that this most generous of Sultans does, indeed, have limits beyond which he will not be pushed.

Chapter 9

A MAN OF MANNERS, PUBLIC AND PRIVATE

This account of a most private man, one thrust, quite literally, onto the throne of his father by force of arms, is being written not with the 'destination' of the subject as the principal objective but that of identifying the 'route' he has taken and, to an uncomfortable degree, been obliged to take to the top.

In many important respects his life has been, and very much remains, a fragmented one, the essential and inescapable burden, perhaps, of an absolute ruler condemned by virtue of that to play many parts, sometimes simultaneously. It was Shakespeare who penned 'Uneasy rests the head that wears the crown' and it has fallen to Sultan Qaboos of Oman to bear witness to its all too often harsh truth. For, even given his life of opulence, 'life on the grandest of scales' in the awed words of a former Minister of the British Crown in the wake of his visit to one of the Sultan's palaces, the life of the Omani monarch is far from being either one of ease or free of many fiercely attendant penalties. In recent years his most striking features have begun to bear the imprint of the many and varied, and, indeed, ever-present burdens of State from which there can be no escape until, of course, his death, or that of those who currently fawn around him, or the unlikely act of peaceful abdication in favour of another, finally grants him relief. There has been evidence in recent years of his willingness to share the burden but, as a Western diplomat formerly accredited to the Court of the Sultan, comments, 'While there are notable exceptions to such an unhappy rule, His Majesty, as yet at least, simply does not have the tools to do the jobs required. He simply does not have the necessary talent at his disposal. He is very short indeed of what could be relied upon to be capable hands.' It is a comment which very much reflects the shortage of men of ministerial calibre, a situation made even more problematic by the fact that those who could so well rise to high office choose to put their talents, and spend their energies, on exercising their business acumen, as opposed to labouring in their Sovereign's service.

Conversely, so many of those who vie for the Sultan's attention, with an eye to the main chance of ministerial preferment, do so for the basest of reasons: social advancement, the very considerable perks of high office and, as ever it seems in the Sultanate, the chance that with ministerial power will come the opportunity to get rich with considerably more ease, and with greater speed, than otherwise would be the case. And throughout such trials and tribulations of the exercise of such personal, unfettered power, Sultan Qaboos has been obliged to maintain a dignity and public demeanour which, for its constant quality alone, can only be a source of astonishment and admiration. Yet the route to such distinction has been a lonely one and particularly so given his constant bouts of self-doubt, which on so many occasions have led to long periods of debilitating prevarication and an all-pervading melancholy, an aspect of his character recorded in 1969 by one of Britain's most able and distinguished politicians. Douglas Hurd, who became Foreign and Commonwealth Secretary in the Government of Margaret Thatcher, committed to his diary his first meeting with the young Qaboos with the observation, 'This melancholy Crown Prince'. Another British observer of the Omani scene commented that the young Sultan, shortly into his reign, appeared to have 'few Omani friends'. Yet what none can fail to take note of, and indeed admire, is the Omani Sultan's courtesy, his innate practice of good manners. And if life at the Sultan of Oman's Court does resemble the power, colour and, on occasions, the extravagances of an earlier age, then, at the very least, he has old-fashioned manners to match.

It was a man of the 'old school' of conduct and expectations, General Sir John Akehurst, a British man of arms of particularly sound judgement and expectation, who passed succinct comment on the sterling qualities of Oman's leader. Sir John, who commanded the Dhofar Brigade during Oman's Dhofar War of the 1970s, wrote of Sultan Qaboos, in *We Won a War* (1982), his account of that desert war and his role in it: 'The Sultan is quiet, intelligent, beautifully mannered, good looking, a lover of Western music and art, diplomatically shrewd and skilful . . . generous, a keen horseman and tennis player.' It is an apt description, in more senses than one: witness the handsome and most distinguished features of the Omani ruler described by a man who was the most professional of soldiers, given neither to sycophancy or to giving a spade its incorrect designation. Yet there are those who, whilst not necessarily disagreeing with the General, do draw, in their judgement of the Middle East's only Sultan, a more Cromwellian 'warts and all' picture. As a former British soldier of the Sultan comments:

> His Majesty has a justifiable reputation for the most excellent manners, and is, without doubt, a man of considerable charm, but in no way can he be described as charismatic, like, for example, his fellow Arab Sovereign, the late King Hussein of Jordan. Furthermore, his many virtues can, on occasions, be erratic, such as the National Day celebration when his principal guest, a member of the British Royal Family, was kept waiting at the Stadium for such a long time for the Sultan's arrival that he eventually walked out.

The Royal visitor from the House of Windsor was His Royal Highness the Duke of Kent, cousin to Her Majesty. But this most likeable and easy-going of Dukes is far from being the only prominent Briton whose relationship with the Omani monarch has been 'strained', as the following episodes so adequately illustrate.

The new Ambassador was resplendent in frock-coat, with gold-embroidered cuffs and epaulettes, cocked-hat held respectfully at knee-length, in full imperial fig . . . in short, he cut a most dashing figure. But this Envoy Extraordinary and Plenipotentiary of a European Royal House, at presenting his credentials to the Court of His Majesty the Sultan Qaboos, delivered his salutation in the most exquisite fluent Arabic. For reasons best known to Oman's 14th Sultan, this was all too much and when the Ambassador had done and was preparing to exit the Royal presence, he was quietly, courteously but most firmly advised that, on future audiences, would he be so kind, please, as to address the Omani ruler in the English tongue.

The Sultan's relationship with his British Chiefs of the Defence Staff were equally 'prickly', a matter of some surprise given the very real bond he feels with men cast in the military mould. This was particularly so with General Sir Timothy Creasey, a notorious martinet (hence his unappealing appellation among his own, immediate staff: 'The Bull'). But in the Sultan he had met his match, causing the senior soldier to describe his audiences with Qaboos as being akin to 'a schoolboy being carpeted by his headmaster'. Another quip to fall from the Bull's lips was that, 'Oman brings out the best and the worst in both men and machines', although whether he included in such a judgement (with which many would agree) his humblings by Sultan Qaboos he never made clear.

The Bull was, however, also bluff and direct (attitudes known to have appeal for the Sultan), as witnessed by his very first interview with Oman's then Minister of Defence, the late Sayyid Fahr bin Taimour Al Said, himself a huge bear of a man, with a heart as large as his kind and generous presence indicated but who did not suffer fools gladly – or appreciate a man's airs and presumptions. So it was when, arriving at the Minister's office, The Bull slapped down his briefcase on the desk and all but bellowed, 'I have a choice: I can either accept the post of the Sultan's Chief of the Defence Staff or take an offer which is on the table from Nestlé. So what's in it for me?', such an opening remark of course bearing witness to his own assertion that Oman invariably brings out the worst in men.

It was a somewhat less than auspicious start to the proceedings yet, in the event, the General's service as Defence Chief proved to be infinitely more successful than his blustering manner suggested. In fact, many were surprised when Creasey's services were requested of London by the Sultan, given his uncompromising reputation and bullying tactics. But Qaboos had not forgotten the most effective and professional contribution made by the General during the Dhofar War, during which, his first tour of duty in the country, he had been Commander of the Sultan's Armed Forces. Indeed, in commenting on the contribution made by Creasey during the conflict, Sultan Qaboos told a then senior Omani courtier, who counselled caution on the Creasey appointment given his not altogether satisfactory reputation, of his 'no small gratitude for what Creasey achieved on the field of battle' and that the General, for all his absence of social graces, not only continued to enjoy Royal approval but continued to impress too.

So Creasey it had to be, an episode which demonstrates the quality of deftness and sound judgement which Qaboos can exercise and his resolve not to be blown off course if his convictions are strong. It is an episode, too, which is a clear contradiction of the Sultan's reputation for wholesale vacillation, an aspect of his character which, to this day, continues to cause comprehensive anxiety amongst his many courtiers.

However, the political skills required in Creasey's overall restructuring of the Sultan's Defence establishment, his principal task in his new role in Oman, continued to be largely absent, with his approach and methods meeting with both the resentment and, indeed, professional disapproval of many senior Omani military officers. As the former British soldier in the service of the Omani Sultan recalls:

> Creasey's 'diplomatic skills' were hardly those required in such a delicate position. He was known, for example, to treat senior defence civilian officials with both scorn and contempt. The words 'bloody civilian' were a common usage. Also, he took upon himself excessive trappings and appurtenances of his appointment, as if he were a latter-day

Kitchener. Such flamboyance may have been acceptable had he been more successful in reining in some of the forces' more blatant extravagances which was, after all, the *raison d'être* of his appointment.

Nonetheless, when his day was done, the Sultan, with his usual unstinting generosity, showered 'The Bull' with riches, both cash and material. His 'loot' was so large that it was loaded into the back of a C130 transport plane and, once back home, he proceeded to buy up half of bloody Essex.

Yet another comment justifying Bull Creasey's remark on Oman and its unwavering tendency to bring out both the best and the worst in mortals. And, as for the 'worst', a former man of arms, who served the Sultan with no small distinction, recalls the General's passage through the Sultanate:

Despite the openly declared purpose of his appointment, as Chief of the Defence Staff, to clean up the 'Augean Stables' of defence procurement, Creasey did not set the example of rectitude that might well have been expected of him. Apart from the generously equipped mansion at Seeb, which, to be fair, was not inappropriate for a four-star General, the more visible trappings included an impressive silver belt buckle, the value of which ran into four figures. His many excursions to Britain on His Majesty's Royal Flight terminated at an airfield in East Anglia, not much more than a stone's throw from his home. And the cost of such sundries as long telephone calls home and postage stamps for personal use were dismissed as mere trifles.

Yet, in substance, this former soldier's lament on the General's free-loading is true of those in similar positions today, as many Omanis are only all too ready to confirm; in short, an Omani lament as to the over-generous nature of their Sultan. But an end to the three years of incessant banter, bluster and bullying of General Timothy Creasey was, however, well and truly on its way, and with confirmation that his successor was to be General Sir John Watts

('Johnnie' to his many friends), yet another veteran of the guerrilla war of the 1970s in the deserts and mountains of Dhofar, there were many who breathed a collective sigh of relief. General Watts was as different in approach and temperament from Bull Creasey as it is possible to imagine: quiet, courteous, brave and professional in all he did, he quickly commended himself to the Sultan and his subjects and, even today, in Oman and elsewhere, is remembered with respect and affection. His bravery extended to advising the Sultan of some facts he would have preferred not to hear and, when venturing into such potentially explosive territory, he went where no man had dared go before. This included constant words of caution as to the country's high defence expenditure, territory which constituted a minefield given the Sultan's attachment to his Armed Forces, and a subject into which so many who should have known better feared to tread. Indeed, Oman's high defence expenditure ranks, among so many senior Omanis, as the single biggest difficulty they have with the manner in which their Sultan exercises his absolute rule, with the phrase 'buying weapons we neither need nor can afford' being the criticism most regularly levelled at the man on the country's throne.

There is, of course, a real, and ever-present, connection between defence expenditure and the second concern so frequently expressed by the Sultanate's rapidly increasing educated constituency: the overbearing influence of those who, animated by the creed of enlightened self-interest, fawn and pander at the foot of that very same throne, many of whom are blamed for persuading Qaboos to embark upon yet another arms spending spree from which they stand to gain huge commission payments. It is this fact, and this fact alone, which has led in the past, and continues to lead today, to the harsh condemnation by so many senior Omanis of Brigadier Timothy Landon, to the exclusion of what would be a justifiable consideration of much else that he has done over the years which has, without doubt, been of great assistance to the Sultan and, therefore, to the country. But, in the case of General Sir John Watts, his wise words of caution on the matter are well remembered and, indeed, appreciated by many in the country, with one senior Omani military figure, now long gone from the scene of military service, commenting, 'Without the General's influence, his constant advice to His Majesty for moderation, things would have been much worse.' Which, with even a cursory consideration of the facts of the matter, is really saying rather a lot.

Indeed, while the Sultanate's defence expenditure, known to consume between 40 and 44 per cent of the State's annual budget (a preposterously high figure for a total indigenous population of two million people), was highlighted by the *Financial Times* journalist Robin Allen as far back as November 1994 (in the wake of a World Bank Report which expressed concern at Oman's 'exceptionally high levels of defence and national security expenditure', describing it as 'among the highest in the world' and warning that, given its unsustainable nature, social and political consequences could flow from it, if not checked), the problem was, even then, far from being new.

As early as 1974, just four years into Qaboos's reign, his determination, under pressure from the cash-cropping cabal around him, to proceed with the purchase from British Aerospace of an integrated Air Defence System almost bankrupted the country. And this was at a point when the oil price was at an all-time high. That year, 1974, was also when the Sultan put in train the purchase of Jaguar fighting aircraft and the Rapier Guided Missile System. On this occasion, however, he was bluntly told by his Treasury that such purchases could not be paid for out of State finances, and that if they were to proceed, they would have to be financed via the raising of costly loans.

In more recent times the purchase of British Challenger tanks has proved far from being practical, even when their high purchase cost is laid aside. They are, essentially, designed for use by NATO forces and as such are better suited by far for the plains of Westphalia than for operations in the deserts of southern Arabia, as the 2001–02 Anglo–Omani joint exercises in Oman, Operation 'Swift Sword', proved, when both Challenger and Chieftain tanks seriously malfunctioned in the desert conditions. Indeed, within weeks of their arrival in the Sultanate, several of the Challengers were in the workshops of the Sultan's Armed Forces at Shaafa, where expensive repairs had to be carried out.

SULTANATE OF OMAN

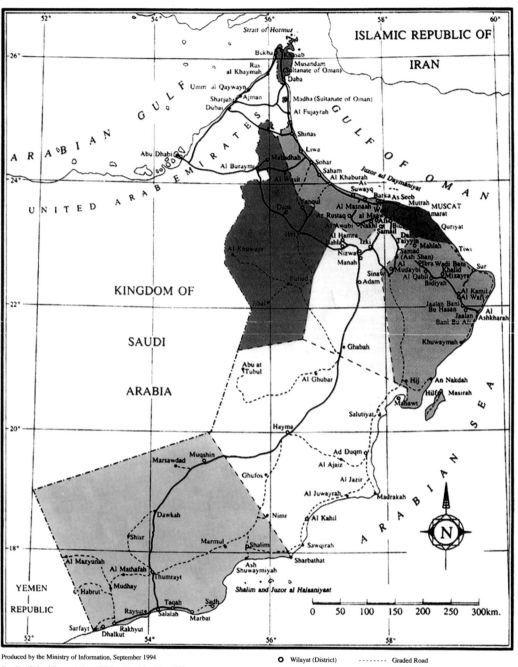

Produced by the Ministry of Information, September 1994

Based on National Survey Authority OR 1, edition 6 dated June 1994

This map is not an authorittty on international boundaries

○ Wilayat (District)	- - - - - - -	Graded Road
● Village / Town	———	Metalled Road
	—·—·—	International Boundary

Old Muscat, pre-coup and pre-oil.

View of Muscat.

SNM 4

The Palace and Customs House in old Muscat.

The British Consulate in old Muscat.

Sultan Qaboos arriving at Muscat, just three weeks
after his seizure of power on 23 July 1970.

The new Sultan just 18 days after the
Palace Coup of 23 July 1970.

A Queen and a Sultan. Queen Elizabeth on a visit to Oman's Sultan
in February 1979, when wind blowing in from the Arabian sea made
its very own unscheduled contribution to the occasion.

The Prince of Wales and his consort, the late Diana,
Princess of Wales, with Sultan Qaboos. This photo
was taken during a private visit to
Muscat in 1986.

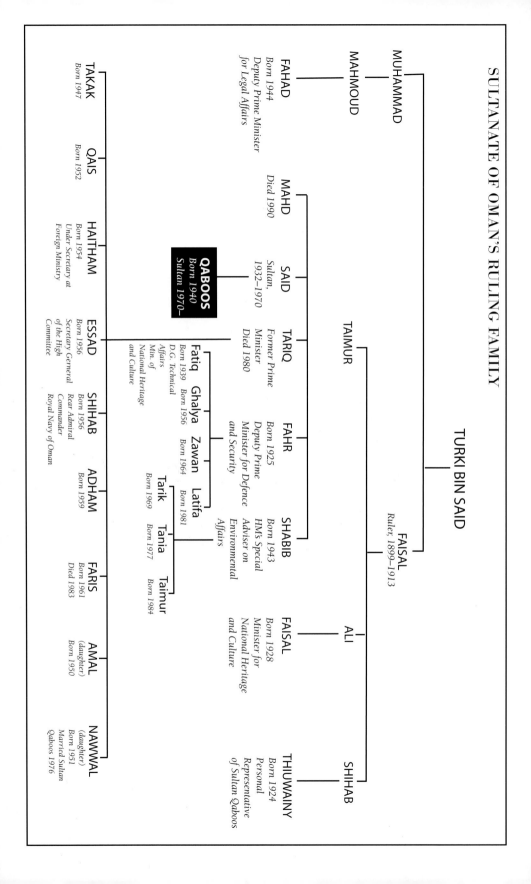

SULTANATE OF OMAN'S RULING FAMILY

TURKI BIN SAID

MUHAMMAD

MAHMOUD

FAHAD
Born 1944
Deputy Prime Minister
for Legal Affairs

FAISAL
Ruler, 1899–1913

MAHD
Died 1990

SAID
Sultan,
1932–1970

QABOOS
Born 1940
Sultan 1970–

TARIQ
Former Prime
Minister
Died 1980

TAIMUR

FAHR
Born 1925
Deputy Prime
Minister for Defence
and Security

SHABIB
Born 1943
HM's Special
Adviser on
Environmental
Affairs

Fatiq
Born 1939
D.G. Technical
Affairs
Min. of
National Heritage
and Culture

Ghalya
Born 1956

Zawan
Born 1964

Latifa
Born 1981

Tarik
Born 1969

Tania
Born 1977

Taimur
Born 1984

FAISAL
Born 1928
Minister for
National Heritage
and Culture

ALI

SHIHAB

THIUWAINY
Born 1924
Personal
Representative
of Sultan Qaboos

TAKAK
Born 1947

QAIS
Born 1952

HAITHAM
Born 1954
Under Secretary at
Foreign Ministry

ESSAD
Born 1956
Secretary General
of the High
Committee

SHIHAB
Born 1956
Rear Admiral
Commander
Royal Navy of Oman

ADHAM
Born 1959

FARIS
Born 1961
Died 1983

AMAL
(daughter)
Born 1950

NAWWAL
(daughter)
Born 1951
Married Sultan
Qaboos 1976

It is such high defence expenditure, allied to those who profit from it, that has been, and continues to be, a cause for mounting anger among so many of Sultan Qaboos's subjects. It is a concern of many, including diplomats such as Ivor Lucas, who was British Ambassador at the time of Margaret Thatcher's visit to the country in April 1981, but who had his concern brusquely dismissed by the Prime Minister. Many senior expatriate servants of the Omani State have also expressed their anxiety at so much of the country's finances being consumed by a 'top-heavy' expenditure on arms and security-related equipment, fearing that it would, sooner rather than later, have inescapable political consequences. One particular senior figure, now retired, spoke of the curious dimension given to the Sultan by such a state of affairs:

> It really is quite extraordinary: a situation that in so many respects defies rational explanation. Here you have one of the most perceptive, intelligent men it is possible to meet, one who has, on most issues, seen for himself the benefits to be won from tempering his absolute power; a realist no less, a ruler who wants very much to do what is best for his people and country and has, by and large, done just that throughout his reign. But on the question of arms, and the high expenditure it invariably entails, all caution, all financial prudence, so evident in other matters, is all too often thrown to the winds. And, increasingly I found towards the end of my time in Government service, woe betide any poor sod who chose to contradict him on defence purchases which, again, is so out of character. His Majesty is not, generally speaking, a man who will not brook debate and, on occasions, a putting of opposing opinions. Again, generally speaking, he not only tolerates a counter-argument but positively welcomes it. It remains a conundrum of his character to which I, personally, never found an answer. And as for those who prance around him with a gut-churning sycophancy, urging him on for purely selfish, personal gain, well, I have never understood why he doesn't tell them to bugger off, that they have enough to be going on with, which would be something of a master

understatement. He acts as if he still is in their debt, whereas it is the very opposite which is the truth of the matter. His indulgence has enriched them beyond what must be even their wildest, most greedy dreams. They are, and increasingly so, the most terrible liability to His Majesty, and, of course, a threat as well. But still they remain. It raises questions, just like the high defence expenditure, to which for now at least, no rational answer is available.

Yet it is not only defence expenditure about which so many Omanis currently vent their anger. Conspicuous consumption, so visibly apparent in the capital area, comes an uncomfortably close second to arms purchases. The outward and visible signs of an 'important person' in the mentality of so many Arabs, indeed in the minds of the great majority, is a simple correlation of 'big man, big house'. 'It is,' says the former senior courtier, 'a philosophy to which His Majesty himself quite rightly subscribes.' Rightly or otherwise, the one immediate impression made upon visitors to Muscat is the proliferation of 'big houses' for, presumably, 'big men', although most of them, often of the most vulgar, ostentatious proportions imaginable, defy the description of 'house' and are both regarded and, indeed, described as 'palaces', ignoring the fact that most of them are not inhabited by members of Oman's Royal Family, some of whom choose to live in the most modest of dwellings. The Sultan himself has two palaces in the greater capital area, one of which, Al Alam, is quite small and used for official functions, such as receiving Ambassadors and bidding farewell to those who present their letters of recall. The other, Bait Al Barka, on the Batinah coast road north of Muscat, is, however, a grander, more opulent arrangement, the lavishness of which has struck dumb many a visiting, usually garrulous, Western leader. It is where the Sultan often entertains and those fortunate to be on his guest list have spoken, and in the case of the British Defence Procurement Minister, the late Alan Clark, written, of the flaming torches lining the final approach to Bait Al Barka, the sweeping, palatial grounds and the heavy scent of frankincense as one enters the many marbled and bejewelled halls of the Sultan's palace. Clark, always ready with a 'catty comment', also went on to write of the Sultan's 'feline' nature but observed, more kindly, his 'high intelligence'. It is here, too, that Qaboos holds his annual New Year party, the guest list serving as a clear indication as to who is 'in' and who is 'out' of Royal favour. Dinner is, as one would expect, of the most sumptuous nature, with the Sultan, an excellent, attentive host, moving between the tables, making lively conversation and making sure, too, that everyone has just what they want. It is, by all accounts, the most splendid of occasions, an evening indeed to remember. And, on one occasion at least, it was an occasion which, later, delivered a sad surprise.

When the crackers are pulled, jewellery of the most expensive kind falls from the brightly coloured paper and, when the plum pudding is eaten, guests are warned to be on the most careful lookout for the gold sovereigns embedded in its rich fruit. Or, at least, that was what one was led to believe, including the Royal host, by the London company who had supplied the precious coins. But upon returning home to England, one guest attempted to cash in his sovereign only to be told in terms both clear and unequivocal that the supposed gold content of the coin had about as much relevance to the metal as embroidery would have in a factory mass producing rubber bath-mats. This is another example of the interests of Oman's Sultan not always being taken care of in the spirit they should be.

In addition to his Royal residences in Oman, the Sultan also has substantial properties overseas, most notably in Britain – Wargrave Manor in Oxfordshire, Grove House in London's Regent's Park (the only property in London, save that of Buckingham Palace, to have a lake in its extensive grounds) and a town house in Mayfair's Upper Brook Street. Properties in Vienna and outside Paris, at Fontainebleau, are also held, together with a truly splendid Bavarian castle in Garmisch Partenkirchen. And to move between these properties, the Omani ruler has his own Boeing aircraft although, according to a former member of the Royal Flight, 'His Majesty is a white-knuckle flyer', and, of course, his fleet of Royal ocean-going yachts.

His Majesty Sultan Qaboos of Oman is very much aware that Sultans, now so rare a breed of men, have, even given the increasingly drab, colourless condition of the 'cut-price crowd', a tradition to maintain and he, for one, seeks on all occasions to both honour and embrace it. Oman's ruler lives in the style and manner befitting his title and, in so doing, has the courage, and of course the means, to meet a Sultan's many and varied responsibilities, not the least of which is to bring colour to an international landscape increasingly bereft of true spectacle. Of course, like the greater majority of leaders in the developing world – and while many would dispute such a designation, that is precisely what Oman is, in that its principal revenue is derived from exporting a primary resource in a raw, unmanufactured condition – Qaboos is only too well aware of the ultimate fate threatening so many in his situation, remembering, perhaps, the fate that befell his own father. Consequently, the personal security with which he surrounds himself is increasingly suffocating.

Long gone are the days when his loyal subjects, still the greater majority of the Omani population, could greet him personally as he rode his horse along the beach in the early morning air or as his convoy of cars made a Royal progress around the country. Similarly, his visits, often made alone and unannounced, to his military units late at night are occasions of the past. It is a situation that many in Oman regret, being of the well-considered opinion that the blanket of security now surrounding the Sultan has led to a serious distancing from the people. As one former Omani diplomat comments, 'All in all, there is a pervasive feeling of increasing paranoia around His Majesty. It is generally accepted that the only military formation in the country upon whose loyalty the Sultan can depend is his Special Force.' This elite group has always been commanded by a senior British officer with a Special Forces background, a link with such skilled practitioners of the military metaphor which dates from the opening hours of Qaboos's reign when a small force of men from Britain's Special Air Service, the renowned SAS, moved into Salalah's Al Hisn Palace to stand guard over the country's 14th Sultan.

Not that manpower alone, however expert it may be, is the only arrangement in place for the personal security and safety of Oman's Sultan. A truly splendid example of the many and varied devices designed to afford Qaboos a swift exit from the country, should the need ever arise, is contained within the perimeter wall of his Bait Al Barka Palace. For within the wall's otherwise solid masonry is an artificial section through which a vehicle, or, indeed, a pedestrian, would easily be able to pass. It is a superb example of high-camouflage and is far from being the sole measure firmly in place to deflect and frustrate any enemies of one of the few remaining Crowned Heads in the Arab Islamic world.

But, and laying aside the necessary preparations for a situation of extremis which may at some future time confront the Omani ruler, within the walls of Bait Al Barka the atmosphere generated by a man of exquisite taste and culture continues to reign supreme. While the palace's halls of marbled splendour reflect the glorious heritage of Islamic and Sultanic design, here, without question, is the influence of an individual whose love and appreciation of art and music and, indeed, knowledge of both subjects, is so evident. Such a fact manifested itself with the founding in 1985 of the Royal Oman Symphony Orchestra, the annual concert of which is a highlight in Muscat's social calendar and which, through the Sovereign's generous funding, has enabled so many young Omanis to train for a career as classical musicians, in both the Arabic and Western genres. It is a unique achievement, one which speaks volumes about the interests and instincts of a most cultured man, one who not only installed at one point his own personal organist at Bait Al Barka, but who himself is also an accomplished pianist and player of the organ, being known to serenade his dinner guests on the latter instrument. His private art collection, too, is, by all accounts, a wonder to behold and when, in the mid-1990s, it was valued by a lady flown in from Paris, it was known to have been the cause of much excited astonishment – although, alas, and in a particularly despicable imitation of the 'gold' sovereign scandal, there were several paintings which, in terms of current market value, bore no relation whatsoever to the price at which the Sultan had been 'advised' to purchase them.

But the matter of abiding concern to so many, both within Oman's establishment and indeed beyond the shores of the Sultanate, is the overwhelming secretiveness which now pervades the life of the Omani ruler, which many regard as but symptomatic of a rapidly increasing tendency of the Sultan personally to isolate himself from his own people. This makes for the justifiable ringing of alarm bells given that this was such a characteristic of his father and which was the justification, in part, for his forced overthrow, a reason which Qaboos himself is known to have expressed.

It is a circumstance which gained momentum as the twentieth century drew to a close, when *The Economist* asked in one of its reports from Oman, 'Where is our Sultan?', a *cri de coeur* believed to have come from an Omani of the most senior rank. The next most vexing question to exercise so many minds, not all of them Omani, is that of the succession.

Unlike the palace coup of 1970, when Qaboos, as Sultan Said's only son, was the sole choice, today, with the Sultan having no heir apparent, indeed having no offspring at all, the matter is one of considerable delicacy and, on occasions, the most energetic speculation.

In theory there are, within the Royal Family, the Al Saids, several contenders and to prevent family feuding, which, over the centuries has been such a feature of Oman's ruling house, in 1996 Sultan Qaboos promulgated what he termed the 'Basic Statute of the State'. Chapter One declares that the Government of Oman will be based on Royal, Sultanic succession, of the male descendants of Sayyid Turki bin Said bin Sultan, the premier scion of the Al Said family. Any future Sultan must be a Muslim and the legitimate son born of Omani parents. When the throne becomes vacant, the Ruling Family Council must assemble within three days to determine a successor to the throne. If they fail to agree, the country's Defence Council will then be constitutionally obliged to confirm the individual designated by the Sultan as his successor. A cardinal condition in the Basic Statute is that the Ruling Family Council is not obliged to approve the Sultan's choice. Indeed, if, after due deliberation, it prefers to choose another, they are at liberty to do so and the Defence Council cannot overrule such a choice.

It will be the duty of the Defence Council to summon the Ruling Family Council upon the demise of the Sultan, as opposed to the Majlis Ashura, as the Council of State. This is a marked departure from Al Said historical practice and, indeed, from Omani Ibadhi tradition. Sultan Qaboos has designated two members of the family as acceptable heirs, with their names having been sealed in envelopes and deposited in two secret locations. Throughout his 33-year-long reign, the Omani

Sovereign has resisted steadfastly to name a Crown Prince. Not unnaturally, the names contained in the envelopes have excited considerable speculation but Omani 'insiders' of senior rank believe that the Sultan's chosen candidates are two of the following:

1. Sayyid Haitham bin Tariq bin Taimour
2. Sayyid Shihab bin Tariq bin Taimour
3. Sayyid Asad bin Tariq bin Taimour

All are the sons of one of Oman's most remarkable men, Sayyid Tariq, one of Sultan Said's brothers, who was appointed Prime Minister at the time of Qaboos's accession to the throne, an appointment which was, in itself, a radical departure, an implied willingness of the new Sultan to share power, but which came all too soon to grief, as conservative and commercial elements besieging Qaboos conducted a whispering campaign against him. Sophisticated, elegant, a polished linguist and a man of the most progressive opinions and intent, it was not too long before he found the obstructions being placed in his way by his political enemies intolerable and, resigning his post, flew out of the country. It is the nature of his radical spirit which, had it been allowed to flourish and blossom, would, without doubt, have led to Oman becoming the first fully constitutional monarchy in the Arab Islamic world, a development that would have guaranteed a premier position for Oman, both in the region and beyond, which, even today, a quarter of a century after the event, may well cause those conservative elements which continue to hold sway in the country to raise questions about the succession of one of his sons to the throne of Oman. Other names which have been mooted in the past are Sayyid Fahd bin Mahmud and Sayyid Faisal bin Ali.

Other inhibiting factors that cannot be ignored in the selection process will be the essential need for any new Sultan to have, or be able to promptly forge, an equal identity with the people of the north and the south of the country, which means that Qaboos's successor will have to court the allegiance of the people of Dhofar, an independent breed of men at the best of times, many of whom resent what they regard as the excessive development of the north at the expense of the south. Qaboos, of course, had an identity with Dhofaris from the very moment of his birth, with his mother being very much one of them.

Sultan Qaboos may well have laid the ground rules with skill, singular care and precision, but given the Omani propensity for argument and intrigue, the succession process could well prove in the event to be every bit as problematic as the Sultan's subjects, including members of his own family, can possibly make it.

There are occasions when the practices of government, of the Sultan's own design and choosing, serve up a menu of complications and difficulties which many of his Ministers not only dread but increasingly find most difficult to digest, with the annual transfer of the seat of government from Muscat, in the north, to Salalah, some 1,100 kilometres to the south, being the principal bugbear. Not since the days of the British Raj in India, when, each summer, the Government moved from the sweltering plains to the cool hill-stations, such as Simla, has such an administrative transfer taken place. When the annual move was first announced, many saw it as a splendid way in which a devolution of power could be brought about, or, in the glib parlance of the age, a 'caring, sharing, quasi-democratic manner of carrying on the business of government' be introduced. It is an opinion which quickly withered on the vine and, today, finds few adherents, with many, indeed probably most, of those who are actually involved dreading the whole extraordinary business. As bemoans a former senior servant of the Omani Crown:

> This isn't just a question of a handful of Ministers shifting from one air-conditioned office to another, but of the whole Government, with all its multitudinous current files, being shipped across the desert. You can have no idea; armies of civil servants deployed just to try and keep track of the stuff. Plane-loads of sensitive papers being ferried from one end of the country to the other. It is truly a nightmare, a logistical nightmare. And His Majesty gets into the most tremendous rage if, at Cabinet, or at a briefing, you can't lay

your hands on a particular piece of paper immediately. It's no good saying that it is in transit or whatever.

The same source said that some Ministers and senior civil servants dreaded the Sultan's annual 'Meet the People' tours for very much the same reasons:

> A deluge of Post-it notes, a storm of bits of bright yellow paper. His Majesty would be harangued by some old desert white-beard at one of these frightful occasions, under the burning sun or in a barren wadi, and before you could say 'action', out would flash the Post-it pad and every man and his brother would be involved in trying to track down details of an arcane land dispute going back several generations. Often, of course, what people really wanted was money. A fistful of rials. And I have to say that latterly, and especially if we were running late on these tours of the deepest interior, money would just be thrown out of the car windows as we drove by in clouds of dust. People would line the wadis outside villages shouting demands. It could all become rather undignified, rather sad. And to add to such an unpromising picture the fact that all of this would, more often than not, send His Majesty into yet another bellowing rage, well, the unhappy atmosphere can be easily imagined.

Indeed, while the tours to Oman's interior by the Sultan appear impressive as a modern-day version of the medieval progress of an Eastern potentate, the occasions have never been, in actual fact, a progress characterised by sweetness and light, as the one-time senior servant of the Oman State so well remembers:

> Those damn Post-it notes! Careers were badly damaged by those demands for instant action. The worst-case scenario was for you, as a Minister or an executive civil servant, to receive a Post-it demanding to know, there and then, why action promised to some scheming petitioner you didn't know at all had not been carried out. If, by any chance, the

petitioner had been able to claim that the action had been sanctioned by His Majesty on an earlier occasion, well, you could see your career going up in smoke in front of your very eyes. It was no laughing matter.

As slightly amusing as such a scene may be, a hapless Minister being called to account by an irate Sultan, such episodes do symbolise in stark relief much about the governance of Oman and the private nature of its ruler. So much of what Sultan Qaboos does and says is so obviously right, proper, fitting and, indeed, generous of spirit. Or so, initially at least, it invariably appears. Yet, not unlike a flawed gemstone, seen in only a fractionally changed light, something very different instantly becomes apparent. Thus 'Meeting the People' degenerated into a money-throwing exercise, which inevitably demeaned all those involved in it. It is a point of view shared by a writer and journalist long familiar with the Sultanate and all its many facets:

> On one occasion, when reviewing a book, a particularly loathsome example of brown-nosed journalism by the publishers of those wretched little pocket guides to this and that in Oman, I wrote that people who should know infinitely better often obscured the real achievements of the Sultan by paeans of quite the most ridiculous praise. There was a real danger, I wrote, of Qaboos being drowned in a treacle tide of sycophancy. Then, I was certain that he truly hated the fawning, the stomach-churning grovelling that went on in print and, indeed, in speech on the radio and television. Now, sadly, I am nothing like as sure. I recall when, quite suddenly, the FM Service of Radio Oman ditched light pop music from its morning and afternoon schedules and substituted hugely heavy classical stuff by, mostly, German composers. Many were dismayed, some of whom plucked up courage to complain publicly. It so happened that a few weeks later I met with the country's Information Minister, Abdul Aziz bin Mohammed Al Rowas, and asked why the change had been made. 'Because,' he replied, 'the Sultan ordered it.' On another

occasion I asked a palace official who in God's name had persuaded the Sultan to take a formal salute at a march-past dressed in a uniform that even Amin or Jean-Claude Bokassa, those two most repellent of African dictators, would have found ludicrously over the top in terms of braid and frogging. But His Majesty himself designed the uniform, I was told. Such examples, I think one has to agree, are not the acts of a man of a truly modest and retiring disposition.

And then, just as this book was nearing completion, in the dying days of 2003, there came, both literally and metaphorically, a shot from the blue, the consequences of which prompted many to question, for the very first time, the contradictions and the conundrums so long apparent to the few of the nature of the Sultan's rule, the fact that so much of the country's governance has had, and continues to have, an unreal quality. At first, like so much in the Sultanate, in a society where all too often the truth has been either wilfully suppressed or distorted, it began as a rumour. But, on this sad occasion, principally because the fatality was a European tourist, the truth of the matter refused to lie down and the bare, bleak facts slowly but surely emerged. In an increasingly violent world and in a region not particularly noted for its docility (to the north of the Sultanate, for example, the Palestinian Uprising continues in the face of the relentless seizure of Arab land by the Israeli state and in Iraq the US/UK armies of occupation continue to come under attack), the shooting of a tourist may not, at first sight, appear to be, in the harsh judgement of news editors in distant capitals, that much of a story. But this was in Oman, a country known for a peaceful domestic atmosphere and, what is more, its pro-Western stance. Yet, in a dramatically changing climate of hostility to both America and Britain for their invasion and occupation of Iraq, it was an image, a reputation, that was now to be badly tarnished. If the act itself was shocking, carried out in broad daylight in an urban area of the capital, the reaction of the Government, its efforts to conceal the facts of what had actually happened was, to the great majority, both Omani and expatriate, more shocking still. It had been a 'hunting accident'. This was, simply put, an evasion too far for so many in the expatriate community and, it has to be recorded, for a great number of Omanis too.

The initial shooting, which took place in October, at about noon, at the approaches to Muscat Private Hospital, involved a British visitor to the country who sustained serious wounds and was, in the event, flown home to Britain for further treatment. It was the Royal Oman Police who, at the insistence of the country's Ministry of Information, described the shooting as the result of a stray bullet from a hunting accident and this is just how it was reported in the State-controlled *Oman Daily Observer* newspaper, even given that the shooting took place in an urban area of the capital, one with steady traffic. While the expatriate community usually confines itself to social gossip of an inherently harmless nature, this tipped many into a nature of speculation based on raw fear, a fear that was given a quite terrible impetus on 2 December 2003, when a German tourist was shot and killed within yards of the British Embassy. On this occasion, the usually cautious and eminently sensible staff of the British Embassy acted with commendable speed, declining to wait for yet further incredible 'explanations' from the Omani authorities. Michael Snell, the First Secretary in the Consulate, issued the following statement on 3 December to British residents in the Sultanate:

> We have just been informed that a European tourist was shot and killed near this Embassy yesterday afternoon. The Royal Oman Police are investigating and we are seeking further details. Further, this is the second such incident in the past six weeks. Another European was shot and seriously injured close to Muscat Private Hospital in late October. On that occasion, the ROP put this down to a stray bullet from a hunting accident. You will understand that we can no longer be so sure, though more information will be required before we can be certain as to whether there is a connection or not. It is important that the community not become unduly alarmed. What we can say is that both incidents took place in broad daylight (one at noon and the other around 0900), in areas with open spaces, but with steady traffic. Both victims were alone at the time of the shooting. Neither was an obvious

target for attack. It is difficult to be prescriptive over the right advice in cases of random shooting but the community will wish to use common sense as they move around Muscat and consider keeping to areas well frequented by pedestrians when on foot, or waiting in a stationary vehicle. Please disseminate this message to the community in unedited form. We have no further information at this time, but will keep you informed of any significant developments.

By now, both the regional press, and expatriate computers, were most decidedly up and running, the latter with a palpable fear. On Thursday, 4 December, the Abu Dhabi-based *Middle East Newsline* ran the following short, sharp report. Under the headline 'Westerners Come Under Attack in Oman', the story ran:

> Another Western national has come under attack in Oman. A German national was killed in what Western diplomats said appeared to be an Islamic insurgency attack. It was the second shooting of a European national in the Sultanate in several weeks. On Tuesday a German national was shot dead near the British Embassy in Muscat. The Embassy said the shooting took place in a busy area during broad daylight. In late October, a British tourist was shot and seriously wounded near a Muscat hospital. Western diplomats said that the circumstances in both shootings suggested an insurgency attack.

With such detail now firmly in the public domain, and with it a wide discrediting of the decoy 'hunting' line from Oman's Ministry of Information, the reporting of the shootings now assumed the usual excitable tone so well practised by the press. Just one day after the more sober storyline from Abu Dhabi, its neighbour, the thrusting pack in Dubai, more than crossed the Ts of the story and dotted its Is. With a dateline of 5 December and the headline 'Two Europeans Shot in Muscat. German Succumbs to Bullet', the local press reported the following:

The 6,000-odd British nationals living in Oman are in the grip of a fear psychosis following a shooting incident, which the Royal Oman Police is investigating. A British national was shot and wounded in October and a German national was shot and killed in December, both in Muscat. Police are investigating both incidents. According to emails circulating among European citizens, a European tourist was shot and killed near an Embassy yesterday afternoon. This is the second such incident in six weeks. Another European was shot and seriously injured close to Muscat Private Hospital in late October. On that occasion the ROP put it down to a stray bullet from a hunting accident, said one such email. Oman has been a peaceful country but the anti-Western sentiment is so strong that the Westerners have been alerted to remain careful in public places. The British/American Schools received threatening calls and bomb hoaxes during the joint US/British Iraq attack.

While, unlike the shots fired in Sultan Said's Salalah Palace on 23 July 1970, the shots fired on the streets of Muscat in 2003 may well have not ricocheted around the world, they do raise the most serious questions as to the direction in which the country is to travel. For just as, for a disgracefully long period, the armed coup which brought Sultan Qaboos's father down was portrayed to the world as an 'abdication' of a monarch who, in any event, was not fit to rule, so, some 33 years later, is the daylight murder of civilians on the streets of the Omani capital portrayed as 'a hunting accident'.

The nature of such blatant and ludicrously designed propaganda by Oman's Ministry of Information, propaganda that would have had the Third Reich's spinmeister Dr Josef Goebbels blushing, does, inevitably, raise the most serious questions as to the grip the Sultan has on his administration and, indeed, on reality. It raises, too, with equal inevitability, the question of which road Oman is to travel as the twenty-first century unfolds, one in which autocracies can no longer control the free flow of information, however inconvenient it may be. Attempts to divert its flow will result in not only reducing the State to an international laughing stock but also infuriate the educated constituency at home to such a point that it will come, with an astonishing speed, to represent a challenge to the leadership itself.

But the urgent question has to be how such a situation can occur when the man wearing the crown is known to be of high intellect, intelligent in virtually every way, a man who knows the lessons to be learnt from the past, an able administrator, a supreme realist with regard to how the world is actually run and, most crucially of all, a leader who has proved that he has courage in abundance to confront unpalatable facts? What, then, is the true nature of the conundrum represented by Sultan Qaboos of Oman? Is it that he has a split personality or that, quite simply, he prefers not to challenge those who disseminate such palpable, unprofessional nonsense in his name, men such as Anthony Ashworth, the octogenarian former MI6 functionary who, for over a quarter of a century, has schooled Omani officials in the dark arts of propaganda – 'Lying for the State', as a senior Ministry of Information official describes the man's work.

As with every situation that defies rational explanation, an irrational answer has to be established. For it would be, in the final analysis, irrational to attempt to be rational in an irrational situation. There are many in Oman who are of the opinion that, with men such as Ashworth, the Sultan continues to feel under an obligation, even though, through his unbridled generosity, he has made both the man and his wife, Margaret, rich beyond their wildest dreams. But it would be as unfair as it would be irrational to lay the blame at the door of a man, a servant of the Omani Crown, for a situation which for far too long has been so apparently as dangerous as it has been ridiculous. For, surely, such a servant of the State could so easily have been apprehended in the peddling of his falsehoods? Yet no such measures have been taken and with such a bizarre fact is the Qaboos conundrum deepened. So an increasing number of Omanis and foreign observers of the Sultanate scene continue to lay the blame, not always justly, at Ashworth's door, with one prominent Omani, well known for the constant quality of his philosophical observations, deliberately paraphrasing a well-worn saying, commenting, 'Look, Omanis, on Tony Ashworth's works and despair.' And in a particularly sombre contemplation he comments further, 'My greatest fear is that the Ashworthian legacy will live on long after he has quit the country.' It is a fear shared by many, from both within the country and, indeed, further afield.

The highway of history is strewn with signs of warning and, irrespective of who is to blame for Oman's long-standing practice of dicing with the truth, the clearest sign is that it is a game that has run its course. Indeed, the time when rhetoric can be deliberately confused with reality is at a terminal end. So a change of tack, a change of direction in the State's dissemination of information, is, for the future credibility of Oman and its people, and its Sultan, too, a development long overdue, one that if postponed for much longer could lead to the most regrettable of consequences.

And, again as this book was being written, yet further evidence gives emphasis to the contradictions surrounding the Sultan's stewardship. To his many credits of being a cultured, sensitive man one could so well add the quality of his humanity, a man who, while given, on occasions, to bellowing away his frustrations at what he often perceives as the greed and incompetence of so many who attend him, is of a gentle nature, one who is well known to be particularly averse to any form of cruelty. Yet, on 17 December 2003, there came a news report from the Pakistani capital, Islamabad, which was as shocking for its content as it was for the fact that the truly horrid events it described are alleged to have taken place in Oman. Under the headline 'Pakistan to Raise Deportees' Torture Issue with Oman', the story, which was confirmed by a senior Government source in Islamabad, ran as follows:

> Islamabad is to take up with the authorities of Oman the allegations made by Pakistanis deported on Wednesday that they were tortured in Muscat jails. As many as 1,025 Pakistanis returned home by sea on Wednesday after they had been jailed for illegal entry and employment in Muscat. Many of them showed the marks of torture on their backs, which they say they received while in jail. Their backs bore large wounds; some with blood oozing, while others appeared to have been lashed. It has been some of the most horrifying footage that GEO television showed, causing outrage against the Omani authorities.

'This matter will certainly be taken up by us with the authorities in Muscat and we will get to the bottom of these allegations and find the truth about this,' Masood Khan, spokesman of the Foreign Office told *The News*. He said there are about 1,000 illegal Pakistanis still awaiting deportation in Oman. 'This is a huge problem for us and we are tackling it as a top priority for Pakistan. Since the year 2000 we have seen 22,000 Pakistanis being deported from Oman.' He said there are inputs and coordination from the Ministry of the Interior, the Coast Guard and the provincial governments but somehow trafficking of humans continues unabated.

Questions being asked include how desperate are these Pakistanis who are willing to risk their lives in search of a better livelihood? This is apparent from the fact that the returning Pakistanis said that when they were climbing the rough terrain to reach Muscat, it was littered with bodies of Pakistanis, Bengalis and Afghans being ripped apart by birds of prey.

It is a bleak, harsh report, one which was received in Muscat with a thunderous silence and one from which many, as in the past, will choose to divert their eyes. For Sultan Qaboos, personally, it will have been an affront and one which suggests that Government measures to review the country's Criminal Justice System, to put in place a judicial system of greater transparency, allied to a range of checks and balances designed to prevent, and punish, abuses of power in the country's police force and penal system, are a matter of some urgency. But, as ever it seems in Oman, those who surround the Omani leader, those who constitute a praetorian guard, a *cordon sanitaire*, will do their very best to ensure that such measures are not taken and, in the process, that their own agendas – the perpetuation of their personal power and the manner in which they wield it – will not be disturbed. Such practices at the top of Oman's establishment have resulted in what is best described as a wilful arrest of the intellectual development of Government, of the evolution of the machinery of the State, which would have made the necessary responses to rapidly changing social expectations held by the country's educated class, which expands with equal rapidity.

For the present, such men can rely upon the Sultan's unwillingness to confront them in any substantial manner, for fear, it would appear, of making enemies who would then plot against him, an attitude which is far from unusual on the Arabian peninsula, one based in substantial part on the premise that it is better by far to have an enemy in your tent, where he can be kept fully under observation, than on the outside looking in and urinating on its occupants. It is, however, a strategy not likely to last, in that, in Oman, the many in the land are becoming increasingly restless, with levels of toleration of such a situation wearing thinner by, virtually, every passing day. A British Ambassador of recent years remarked, at an Embassy dinner party, 'Oman is indeed a police state, but as long as Sultan Qaboos remains in charge it will continue to be benign.' It is an observation with which many will, with considerable degrees of justification, agree.

And, for the past 33 years, this, indeed, has been the case. Oman is, in regional terms, governed well, ruled by a man who would be regarded as outstanding in almost every way, humane, cultured, intelligent and, when the situation demands it, provocatively brave. Yet – and here again is the essential burden of the conundrum presented by his personality – why does he, on certain occasions, choose to abdicate his widely admired qualities and exercise instead those which damage the fluency and quality of his reign? Such a man must surely know that the hour is late and that there are many who seek full answers to the questions about his rule, which are, ever more stridently, being put. Not least men such as those Pakistanis whose taste of Oman, even given their illegal status in the Sultanate as workers (a system to which, for decades, senior Omanis have chosen to turn a blind eye, given that it has resulted in them being able to employ men on disgracefully pitiful wages), ended in the pain of the jailer's whip. The future of Oman as a peaceful, progressive country will depend on one of the world's last Sultans and the manner in which he reacts to an increasingly hazardous situation in the land over which he has so successfully reigned for so many years.

Chapter 10

CATASTROPHES FROM A TERRACE

When that distinguished man of letters, Jean Giraudoux, wrote, 'One of the privileges of the great is to witness catastrophes from a terrace', he could well have had the autocracies of the Arabian Gulf in mind. Of course, to be considered 'great' and to have, therefore, a privileged place on a terrace with a commanding view from which to observe the all too often irreverent passing parade of history, clearly establishes in the Arabian Gulf that history itself, with just a little tweaking here and there, has been at your command. And if unbounded riches spell power, it is doubtful that at any other time in the history of the human race have so few men been the recipients of such a huge transfer of wealth, in such an astonishingly short period of time, as the leaders of the Gulf, most of whom, in terms of geography and population, preside over the national affairs of what are termed 'pocket states'.

Indeed, from 1973, when the cartel of oil-producing nations, as represented by the Organisation of Petroleum-Exporting Countries (OPEC), placed the Western world over an oil barrel and rifled through its pockets for somewhat more than loose change, to 1986, when the price of crude oil began its initial descent on world markets, the amount of treasure which passed from the industrialised world to what a celebrated columnist of international stature described as 'a handful of desert nomads, more used to driving goats than Cadillacs' was phenomenal. It is improbable in the extreme that the world will ever see its like again and the changes such an enormous transfer of wealth wrought on, basically, a nomadic people, is worthy of an account all of its own. People did indeed go from herding goats across desert wastes and riding camels through towering sand dunes, to driving Cadillacs down multi-lane highways and across soaring fly-overs, and did so in well under a generation. As with the ruled, so with the rulers too, who harvested riches from 'black gold' way beyond the most extravagant dreams of avarice, men who, without exception, owed their thrones, their commanding positions on their respective national terraces, not to the decision of a national franchise but to the accident of birth, a tribal paramountcy, aptitudes and appetites for the exercise of raw power, a readiness to hasten history down its precarious and uncertain path via a little plotting and, of course, a compliant people. It was, and in many respects remains, at once both gaudy and gorgeous, morbid yet magnificent. For who with any imagination can fail to have their senses quicken at the sight of a Royal progress of Gulf leaders: the gold-trimmed robes, the dignity that can only come from Arab courtliness, the many genuflecting servants, the flash in the sun of a bejewelled hand, the graceful salutation of placing the left hand upon the heart? The leaders of the Arabian Gulf may, indeed, preside over the affairs of 'pocket states' but they do so with the style and manners of the rulers of the ancient world, and for all its ostentation and, on occasions, pretence, it remains, in the contemporary world at least, a sight to behold and, for the less grudging, to marvel at.

There is, of course, a national 'profit and loss' balance-sheet aspect to such dramatic social change, with the 'get rich quick and easy' syndrome of oil having resulted in a truly devastating effect on the Arab consciousness, as well as having laid low its manners and, all too often, warped the attitudes of its people. Now, the admirable courtesies so evident, for so long, in Gulf society have been replaced by an all-pervasive greed and arrogance and a nature of amorality of the most corrosive kind. Edward Gibbon, in his

Decline and Fall of the Roman Empire, wrote, 'Let the slaves of domestic tyranny exalt in their independence but the Arab is personally free.' Today, not only have so many in the Gulf States proved themselves to be slaves to materialism but they have also made the tragic assumption that from the money which makes acquisitions possible comes power too. Gone are the previously internationally admired and comprehensively respected virtues of the Arab race, central to which was the importance of honour and reputation. They have been replaced, as a result of an abdication of such values, values which had been nurtured down through the generations and made the race so impressive, by a range of social practices of the basest kind, which has been truly hideous, and painful, to witness. Such a social transition is most evident, to exercise the contemporary idiom, on the Arab street. Muscat, for example, has long been admired and rightly so, with a catalogue of praise ranging from 'The most Byronic of ports in the world', which indeed it is, to more prosaically, 'The most beautiful port in all Arabia', and it is that too. Yet, today, its graceful streets are so often assaulted by convoys of roaring, insanely careering cars, dangerously driven for effect alone, streets that, without the silent, long-suffering sub-continentals who sweep and clean them daily, would, within the time that it takes for the sun to rise and set, be similarly assaulted by a rising tide of rubbish, the flotsam and jetsam of both an affluent and an effluent society. And, in the city's otherwise splendid shopping malls can be seen the indolent manner in which groups of bored young men inspect merchandise, tossing items aside with a casual flick of the wrist and the insulting, disdainful manner in which staff, mostly from Asia, are treated. Such daily cameos of Gulf society demonstrate that while so much good has come from the wealth derived from oil, it has been accompanied by a frightening corrosiveness of a people who were for so long, and so rightly, regarded as nature's gentlemen, yet who have been coarsened by the very product that has, simultaneously, afforded them the salvation of education, medicine and the liberty of modern communications.

None of this, of course, has gone unnoticed; the collapse of a value system is known to have pained many, from the observation of Oman's leading intellectual commentator, a constant in his provocative bravery, Kamal Abulreddha Sultan, on the 'Coca-Colanisation of a natural way of life' to the Omani monarch himself, who personifies the qualities traditionally associated with the Arab race, the passing of which among so many of his people is an increasing cause for lament both far and wide but which even his autocratic rule has been quite unable to prevent. Yet once again, and in a different context from that which usually dominates discussion on the fabric of the Sultan's reign, it signals that even his absolute power over his subjects is vulnerable to social forces which, with the installation of modern systems of education – one of the most beneficial and, in its scope, remarkable aspects of his rule – have made him very much a hostage to fortune.

The pain and discomfort of the Sultan, born of his awareness that he has presided over a collapse in personal conduct by so many of his subjects; that his aesthetic sense, so apparent in numerous public works projects throughout the land, counts for little or nothing with the greater majority; that there is, in terms both pure and simple, an abandonment by so many of national decorum, is well known to a limited number of his inner, immediate circle. Of course, Omani society, its community of tribes, with its many strata and origins of its people, who inhabit a range of social and economic conditions, is little different in terms most basic from what has come to pass across the social expanse of the Western world. But what is of such fundamental significance in Oman's case is not just that such a radical and, to its ruler, distasteful downward spiral of values represents an irreversible social transition but that it has taken place in well under two generations and at a time when he was ostensibly setting the national scene in which the revitalisation of his people was being heralded, ad nauseam, as a 'renaissance' of the nation. It was a deliberate abuse of a term by the country's spin doctors which, given no artistic or intellectual circumstance was actually taking place in the Sultanate, has come to haunt them.

Just one aspect of a practice of Arab culture at its very best proves such a sad point. The design and construction of that beautiful 'queen of the seas', the dhow, has a special place in Oman's history, for here, in this ancient land, some of the finest sea-going craft of its type, with their sweeping, classical lines, were built. But, today, should one travel to the home of dhow construction, Sur, at the Sultanate's eastern extremity, one will find craftsmen from Bengal and Bangladesh patiently, skilfully constructing 'Omani' dhows. With the age of easy money from oil, so many Omanis have come to regard any kind of manual labour, even if it entails work of high craftsmanship, as demeaning and as such quite beneath them. The one person who knows both the truth and the pain of such a circumstance is their ruler, Sultan Qaboos, who, in private conversation and without in any fundamental manner diluting the very real affection he has for the people who are at once both his subjects and his compatriots, speaks of his despair at 'the road so many of the people have taken', whilst maintaining his faith and belief that, ultimately, a sizeable minority will seize the benefits and advantages given to them by the institutions of education which he has put in place. He is also well aware that it is those very same institutions that make him a hostage to fortune, a philosophical turn of mind which echoes the caustic, dismissive remark of his father all those years ago to the British Minister of State, Julian Amery, that most polished of courtiers, that if you educate a people they invariably turn against you, using as their principal tools of destruction the very education which has been made available to them! 'There is little gratitude given to those who lead,' the Sultan laconically observed to an English lady friend, herself not having been immune to the ingratitude of public service. To which he could so well have added, 'particularly when one is an absolute ruler', for in the final analysis, the people have no one else to blame.

Yet the picture which portrays so vivid a metamorphosis of public manners, a system of values gone berserk in the hard face of Western-sponsored materialism, where 'rich' equates with 'quick and easy' is, in Oman, not entirely black in colour. Indeed, Omanis remain, generally, one of the most courteous of people in the entire Arab world, with the independent spirit of hard, innovative work and mercantile spirit being regarded as the key with which to unlock personal success and social progress.

In 1986 John Wright, already a banker of no mean achievement and a particularly good representative of Scotland, was invited to the Sultanate to be the Chief Executive of the Oman International Bank (OIB), the brainchild of Dr Omar Zawawi, an Omani of well-established reputation as a businessman with the shrewdest of instincts and a pioneer in his field. Arriving in 1986 with his wife Christine, John Wright embarked upon what he now regards, at home, in retirement in Scotland, as 'the most remarkable experience of my career'. His story is of particular interest and significance in that it relates, in a most telling manner, the spirit of adventure, endeavour and opportunity which the reign of Sultan Qaboos spawned, an atmosphere where virtually everything and anything seemed possible:

> OIB was to be, as envisaged by its founder, Dr Zawawi, the country's very first 100 per cent Omani-owned bank, and we all set to with a will to ensure its success. During my time OIB grew from 14 branches to a national network of 63, far and away the largest in the country. In balance-sheet terms we were number three in 1986 but by 1991 had achieved the first spot. The commitment of our very young Omani workforce, simply put, made this possible. They worked all the hours God gave and were happy to be on duty at any time, real pioneers of the 24 by 7 by 365 culture that prevails in today's banking industry.
>
> We opened branches which served the remotest communities, some of them many hundreds of kilometres from the nearest town of any size. Those sent to establish these outposts were often very young and inexperienced but faced up to the demands of the environment and the job with equanimity and enthusiasm. We sent Nasser Rahbi to open the Wadi Tayeen branch. Tayeen, whilst an important agricultural area in the mountains, had very little in the way of a formal infrastructure and was accessible only by four-wheel drive, for some 75 kilometres through the mountains and over boulder-strewn river beds. The branch opened in the heat of summer but there was no power or other amenities so Nasser rolled himself in his dish-dasha and slept on the ground for many weeks until the weather became cool

enough for him to use the room that had been rented for him! Every week he made the trip to the nearest computerised branch to do his posting and to collect and deliver mail.

Such a will to succeed did have, on occasions, an amusing side to it. Nasser Al Hinai, an enormously enterprising and charismatic character, was the manger of our Rostaq branch, in the interior. Our competitor in the town, the National Bank of Oman, telephoned me to complain that Nasser had taken to standing outside their bank soliciting their clients to change to OIB, as they arrived and left the branch. He later became famous for the way in which he developed the market with the schoolteachers in the area, many of whom were Egyptian, working on two-year contracts. From his own pocket, Nasser rented buses which he and his staff drove down to Seeb International Airport, collected all the Egyptian schoolteachers, opened accounts for them on the bus and then delivered them to their destination!

His most famous exploit was, however, his formation of what became known as 'Al Hinai's Volunteers'. He mobilised teams of young people from all the branches in the area, which covered hundreds of kilometres, and at all meeting up in a designated town, they spent the weekend knocking on the doors of every house soliciting business. Would that we could see such enterprise in Scotland!

Another extraordinary tale involves the establishment in 1989 of a branch in the Shawmia, at a place called Al Hijj. At the time, Al Hijj was simply a newly created Government centre with a clinic, a police post and a handful of basic services. There was provision for a post office but postal services had not yet reached the Shawmia, so we used the post office building as our branch. The main business was fishing for tuna, very high-quality fish, with a high value, which was shipped to Japan. We discovered that the branch was some 60 kilometres from the fishing grounds and indeed during the season the fishermen tended to remain out at sea and the buyers who had travelled for several hundred kilometres over graded roads would have their own boats and go out and actually buy the catches at sea, transferring them straight on to their small, refrigerated four-wheel drives for transportation to the airport. Our first manager there, Said Al Bathary, a very enterprising individual, decided that he needed to rent a boat, which he duly did, and with his OIB-liveried Toyota Land Cruiser, he set up his stall on the beach, went out with the buyers, collected the cash, no receipts mind, took it back to the four-wheel drive, counted it, checked it, recorded it and once a week would drive the 300 kilometres to a computerised branch in one of the oil fields where he would post all the entries, post the passbooks and return the following day with the passbooks duly made up. Over a million pounds in savings deposits were generated in this way, with complete trust on either side. And like Nasser at Tayeen, Said spent many nights sleeping in the open.

One of the nicest illustrations of honesty that I can recall ever seeing in my career was at our old branch in Sinaw, yet another branch which was reached after a very tortuous 100-kilometre trip across the desert on a very rough graded road. By contrast you can now reach Sinaw in two hours from Muscat over a splendid highway. On my first visit to the branch I was having coffee with the manager when I became conscious that there was traffic in the branch through the front and their back doors. On closer scrutiny I found that at busy times customers would come in and if the lone teller was busy they would simply put down their withdrawal slip, or their cheque, and take the cash from the till themselves. This system worked beautifully and the cash always balanced!

Dhofar province, that legendary land, gave us its very own incidents, to recall and take delight in. A Dhofar gentleman, who had sold a camel, brought the proceeds into the main branch in Salalah. He had wrapped the banknotes in his headdress and because it had been raining some of the dye had run from the headdress into the notes, colouring them with a red dye. The transaction was duly processed and he was issued with a passbook. A couple of weeks later he returned to the branch and demanded to see his money. The staff produced the amount of cash from the strong-room, at which he flew into a rage, claiming that this was not his money because it did not have the red dye running through the notes!

Of course, I do have, today, my own personal perceptions and concerns about the economic future of Oman. There is no doubt that the country's history since 1970 is a remarkable story of economic and social development, built on strong historical and cultural foundations stretching back over many centuries. However, like any large company that has become set in its ways and has moved in the same direction for a considerable length of time, some significant change is now required. The analogies between the Sultanate and large companies are, I believe, relevant and unless His Majesty and his Ministers are prepared to actually undergo a programme of classic change management, I worry for the future of the country. Too little has been made of the country's geographic advantages for entrepôt-type trade and for manufacturing. Dubai has well and truly eaten Oman's lunch, to say nothing of its breakfast and dinner! This applies also to tourism, where there have been only half-hearted attempts to develop the industry in the Sultanate, with a strong dichotomy running between those espousing tourism and those advocates of national security. The end result of all of this is that Oman has a substantial, educated population of young Omanis who, essentially, are either under-employed or unemployed. The level of the dissent that this breeds is palpable and unless this is addressed expeditiously one fears for the future of the country. It would be a classic tragedy if the tremendous steps made since 1970 were lost at the finish.

Those who, throughout his reign, have commented on the Sultan's melancholy have invariably done so in the spirit of concern, matched by a sense of bewilderment as to why it should be so. For he is, even by the standards of the most demanding, the most likeable of men, kind, modest in his approach, generous to a fault, slow to condemn the faults and foibles of others and quick to forgive. While there were many who, in the opening months of his reign, grew increasingly concerned that he was, to quote a contemporary, 'infirm of purpose', and those who, subsequently, became concerned at his indecisiveness, there are few, today, who would question the resolve of the man at times of crisis. Yet so little observed and commented upon is the ever-present fact of the appalling loneliness of his position, a pressure to which so many men, as the years ran away, hastened by unrelenting demands, would have succumbed a very long time ago. Such sterling qualities as now identified have won him discreet admiration. While it is the usual practice of Her Majesty Queen Elizabeth to invest other heads of state with honorary knighthoods, few have received such accolades from Britain's Sovereign as Qaboos of Oman. Indeed, he has three. He is a Knight Grand Cross of the Order of the Bath (GCB), the Order of St Michael and St George (GCMG) and the Royal Victorian Order (GCVO). For a ruler of Royal rank, the Sultan's uniforms bear a considerable number of decorations but he is known to take a special pride and pleasure in the investitures from his British counterpart and, allied to an interest described by an Omani courtier as 'intense' in the badges and uniforms of his own Court and Armed Forces, wears them with particular relish. A peacock in the desert.

Indeed, many of those badges and uniforms have been personally inspired and designed by the Sultan, with the 'intense' nature of his interest in the minutiae of the matter leading to many frequent changes. But such an interest, such Royal, solemn concern for the appearance and the welfare of his Armed Forces, is, on occasions, far from being respected by some expatriates who have taken, in military parlance, the 'Sultan's Shilling' and are thus bound by an oath of allegiance to his service. While such men bray their 'loyalty' to the person of His Majesty in the loudest of public terms possible, some of them, ignoring the widely used and affectionate expatriate appellation for Oman's ruler of 'Super Q', stoop to the also widely used nickname of 'Sooty'.

Yet such a fact does not diminish the attendant detail that, for every expatriate officer of doubtful conduct, many of whom arrived in Oman just about as far as possible as it can be from the conventional military route, there are a greater number by far who have served the Sultan, who were prepared to give their lives for him and his throne, with raw courage, bravery and the best of honour, men such as Brigadier Colin Maxwell and Major-General Geoffrey Harcourt and a legion of others quite literally too numerous to name.

And if Qaboos has inspired both respect and affection in Britain, from the British monarch to British individuals who bore arms for him, they are human attitudes reciprocated by Oman's Sovereign. If imitation is indeed the sincerest form of flattery, then a desire to reside in the land of one's affections must, surely, come a pretty close second. Earlier in this book the Sultan's considerable property holdings in Britain were mentioned, with his first purchase of a countryside property being identified, Wargrave Manor, in the Thames Valley, a quite splendid house overlooking the river. Then, in a perfect combination of his affection for Britain and for Western classical music, he made his more recent purchase of Grove House, located on the northern fringes of London's Regent Park. This most striking house was built in 1823 by Decimus Burton for the noted scientist of the time, George Greenhough. During its 180-year life, Grove House has passed through the hands of various owners, one of whom in more recent times converted the main drawing room into a music room, which is used by its present owner for occasional private concerts. And so, for the moment at least, the music does indeed play on.

Just as there were those who, at the outset of Sultan Qaboos's reign, questioned whether or not he would, in the event, prove to be 'up to the job', being, in turn, both saddened and then alarmed by his apparent infirmity of purpose, that he was plagued by persistent indecisiveness that stultified his grip on power, there are those, today, who are similarly troubled by the equally apparent contradictions in his character. It is not difficult to see why.

No one doubts for one moment that here is a really quite

extraordinary man, one whose intellect, creativity, imagination and sense of purpose would be considered exceptional even without the dimension of one who has had the courage to take upon himself the role of national leader bequeathed him by birth and history. Yet alongside his shrewd political instincts and courage sits his continuing inability, for example, to rein in the more base, greedy and vainglorious appetites exercised by so many of those around him. The Sultan's unwillingness to confront this situation constitutes, in the words of a courtier, 'a scandalous tolerance' of those craven individuals to whom he believes, quite erroneously (for he has long stuffed the mouths of such men with gold to the point of suffocation), he owes some sort of debt and those whom he fears will create trouble for him if he dismisses them from office. This is all the more perplexing to those, the great majority, who fear for the reputation of his rule given that by continuing to allow such individuals access to him, the quality and, indeed, the duration of his time upon the throne of Oman is called into public question. This courage and conviction, so well demonstrated and recorded, as opposed to an abiding contradiction of vacillation, indecisiveness and intimidating fears where none should ever be allowed to exist, remains the essential conundrum in the Sultan's character. One of the more basic examples of the damage this has caused, and continues to cause, is in Government policy relating to the publication of information, with the result that many young, educated Omanis regard such a policy as a humiliation difficult to bear and that the only solution is for the Ministry of Information to be completely shut down, abolished and some of its functions carried out through the Heritage Ministry. It would not be a measure without precedent in the Arab Gulf.

Shortly after taking over from his father on 27 June 1995, in a bloodless palace coup, the Emir of the oil-rich state of Qatar, Sheikh Hamad bin Khalifa al-Thani, took the decision to disband the country's Ministry of Information and thereby end press censorship. Once this unprecedented measure had been taken, others of an equally progressive, liberating nature quickly followed, with Qatar blazing a trail of politically inspired progress which so many had hoped Oman would pioneer, not least many of its own people. A draft constitution, enshrining the principle of universal suffrage, which will put Qatar firmly on the road to parliamentary democracy, was ratified by some 96 per cent of the country's electorate in a national referendum. Women enjoy full and equal rights with men and are encouraged to take their place in the political and economic life of the country and to take full advantage of the country's rapidly expanding academic institutions.

In the arch-conservative atmosphere of the Gulf, Qatar's pioneering path of political progress is regarded as little short of revolutionary, although four years earlier, in 1991, Oman's Sultan had taken the first cautious, controlled steps towards laying the foundations of parliamentary government with the creation of a Majlis Ashura, a consultative body, on a partially elected basis. The Majlis includes women in its number, although throughout the Sultan's reign women have been actively encouraged to take their place in the civil service, the professions and the commercial life of the country. The introduction of such an institution into the body politic of the Sultanate was designed to meet the rising expectations of so many to have a greater involvement in the governing of their country, although its consultative role was, and indeed remains, severely restricted to simply suggesting laws and regulations to the ruler, with it being expressly forbidden to debate three of the most crucial matters of State: foreign policy, the financing of the country's Armed Forces and the running of the State-owned oil and gas industry. These are limitations which have inevitably led to widespread disillusionment among Omanis, so much so that, in the words of *The Economist* of 9 August 1997, the Majlis is regarded as being 'ineffectual'. Further elections were held to the body in 2003 but the public's disenchantment with and consequent apathy towards the institution, which in 1991 seemed to promise so much, has only intensified. Indeed, so much so that of the 800,000 Omanis deemed eligible to vote, less than 25 per cent of this number went to the polls. Furthermore, the 500-plus candidates were forbidden to hold public meetings and, if this was not enough in the inhibition stakes, a notice prominently displayed on the Ministry of Information's staff noticeboard declared, 'No one is allowed to talk to any of the candidates standing for election on any of the programmes.' It is an injunction with which Josef Stalin of Soviet Russia would have had full and ample sympathy.

The Sultan, again demonstrating his ability to command bold initiatives when circumstance demands it, had, in November 1996, issued a Decree establishing a Basic Law, in effect an Islam-inspired constitution, with a Bill of Rights guaranteeing press freedom, religious tolerance (for so long an admirable human quality of both the ruler and the ruled in Oman due, principally, to the spirit and tenets of Ibadhi Islam, to which the greater majority of Omanis adhere) and equality of race and gender in the eyes of the law. An assurance was also made that the provisions in the Basic Law would be protected and, when required, interpreted by an independent arm of the country's judiciary. But, as a senior observer of the Omani scene has commented, as with so much with Sultan Qaboos, the initial promise of a State initiative, from a crackdown on corruption to an end to press censorship, never actually comes to pass, as recent events on the streets of the capital – the gunning down of individuals being described as a result of a 'hunting accident' – all too sadly prove.

The 'Shadows' and 'Substance' factor, as a reflection on the character of the country's 14th Sultan, has, by force of circumstance, to take a principal place in any legitimate account of his life and reign. This conundrum has led, more disturbingly, to at least two known planned attempts on the life of the Arab Islamic world's most extraordinary leader. Both attempts were thwarted, the first, in the 1970s, thanks to the alertness of an officer in the Royal Oman Police, the second thanks to Egypt's Security Services, which picked up on the plan from their own home-grown operations, prompting President Hosni Mubarak to advise Sultan Qaboos, who then took with equal promptness the necessary measures.

Central to the plan was the assassination of the Sultan as he attended the country's 24th National Day celebrations in the ancient former capital of Nizwa on 18 November 1994. The assassination was to be accompanied by explosions in three of Muscat's shopping malls, designed to cause chaos, confusion and public panic, during which the reins of power would have been seized. During a series of nationwide arrests in May 1994, over 200 were arrested on suspicion of being involved in the plot of murder, mayhem and treason, of which some 131 were brought to trial. Among their number were a limited number of Royal Oman Police officers, together with members of the Armed Services and a small number of senior civil servants. Of the 131, two received the death penalty, while the remaining defendants received prison sentences ranging from three to fifteen years.

While the Sultan commuted the death sentences to terms of imprisonment, the United States 1994 Human Rights Country Report for Oman, issued on 1 February 1995, recorded its own verdict on the trials: 'The defendants did not receive a fair trial by international norms.' It further observed:

> Oman is an autocracy in which the Sultan retains the ultimate authority on all important foreign and domestic issues. The country has no formal democratic institutions and its citizens do not have the ability to peacefully change their leaders or the political system.

In a country with such a tightly controlled press and broadcasting service, the wider questions as to what may have motivated such men to conspire against their Sultan with such murderous intent were not allowed to be discussed, even when, in November 1995, he decreed an amnesty for those who had been taken into custody 18 months earlier, with a brief Government statement referring to those now being given their liberty as 'having been convicted of involvement in illegal activities and organisations'.

But still the embers of dissent continued to burn. In the autumn of 1997, the former US Secretary of State, Madeline Albright advised the Sultan's Government of security information which listed a number of Omanis who were making financial contributions to Islamic organisations which were using funds to assist that most feared group, Hamas. As a result of this, a further round of arrests were made. Such a development put the burning question once more to the fore: what, exactly, was the human chemistry that prompted men of previous goodwill and, up to that time, undoubted commitment to their ruler and country, men of considerable intellect, to plan to take up arms against a system from which they had personally derived great benefit? Was it religious fervour alone? Hardly, for the facts fail most comprehensively to justify such a belief, although this was, of course, propagated in suitably muted coded tones in Oman following the arrests of May 1994.

However, and in a yet further demonstration of the quality of moral courage at his command, Sultan Qaboos did take the opportunity of his annual address to the nation on 18 November 1994, in the stadium at Nizwa, the time and the place at which his assassination was planned, to warn his people against a subversion of the spiritual message of Islam. In a speech that impressed many, he warned Omanis of 'extremism under whatever guise, fanaticism of whatever kind and factionalism of whatever persuasion'. It was a speech which constituted a defining moment of his reign and he continued:

> The backwardness of Muslims in recent times has rendered them incapable of making use of their inheritance, resulting in weakness among the Muslim nation which has brought about fanaticism based on a lack of knowledge about the correct facts of the religion. It has been exploited by some to perpetuate violence and propagate cases of difference that lead to discord and hatred.

If, indeed, it was a speech that took courage to deliver and was of sufficient merit to resonate around the international family of Islam in 1994, it is, in the tragedy-torn world of 2004, one which deserves to ring around the globe, not just to warn law-abiding Muslims of the danger they continue to face, the danger of having their faith distorted, but also to warn the wider international community of the danger they continue to conjure for themselves, particularly the Western world, by continuing to ignore the cruelty and injustices being perpetrated against the people of Palestine, the cause of which has led so many of previous good intent to take up arms in an attempt to seek justice and restitution. And, post-11 September 2001 and the US/British invasion and occupation of Iraq, there is a strong need for both Washington and London, in particular, to act urgently not just upon the effect that such injustice and dispossession gives rise to but also upon the root of its very cause. In such a necessary exercise it would be salient, too, for Western leaders to remember that it was one of the world's very last autocratic rulers, the leader of an Islamic nation, who had the insight and the moral courage to deliver a clarion-call as to the dangers of 'fanaticism' and 'factionalism', hardly the practices of Arabs and Muslims alone, which has as much relevance to those to whom it was addressed a decade ago as it has to all who have the courage to recognise the injustices of the past and, in so doing, nurture a care for the future.

As early as nine years into his reign, Sultan Qaboos demonstrated his very own brand and spirit of independence when, in 1979, Oman was the only state in the Arab world to recognise Egyptian President Anwar al-Sadat's accords with Israel. According such recognition was a provocatively brave move which, for many years, served not just to isolate the Sultanate from the mainstream of Arab Islamic politics but led to Oman's ruler himself becoming something of a 'whipping boy' for those to whom the Egyptian–Israeli Agreement was anathema, the very work of the Devil, no less. But the Sultan held firm and though the passing years were often difficult – not least with the assassination of President Sadat in 1981, when a member of Oman's military delegation attending the fateful parade was also killed – it was a foreign policy decision which, in time, was vindicated, with much of the Arab Islamic world eventually following the Sultanate's example.

Interestingly, one of the most commonly heard criticisms expressed by Omanis of their Sultan is that the country's foreign policy is too pro-Western and has isolated them from the Arab Islamic mainstream. It is, they say, a situation similar to that which existed under the rule of his isolationist father. As one Omani student remarked:

> The causes are different, with Sultan Said just having
> wanted to keep the outside world away from the country
> while Qaboos is just too pro-Britain, too pro-America, for the

liking of many of my generation. We want him to speak out
more for the Palestinians and not always allow the British
and the Americans to use the country for their own military
purposes.

Even when the natural enthusiasms and political indiscretions of
youth are laid aside (the counter argument put in response to such
assertions – 'Yes, but in 1991 the US/British military initiative freed
the Kuwaitis from Iraqi occupation' – having been met with a
fatalistic shrug of the shoulders), it is a valid point to take into
account when a consideration of Oman's foreign policy, under the
rule of Sultan Qaboos, is being considered. And it is valid simply
because the criticisms implicit in the student's comments are, as a
considered point of view, entirely legitimate.

Yet had Omanis, and indeed so many in the wider world, had
sight of a report of an interview Oman's ruler gave to the
distinguished American author and journalist, Judith Miller, in
February 1997 at his Muscat Palace, then a different view of his
political deftness – and, indeed, his courage to take an independent
path, one shorn of dogma and stripped so comprehensively of self-
serving propaganda – and a different public opinion as to his
nature and political intent, may well have prevailed during recent
years. Indeed, Judith Miller's report, hitherto confined to
publication in the US Council on Foreign Affairs journal, *Foreign
Affairs*, for May and June 1997, is regarded as being of pivotal
importance in that it reveals as much about Qaboos as a ruler who
clearly thinks for himself and exercises a keen intellect in a
particularly effective manner, as it does about the quiet,
determined nature of Qaboos the man. Such interviews are rarely
granted and the event was additionally notable for the fact that it
was of three hours' duration. While the interview took place some
seven years ago, it has an even greater relevance now, post-11
September 2001, the second Iraq war and the collapse of the
Palestinian peace process, than it did then.

Judith Miller began the interview by asking the Sultan if he had
any concerns about Washington's policy of 'dual containment'
towards Iran and Iraq.

Nations should be talking to one another. Iran is the largest country in the Gulf, with 65 million people. You cannot isolate it. You can be frank in expressing your grievances, and we are. I don't mince my words. I tell them that the whole world is beginning to work together, that they can't sit apart and go on without the rest of the world. They can't survive if they do. When I talk to some officials, I'm encouraged by their response. The issue is whether they can impress the others sufficiently. Iraq is a different matter. Economic sanctions must remain until Iraq completely abides by the UN resolutions adopted at the Gulf War's end. Iraq violated the international code of conduct by invading a neighbour and by amassing weapons of mass destruction, far more than what was needed to defend itself. So no violation of the resolution, no detail can be overlooked.

The question was then put on Washington's justification of sanctions against Iran by citing Tehran's support for terrorism, its opposition to Arab–Israeli peace and its own intensive efforts to develop weapons of mass destruction. 'Europe has failed in its quest for constructive engagement, why not try isolation?' asked Judith Miller.

The Sultan's reply was so obviously based on personal experience, not all of it easy:

I know that dealing with Tehran can be very difficult. Iran has different factions in its leadership. There are those willing to try to make Iran do what is needed to take its rightful place in the international community. But there is another side that lives in its own world, not in ours. Then there is a third faction that waits, and whose exact views are unclear. There is a hidden power struggle. My view is: if the Government can bring itself to take a different approach to the West, one that produces benefits, then the third faction might support greater pragmatism. But there is no easy solution. Time will tell.

As to his views on the Arab–Israeli peace process, Oman's ruler was no less explicit:

> The Palestinians remain the core of the problem. The second line is Syria and Lebanon. For Lebanon, the issue is one of security since Israel has not annexed any Lebanese territory. For its part, Syria wants to restart talks where they left off, which is not an unreasonable request. They don't want to return to square one all the time. Based on my conversations with Syria's leaders, I'm convinced they want peace, a comprehensive peace. There is no doubt. So once the Golan Heights issue is solved, there shouldn't be any problem with Syria. But the big issue for us, particularly in the Gulf, is Jerusalem, guaranteed access to the city's holy sites, which is crucial for us, and the separate issue of who lives where. I don't want to speculate about how Jerusalem should be tackled or settled. That should be left to those concerned. Each side is aware of the other's political constraints. The rest of us should not intervene or pressure. Oman will support the Palestinians in whatever agreement they reach with Israel.

Judith Miller then raised the question of the threat of senior Arabs to resume the economic boycott of the Jewish state. The Sultan, in his reply, made plain that his Government did have direct dialogue with the Israelis and had not succumbed to the virus, so sadly apparent in so many Arab moves, of quite the most terrible acts of self-delusion:

> We watch the political thermometer closely. When it's hot, we make our views known to the Israelis. But a resumption of the boycott is not a possibility, happily. And quite frankly, I hope it is not on anyone's list. The boycott never worked anyway. We have walked so many kilometres towards peace that it would be tragic to start going backwards now.

Referring to a car accident in 1995, in which he could so easily have lost his life, and in which his Finance Minister was killed, the question was then asked if such an incident had prompted him to introduce plans for a Basic Law, based on a concern for the succession process in the event of his death. The reply is particularly revealing:

> We used to be governed in a very traditional way. When I was entrusted to be the Sultan, I already had some views about how the country should be ruled. I had spent six years in Britain [1958–64] experiencing work in different sectors. That background gave me a good basis for thinking about things differently. I had promised on the first day of my rule to create a modern government. But I knew change had to be entered into slowly, very slowly. The level of education had to reach a certain point so that people would know what we were talking about. We went from almost zero schools to more than 1,000 and a university in 25 years. I had already established a Consultative Council, but one whose members were appointed by me, not elected. But it was all coming together. As I approached my silver jubilee, I said to myself, this is the time. So I got together four of my most trusted people, all Omanis. I sat with them and told them exactly what I had in mind. I gave them a year to formulate it in a legal document. Then we had a second review, and then a final session. I announced it on my annual 'Meet the People' tour, while encamped in the desert, in the heart of Oman. Then I waited for the reaction, which was very good. Now the Basic Law is being implemented through laws and regulations. I had hoped that this could be done within two years, but that period may have to be extended for an additional year. We'll see. By the year 2000 I want it implemented. My first priority is to establish a judicial system, a Supreme Court and other judges and courts. The Supreme Court will be the guardians of the law. Without that you can't have a proper government. They are the ones to say what is right and wrong. My role is to see that the interests of the people are taken into account. It's not my role to

interpret the law. Only if certain, basic things go wrong would I intervene, as would any head of state. And I will appoint the judges.

Judith Miller, obviously now emboldened by the Sultan's directness and complementary candour, decided to raise, albeit delicately cloaked in the most diplomatic of terms, the question of ministerial corruption, so long a particular bugbear with which Oman's ruler has been obliged to wrestle. The Monarch's reply was no less diplomatic:

Islam gives people the right to own private businesses. But no Minister should use his public post for private gain. So those who hold senior public posts should resign from their private boards. We'll also look at whether their family members should also resign. The people I chose were selected because I trusted them, not because they are my friends or relatives. If they go astray, I'll find someone else. I feel strongly about this.

At this point Judith Miller, true to the democratic instincts and political arrangements of her native United States, raised the key question: what about the future of the Majlis, the Consultative Council? When will its members be able to take their seats not via the ultimate sanction of their Sultan but via the election of the people, and be able to make laws as opposed to merely reviewing them and suggesting amendments? And when would Oman's Sultan hold office via universal franchise? At such a delicate point of the conversation, Sultan Qaboos obviously thought that a little gentle education was called for, in the ways and means of Arab democracy:

At present, people throughout the country meet in their districts and select two or three Majlis candidates and we choose among them. In the long run, the Majlis will be elected, yes, by all Omanis. And the Majlis powers will expand with time, but slowly, so there are no earthquakes. But we are still largely a tribal society, and it's still the

Government's duty to defend the country. The man in the street often doesn't want or know how to deal with foreign governments or defend the country. He trusts me to do it. That is why these areas have been excluded from the Majlis debate. In this part of the world, giving too much power too fast can still be exploited. Elections in many countries mean having the army prevent bloodshed. Is this democracy? Are these happy countries? Do such elections give people real choices? No. They are really just power struggles. I'm against creating such situations when people are not ready for them. As for the Sultan, he is already elected, but not in the way you know. In Oman, you have to earn kingship. We have no heirs apparent. I myself did not become Sultan until a week after the event [deposing his father]. I was only Sayyid, that is, roughly, Lord, until key members of my family and the other leading tribes approved me. As for a successor, the process, always known to us, has now been publicised in the Basic Law. When I die, my family will meet. If they cannot agree on a candidate, the Defence Council will decide, based on a name or names submitted by the previous Sultan. I have already written down two names, in descending order, and put them in sealed envelopes in two different regions.

The question was then put as to the nature of the measures he had taken since becoming Sultan in which the greatest pride is taken. Here, Oman's 14th Sultan, ever anxious, and rightly so in a world in which so much wilful misinterpretation of Islam abounds, took no hesitation in identifying a priority which so ably proves his particular propagation of progressive Islam:

> I congratulate myself for some things, such as the progress women have made. I never said you must do this or you can't do that. I offered services, such as education, and let the families decide. And more of them than I expected chose to accept schools for girls from the beginning. So we have been able to make progress and safeguard tradition.

Judith Miller asked, by way of conclusion, why his more radical provisions in the Basic Law, such as equal rights for women, hadn't been challenged by militant Islamists as 'un-Islamic'. The Sultan responded with what can best be described as 'home truths', so often ignored in the wider world when the subject of Islam comes under debate:

> Islam is not opposed to progress. You can't stop evolution. And while we believe that certain traditions should be observed, Islam provides for ijtihad, for everything being reviewed and interpreted in the time and context of the moment. Those who argue differently are using Islam for their own political reasons. They twist things and they give our religion the wrong image. There is nothing in Islam that prevents a society from living in its day within a framework of tradition. Even in the time of the Prophet, women took their rightful place in society. There should be no discrimination against working women. They should have the same job titles, salaries and benefits. The problem now is that more and more ladies want jobs. So men are feeling the heat. They are competing with us! I say, why not? We have some senior ladies in government. I hope we'll have some more senior women in government soon. We're making progress, but quietly. Slowly. I believe in evolution, and not a sudden evolution. But the progress we've made is irreversible.

In terms of an executive head of state setting out his stall for the future of the country in his command, the interview was little short of brilliant. Indeed, the State-sponsored practice of equivocation, which has deliberately, and for no rational reason whatsoever, obscured so much of Oman's past and obfuscated its future, was, in an open and candid manner, cast aside. It was, for the Sultan, a triumph of his own will and, for Judith Miller, witness to a most professional job. And it demonstrated, too, that, flying in the face of the widespread suspicion and misrepresentation about the Islamic world and its leaders, here were the words of a ruler who rendered them to be the falsehoods they so patently are and explained, with tact and eloquence, that the woeful ignorance, the wilful fabrications and the gross generalisations so often peddled in the West about the Arab Islamic world can be discounted.

All of this being so, how totally counter-productive was the pressure brought by officials in Muscat, when they caught sight of Judith Miller's text, to ensure that the detail so freely and openly expressed by the Sultan should not be allowed the light of day beyond publication in the US *Foreign Affairs* journal. The 'reasoning' behind such pressure not only beggars belief but speaks volumes on the malignant influence of Sultan Qaboos's praetorian guard and the damage, over the years, they have been able to inflict upon his name and, therefore, the reputation of his rule. But that is exactly what came to pass and, until the writing of this book, this illuminating interview has gone unheralded in the wider world.

Of course, there will be those who choose to decry the Sultan's continued belief in the validity and, therefore, the relevance (even in an Arab Islamic society) of Sultanic rule, that the ethic of 'father knows best' ('The man in the street often doesn't want or know how to deal with foreign governments or defend the country. He trusts me to do it.') is right for the Omani people, for now at least. While there is considerable truth in such an observation, one not confined to Oman – consider the appallingly high numbers of those in both Britain and the United States who simply don't seem to want to know, or care, how their respective countries are governed and thus fail to cast their votes – it is an observation which has a decidedly uncomfortable ring when set alongside the attitude of his father for, in that respect, they are alarmingly similar, and it was just such an attitude, in important part, that was cited to justify his overthrow. And given the speed with which Oman's educated constituency grows, it is a belief with the most limited application. Such a writ cannot run for much longer. Yet even here the Sultan was all too ready to confirm his belief in the evolutionary nature of society and that the reforms of his rule were 'irreversible'. Indeed, the interview reveals as much about the temperament of the man, the inner workings of his mind, as it does about his instincts and inclinations for the future. This is of importance simply because there can be few countries where the personality, the character of its leader, has been so closely bound up and identified with its head of state, as the Sultanate of Oman. There can also be little doubt that it is because of this very aspect of his rule that so much, particularly during the first quarter of a century of his time on the throne of Oman, was, in material and physical terms, achieved.

The country's Ministry of Information has been doubly disingenuous in propagating the belief to the outside world that, under Qaboos's rule, a 'modern government' (it is interesting that the Sultan used such a term in his interview with Judith Miller) has been achieved. It is an assertion which is blatantly untrue, given that even the most cursory examination of the facts tells a quite different story altogether. The country, with its soaring office blocks, flyovers, schools, hospitals and a university, may well present a face of modernity to the contemporary world but the actual machinery of government remains feudal, if not medieval, in design and practice. The Court of the Sultan particularly, which revolves around preferment within his gift, is most certainly feudal in both content and character and it is this which an increasing number of Omanis find so unacceptable. They also, again increasingly, regard the Sultan's ultra-cautious moves towards, for example, adult suffrage, as an impediment to an eventual peaceful, non-revolutionary progress to representative government. With regard to the Sultan's cautious approach to the future – 'You can't push things too far or too fast in the Gulf', he so often remarks – he demonstrates a sad lack of awareness, just like his father, that time is not necessarily on his side and particularly so given Washington's most recent and, to some, alarmingly dramatic change of tack on its commitment to forging, in the words of President George Bush, 'democratic principles throughout the Arab world'.

This is, however, for tomorrow and while time is limited to effect change in the Sultanate of an evolutionary nature, it would be as well to recognise that the clock has begun its unstoppable revolution to midnight for the Arab world's remaining autocracies. For the present, Sultan Qaboos should be accorded every right to savour the scope and scale of progress in Oman of which he, himself, has been the instigator. And while it may be principally of a material nature, what a journey it has been!

In another interview, conducted for this book, the writer and journalist Ian Cummins, for many years a resident in the Sultanate, offered his own insights into the country. He began by chronicling an account of the situation in the land at the time of the country's 'new dawn', the ascendancy of Sultan Qaboos to the throne, which illustrates in a particularly evocative manner a 'then' and 'now' picture:

> It was utterly and starkly different then. When Neil Armstrong was bunny-hopping across the surface of the moon, men in Oman were still wrestling with antique systems of taxation and import duties of such dazzling complexity that few, if any, outsiders could even begin to understand them. Currency and trade transactions in the Muscat souq were, at the time, subject to a truly startling array of imponderables and complications. For in daily use within the memory of those currently middle aged were Omani and Dhofari baizas, Maria Teresa Dollars (MTDs), divided into 120 Omani baizas but actually traded at the rate of five rupees (which did not, of course, officially exist) to the MTD, while exchange rates in general were formally fixed in terms of the Kuwaiti dinar. The extraordinary thing about all of this was that such Byzantine complexity was in direct inverse proportion to the Sultanate's provision of the most basic amenities of late twentieth-century life. There was schooling only for nine hundred male children in only three establishments in the capital. There was one, rudimentary, hospital. There was no electric light, no mains water and, in the entire country, fewer than ten kilometres of paved road.
>
> What Oman did have in abundance was a mind-rotting, soul-destroying obsession with regulations, usually by way of outright prohibition of even the most minor comforts of day-to-day existence. Travel outside the Sultanate? Absolutely forbidden in general and only most rarely

permitted and then only by the Sultan in person. The wearing of sunglasses? Forbidden on pain of arrest and incarceration in Fort Jalali, the prison in the capital. Nobody, least of all those who had done time in the Fort, made jokes about prison in Oman.

Muscat was a gated city. If you had been outside the capital, buying, let us say, fodder for your donkey, everyman's taxicab, you had to be back by 9.00 p.m. and carrying a lantern. If you were late, you were locked out. And if you had the temerity to turn up without a lantern after dark, you were locked up. If you lived in Oman, you were trapped in a barbed-wire filigree of petty controls. And all of this aggravation did not come to an instant end on 23 July 1970, with the coup that rammed Sultan Qaboos bin Said onto his father's throne. The official version, spelt out in a succession of nicely produced booklets aimed at journalists and other opinion-formers for 'guidance', is that Qaboos sprang fully loaded, so to speak, onto the stage, waved a wand (burgeoning oil revenues, actually) and transformed his country overnight. That is simply spin and nonsense and, as it happens, seriously devalues the hard work and very real achievements of a complex, many-faceted man who has changed as greatly as his country over the decades.

For a start there was not universal rejoicing about Qaboos seizing power. There were other contenders, some of whom, together with their main supporters, still languish under a sort of house arrest. There were also those who wanted an Islamic republic, a full-blown theocracy such as has been established in neighbouring Iran, while others, especially in the south, in Dhofar, favoured a hard-left, Marxist government of the sort that came to hold power in the state next door, the People's Democratic Republic of Yemen. These people were more than marginally important since they managed to get a vicious insurrection under way in Dhofar, which was to cost much in terms of blood and treasure for more than five years. And, of course, there was the Sultan's uncle, Sayyid Tariq bin Taimour, who had been appointed

Prime Minister and who favoured the establishment of a constitutional monarchy, which would have given the country an historic, honoured place in the world as the very first Gulf state to institute parliamentary rule. Of course, this was not to be, as so many who had the Sultan's ear, not all of them Omani, intrigued against him and by stealth and fabrication made his job so impossible that he resigned and left the country. It was a tragedy for Oman and a lost opportunity of historic proportions for which, even now, the Sultan and, indeed, the country, could well pay dear. Nor, contrary to the official line, was there always the 'unanimity of purpose' so beloved of the Government's spin doctors. Those closest to the man in the driving seat have said that the early cabinet meetings were liable to become tempestuous very quickly. Moreover, given that the climate of pettifogging regulations drove out a great many of the best and the brightest, many of whom went on to constitute a highly effective and vocal overseas opposition, the pool of talent shrank. Indeed, Qaboos was not blessed with a huge array of talent from which to choose Ministers. One glance at the number of portfolios he claimed gives some idea of the scale of the problem.

To be sure, huge and radical changes to the fabric of Oman in general and Muscat in particular came thick and fast. Mountains were, quite literally, moved to make way for roads and houses; wadis were tamed, more or, sometimes, less; schools appeared at a famous rate; and more and more Omanis, not all of whom were immediately appreciative, were able to sample something approaching modern health care.

The high point in the process came, in my view, in 1985. In a survey to mark the 15th National Day celebrations, I wrote that Qaboos had substantially succeeded in honouring the bulk of the promises he made in his first ever speech to the Omani people. He had, I concluded, laid the foundations of an excellent infrastructure and the basis of a modern government. But it has to be said that even then there were many people who, while publicly throwing their hats in the air, harboured severe reservations.

Qaboos, in his first years in power, was famously impatient. He wanted change. He wanted it in all sorts of fields and, above all, he wanted it now. By 1985 there were bright young Omanis, most of whom had graduated from Western universities, asking when, not if, they were going to get some sort of political say in the running of the country. Government by Sultanic Decree was already beginning to look decidedly authoritarian and unattractive by the last quarter of the twentieth century. To be sure, the economy was booming and there was a general sense of well-being. But there were already mutterings in and out of the mosques about oil having been given by Almighty Allah for the benefit of all in Oman and not exclusively for the man in charge to dispose of as he thought fit. I was surprised to hear this opinion being voiced in some of the most conservative villages in the interior. In the hamlet of Qantab, a fishing settlement on the fringes of the capital, I asked an old man what difference the coming of Qaboos to power had made to him. He thought for a while, spat reflectively, and said, 'Before, we used to go to bed when it got dark and we got up when it was light. It was God's will. Today, we have electric lights. Otherwise, it's the same.'

It was when the economy, with violent suddenness, stopped booming in the great oil price crash of 1986 that the cracks in Qaboos's smooth public relations facade really opened up. I think most fair-minded commentators would agree that the events surrounding the collapse of the price to $7.50, and less, per barrel were amongst the most unedifying in Oman's recent history. The spin machine went into overdrive and, with fantastic stupidity, managed to style Oman's hasty, and highly unnecessary, devaluation as a 'revaluation'. This, not surprisingly, produced a blizzard of telex messages and phone calls from bankers, brokers, wire services and increasingly bemused money men demanding to know, in very short order, what the hell was going on.

Also, Oman's formerly iron-clad credit rating began to be eroded and, for the first time, finding syndicates to provide big loans to the Sultanate began to be problematical. But what sticks in the minds of many is the behaviour of some of Oman's rich and powerful during the crisis. All semblance of dignity was cast aside in the rush to bury snouts in what remained of the devalued public trough. Huge amounts of money flew out of the Sultanate, to seek refuge in non-devalued overseas accounts and, for the first time, Oman's progress to the promised land looked a lot less certain.

Also for the first time, aspects of the Sultan's private life began to be discussed regularly, if not entirely openly. It was one of those moments of extraordinary beauty in Oman, when an operatic sunset on the western rim of the horizon, far out to sea, coincides with the rise of a brilliant moon over the saw-tooth mountains surrounding the capital. I was fishing with a friend, a bright young civil servant we shall call 'Mohammed', when I asked, 'Does it really matter?' There was no need to dot the Is and cross the Ts because Mohammed knew that I was enquiring about the ruler's much talked-about penchant for young, male company.

'A couple of years ago I would have said "No." Now, well, I rather think it does. You know, a lot of young people are rediscovering Islam. And there are others who, like me, have been educated, at least in part, in the West. It seems to many of us that if we are going to be a Western-leaning country, with a Western-dominated culture, we ought to have a Western-style participatory democracy. For myself, I would prefer an Islamic government,' Mohammed continued, 'and you know, I am sure, that homosexuality is haram [forbidden] to Islam.' Interestingly, Mohammed was now dressing in a shorter dish-dasha, which barely covered his knees. In Oman, as in one or two other Gulf countries, you could learn much about the vehemence of a man's religious views by the length of his dish-dasha. As an accurate rule of thumb, the shorter it was, the more radical the wearer. When I first fished with Mohammed, he twice brought his wife along. Now, she stayed at home and, when in public, wore the veil.

It is my submission that since National Day 1986, it has been all downhill for Qaboos. And his relationship with the young in his country took a fearful battering over his support for the Western coalition in the first war with Iraq. There were many protests, which were not, of course, reported in the domestic press. Another factor is the ever widening gulf between the 'haves' and the 'have nots' in Oman. When I first visited Muscat, there was a faintly puritan air about the place and after, say, Kuwait, a pleasing reluctance to flaunt ownership of absurdly expensive cars, gold-plated bathroom fittings and the like. Now, alas, consumption is all too conspicuous.

Similarly, in the late 1980s, I wrote a book review in Oman in which I said that Qaboos was in danger of 'being drowned in a treacle tide of sycophancy' by assorted crawlers, all apparently seeking some sort of preferment or other. The implication of what I wrote was that I firmly believed at the time that the object of such nauseous veneration hated it. Now, unhappily, I am nothing like as sure. Indeed, much that has happened recently indicates that Qaboos, like many another absolute ruler, has come to believe his praise-singers.

The essential, sad truth is that Sultanic rule and with it the need for people to turn to the official *Gazette* to see exactly what their ruler has seen fit to decree for them has no place at all in the twenty-first century. Once, and not long ago, Qaboos and Oman were seen as leaders in moves towards modernity in the Gulf. Now, the real pace is being set by the likes of Bahrain and Qatar. Fiddling about with half-baked and entirely tame assemblies, effectively debarred from conducting any meaningful debate on any public matter of importance, just won't do in these days of the Internet and Osama bin Laden. There really is no future in resisting global change. For proof of this, Qaboos only has to recall what he himself was doing on the afternoon of 23 July 1970.

Leaders who succumb to the wiles of their very own propaganda invariably come, in time, to believe in their own immortality. As Elias Canetti wrote in his seminal work, *Crowds and Power*, 'To circumnavigate death, to evade it, is one of the oldest and strongest desires of rulers.' Yet, from the harshness of reality there can be no escape, no evasion, even for the world's 'Good and Great'. Indeed, in a contemplation of events which are all too often companions of those who dance with an attitude of invulnerability, Geoffrey Chaucer, England's thirteenth-century chronicler of time and manners, wrote: 'Pride goeth forth on horseback, grand and gay. And commeth back on foot to seek the way.' And the one abiding lesson history teaches is that we do not learn from history. It is an eduring truth, one with a particular resonance when Oman and its principal characters come under consideration, given that virtually all of the country's 'Good and Great', native and expatriate alike, have confused power, position and wealth with invulnerability.

Such observations have both little and much to do with the Sultanate of Oman and the man who has chartered its considerable progress since the drama-laden days of 1970. Autocratic he may be, but, as has been demonstrated in this book, he is the most humane, cultured and intelligent of men, gentle to a fault and an individual to whom the concepts of honour and integrity remain, in a world that has all but abandoned such aspects of the human condition, cardinal principles of life. He is, in actual fact, that most genuine breed of aristocrat, an aristocrat of the kind to which can be attributed a most generous and forgiving nature. He is, however, a complex man and, as has been observed in these pages, 'many-faceted', and an individual with demons a'plenty to quell. His melancholy nature, recorded by a Whitehall mandarin some 38 years ago, remains with him still. It is as if he knew from a very early age that the burdens of kingship would bring him little happiness or peace of mind or, even, a sense of satisfaction in achievements of State to which, both by right and personal effort, he would be so well entitled. His life would be characterised by a constant need for self-justification and such a requirement would be as demeaning as it would be demanding.

Of course, such an aspect of the Sultan's reign has been something of a necessity in the light of the events which catapulted him onto the throne. While he keeps his thoughts on this very much to himself, it can now be confirmed that just prior to his father's death there was an exchange of correspondence in which, in effect, the son sought his father's pardon and approval of the 'fast forward' policy of Oman's astonishing development. Most certainly, those who know him best, that is members of his own family, confirm that had he been left to his own devices, though his frustrations with his father's conservative rule of the country and himself were real enough, he would not have conspired in his removal from the throne by force. Of course, in the event, that is just what he did, with the constant need from that moment on for a litany of self-justification.

Indeed, in its feudal character, Oman's Palace coup of 1970 had much of the duplicity of the Tudors about it. Most certainly the propaganda generated by that Royal House to justify the 'blacking' of Medieval England's last true and undoubted king, Richard III, was the most dishonest aspect of the whole sad and shaming affair, save the dragging of his naked body through the streets of Leicester following his death at the Battle of Bosworth Field. Yet, and with an almost disturbing similarity, the post-coup character assassination of Sultan Said bin Taimour by the Government's spin machine is now comprehensively regarded as quite the most disgraceful exercise and an indelible blot on the record of his son's reign. What is similarly true in the account of such dramatic events as the death and discrediting of a King, and the shaming of a Sultan summarily dismissed from his throne, is that the 'victors' write the history of the matter, an exercise in which truth is, indeed, the very first casualty.

This book has not been written, neither is it presented, as an academic work. It is an account which attempts to pay as much attention to the path to power of Oman's 14th Sultan, the route his rule has taken, every bit as much as his ultimate destination. It has been, and to some extent remains, an extraordinary journey of a really quite extraordinary man and, as such, contains contradictions, not least in the various comments from individuals who are well placed to make observations on the life, times and work of Sultan Qaboos. This is so because the man who is Oman's Sultan is a mass of contradictions, some more apparent than others. At one moment he displays patient understanding of the frailties of others, courteous to a fault, the next he is bellowing with ill-concealed rage, a repertoire which includes the meaningful caressing of his constant companion, a revolver, always concealed about his person, while a hapless, and increasingly terrified, Minister or senior official cowers in the face of such Royal rage. Such 'Panics at the Palace', as a former courtier puts it, 'are a result of the general incompetence of so many who serve His Majesty. For so much of the time he simply doesn't have the tools to do the job at hand with the professionalism he seeks to bring to all he does.'

He is a man, too, of considerable personal courage, yet is known to be a 'white-knuckle' flyer, only taking to the skies in his very own personal Boeing aircraft after consulting palace soothsayers and, indeed, taking their advice as to what libations should be poured to ward off in-flight fatalities. In one such recent incident, a State visit to India was postponed at the very last hour (the red carpet at New Delhi Airport was in place on the apron) because of a palace soothsayer's dire predictions. Not that much has been left to chance as regards engine or navigational failure. The centrepiece of the Royal Flight, a Boeing 747SB, is an ultra-long-range aircraft with the capability to fly from Muscat to Los Angeles non-stop, a device, it is most reliably believed, to keep the plane in the air for the maximum amount of time should a landfall be being sought in the wake of an emergency post-coup exit from Oman by its executive head of state. For such a capable and luxurious plane, its interior has a relatively small cabin, the reason being that so much space is required for a truly vast amount of very sophisticated avionics. However, as an alternative means of transportation, there are always the luxurious vessels of the Royal Yacht Squadron to fall back on should taking to the air be deemed too hazardous. Here, too, everything has been thought of. The support craft to the principal *Al Said*, the *Fulk a'Salamah*, carries in its cavernous holds cars of classic design, including a Rolls-Royce, together with those of lesser size but all equipped with the very latest gadgetry, thus ensuring that when Oman's Sultan makes a Royal progress, under whatever conditions, all is done in the best possible taste and in the very finest traditions of Sultanic rule.

He is a man of the most exquisite manners, yet his habit of keeping theatres and stadiums waiting for, in some recorded cases, hours, can only be described, and has been, as 'a sad abuse of majesty'. He has the political courage to institute a Basic Law which promises an end, among other liberties, to press and book censorship, yet the practice continues. Then there is his undoubted intellect. Qaboos of Oman is a man of discernment, of keen intelligence and an excellent judge of character. Yet, and the evidence is in abundance, he continues to tolerate to a dangerous degree a cast-list of characters whose craven, self-serving, sycophantic antics well mark them out for what they truly are, the most terrible liability. It is a situation which, in the words of the former senior Courtier:

> . . . really does the most dreadful damage, not just to the personal reputation of His Majesty and painfully so in the eyes of his own people, who are furious at the huge amounts of money such men have received from his hand, but also to the international reputation of the country. The term 'Muscat Mafia' is now pretty widespread.

It is a situation, too, not without danger to those who have been the recipients of the Sultan's largesse, for as the closing words of this book were being written in February 2004, there came confirmation from Muscat that so fearful of 'the people's wrath' has the Sultanate's spin-master-in-chief, Anthony Ashworth, become that he now has, in the Omani capital, a 24-hour armed guard, while his wife, Margaret, resident for most of the year on the Isle of Man, is in receipt of similar round-the-clock protection. It is not the first time such a fear has burdened the man. Indeed, during his days as a Government 'Information Officer' in Aden Colony and Protectorate, there was an attempt on his life – an incident when the bullet came very close to its target, as he left a hotel in the Crater District of Aden City.

Sultan Qaboos is a man with an abiding respect for the past, a man with a keen eye for the detail and significance of history. Yet at the respective deaths of Brigadier Colin Maxwell, Deputy Commander of the Sultan's Armed Forces and Jim 'Mac' Maclean, Sultan Said's loyal Private Secretary, he ordered that both men's diaries be destroyed. Consequently, an enormous amount of significant historical detail was lost for all time. Which prompts the question, just what is it that makes Oman's Sultan so frightened of his country's past?

To all of this, however, Sultan Qaboos appears to be impervious. Indeed, there is increasing evidence, as 2004 dawns, that he grows ever more impatient with any nature of criticism and with such an attitude becomes increasingly isolated from the day to day governance of his realm, as members of his Court grow ever fearful of taking news to him which he may not particularly wish to hear. 'It is,' laments a most senior Omani official, 'a classic case of "shoot the messenger, not the message".'

In the summer of 2003, there came a development with direct bearing on the Sultan's governance of Oman, one which gives considerable weight to the widely held belief that he grows increasingly wary of those around him at his Muscat Court and towards whom he now entertains an almost terminal disillusionment. For, during his summer visit to Britain, in a move that is as poignant as it is telling, he appointed a British-based Privy Council to guide him into the future. It is a Council principally constituted of Britons in whom, it should be recorded, he can well invest trust, having been known to him for a considerable number of years and whose loyalty cannot be called into question. Yet for all of that, and it is a most considerable 'that', it is a development that many, both in Oman and beyond, will find the greatest difficulty in accepting: that a national leader so undoubtedly committed to the advancement of his own people (witness his Government's strenuous efforts pursued over a 30-year period, whereby they would replace expatriates in both government and the private sector) should appoint, beyond the shores of the Sultanate, an advisory group made up of individuals of a race and nationality different from their own. It is a contradiction, the act of an enigmatic man, writ large.

Yet, and casting aside the crude instruments so often reached for by those who deal in political tactics, so very different from dealing in strategy, there is inherent in the Sultan's continuing allegiance to his British chums a touching faith in those qualities which, particularly during the years of Empire, prompted many an Oriental endearment of Britons, an acceptance that if there was to be a Master of the International House, then, pray, let it be them. It is a trust, an abiding confidence so well expressed by one of America's foremost intellectuals, George Santayana, who wrote of the British Empire, 'Not since the heroic days of Greece has the world had such a sweet, just, boyish master.'

And as the writing of this book drew to a close came information which gave a whole new dimension and strategic significance to the Sultan of Oman's 'British connection'. The essential burden of such detail was that, just a few short years ago, he approached London with a proposal that an 'all-encompassing' Defence Pact be established, one that would have gone further than any contingency plans already in place and would go further than any bilateral arrangement which had existed in the past. In short, the Sultan's proposal would have provided as much for his own, personal safety in the event of any coup (once, presumably, the false section of the wall at his Bait Al Barka palace had been successfully negotiated) as for the defence of the country from domestic or foreign aggression.

With regard to the former, that any attempt to unseat him from his throne would be met with a swift, armed response from Britain, was an important aspect of the proposal. It was one the Ministry of Defence in London viewed, even given its long association with Oman and its Sultans, as constituting a possible involvement too far and, accordingly, advised the Government that the proposal should be declined. In view of what has subsequently come to pass in Iraq, which has all the sad promise of involving Britain in a long and costly (in more than the financial sense alone) quagmire, the strategic decision taken by the Chiefs of Staff at Britain's Defence Ministry may well have been prudent, if disappointing. But such a proposal will remain, at least to those who are inclined towards the romantic perspective of history, not always the most practical of approaches, as one that it would have been honourable to accept, as an honourable assurance to give and, even laying aside the *Boy's Own Paper* element ('British troops rush to aid beseiged Sultan in his desert palace'), there will be many in Britain who will keenly regret that their country can no longer give such assurances to its friends and particularly to a ruler who acted, by making such a proposal, in good faith in Britain's so often expressed, especially towards the Sultanate of Oman, very good, very best of intentions.

It was also the act of a man whose continuing sense of isolation at home is not without political connotation, one with consequences for the future of his throne and his realm and is, of course, an attitude of mind, a turn of Royal conduct, which is not just an enigma but also a clear contradiction of character. It is inevitable, it would seem, that when assessing the character of Oman's 14th Sultan, the conflict of 'Shadows and Substance' is destined to make a marked contribution. The contemporary world is not, if the truth is to be told, one for Sultans and most decidedly not one in which Sultans of absolute rule can continue to flourish. For time is against them, a commodity which Sultan Qaboos's father ran short of almost 34 years ago. But there will come a time when it will be said with pride and a painful nostalgia, 'I lived in the reign of Sultan Qaboos and it was good.' For that and for all the spectacle Sultans provide, there should, in an increasingly colourless world, be some appreciation, even if they only provide a living, colourful connection to a past gone for ever. No more is there such a thing as 'the Divine Right of Kings'. Or Sultans. It all hangs on a thread. This is not a prophecy. Indeed, in a world growing increasingly sick (in more senses than one), sickeningly tired, in fact, of today's anaemic leaders, those craven peddlers of promises, it is a warning.

Forward, yes, to the 'broad sunlit uplands' so beloved of Oman's masters of spin, forward, yes, with those whose power is born of public consent; but forward, too, on occasions, with a Sultan.

Appendix

THE CROWN JEWELS

THE EICKELMAN PAPERS

There comes a time in the life of a state, government or administration when its fate turns on a particular written work. The halls of history are littered with such potentially explosive examples. In Britain it was the Magna Carta that ignited the blue touch-paper for radical social and political change; in the United States of America, the Declaration of Independence; in Imperial Russia, *The Communist Manifesto*, aided by Karl Marx's *Das Kapital*; and in the Germany of von Hindenburg, Adolf Hitler's *Mein Kampf*, which itself had been made inevitable by yet another document of political folly, the Treaty of Versailles. And, in an American context of more recent times and with a closer approximation to the subject at hand, parallels can be drawn with the 1971 political and constitutional drama caused by 'The Pentagon Papers', a litany of lies on US Government policy in Vietnam, brought into the public domain by Pentagon official Daniel Ellsberg, which led to the Watergate affair and to the eventual departure from the White House of President Richard Nixon. Not that the papers at hand constitute an untruth, quite the opposite in fact; indeed it is because they detail an abiding truth on Oman's political and constitutional past that they are regarded as being of such relevance and particularly so given that, in the Sultanate, their publication has been for so long suppressed.

While in the case of the Sultanate of Oman, any written work that does not strictly comply with the State's position on any given issue is immediately cast into outer darkness, declared, that is, to be a prohibited publication and consequently banned from public gaze, the range of examples are far from being either abundant or, for reasons obvious, available for scrutiny. This being so, those documents which have been written and permitted to survive, albeit while continuing to be banned in the Sultanate itself, are not just little known beyond the higher echelons of the established order but usually also extremely difficult to obtain access to. Unless, that is, the work in question was written beyond the borders of the country and survives in its original form.

One such body of work is what became known in Oman as 'The Eickelman Papers', and in limited circles, principally among those very few in the country who had read the essays by Professor Dale Eickelman and appreciated that here was a work of outstanding academic scholarship with potentially significant implications for the Al Busaid dynasty, they came to be referred to as 'The Crown Jewels'.

The two essays, written in the wake of considerable field work in Oman by Dale Eickelman, with the express permission and cooperation at the time of the Sultan and his officials, were published in 1984 and 1985 by, respectively, America's Middle East Institute's *Middle East Journal* and by the *International Journal of Middle East Studies*, both of which enjoy a justifiably high reputation for works of academic excellence.

The essays were, however, a cause for consummate concern and considerable anxiety to Sultan Qaboos, for reasons far from difficult to comprehend. In his essay 'From Theocracy to Monarchy: Authority and Legitimacy in Inner Oman', Eickelman deftly demonstrates the marked contradiction between the nature of autocratic, hereditary rule as personified by the Al Busaid dynasty and that practised by the country's majority Ibadhi Muslims, who practised, and indeed continue to believe, that a ruler should only be confirmed in his role in the wake of public approbation. A theocracy Oman's Imamate may well have been, until, that is, its assimilation in 1955 into the rule of Sultan Qaboos's Father, Sultan Said, but it did epitomise the practice of Islamic democratic rule. Central to such a practice was, and remains for Ibadhis, the principle that the Imam, 'one who is just' and is both a spiritual and temporal leader, should be nominated from a field of candidates and then elected by consensus and public acclamation. In short, a democratic system of rule via the consent of the governed but one markedly at odds with dynastic, autocratic, hereditary power. While Sultan Said's success in unifying Oman is justly regarded as his most significant achievement, from which the country, with the advent of revenues from oil, derived great material benefit, the fact remains that the contradiction in the two systems of rule represents a potential threat to the nature of absolute power, which Sultan Qaboos represents, while the instincts of the greater majority of his Ibadhi subjects tell them that there is indeed an alternative.

However, it has been the material benefits made possible throughout his reign which have prevented Ibadhi dissent from constituting a challenge to the autocratic rule of Sultan Qaboos. As was observed by Karl Marx, 'The ideas of the ruling class are in every epoch the ruling ideas, i.e., the class which is the ruling material force of society is, at the same time, its ruling intellectual force.' It was, of course, quite beyond Sultan Said's means to provide material benefits on any significant social scale to his people, given the pitiable nature of the State, a fact to which Eickelman, most surprisingly, makes no reference at all in his essays. Neither does he record that on 1 January 1968, just five months after the oil revenues began to flow into the State coffers, Sultan Said posted a public notice detailing the reasons for the country's lack of social infrastructure and setting out his plans for comprehensive development, much of which had already commenced. Such an absence of relevant detail in the Professor's essays could be seen as an attempt to justify Sultan Said's overthrow by his son but, nonetheless, the papers were still considered to be just too inflammatory and were consequently banned from publication in Oman.

In his essay 'Kings and People: Oman's State Consultative

Council', Eickelman demonstrates that Sultan Qaboos's 1981 initiative in establishing a Consultative Council was just another device in a list of similar initiatives taken by the world's few remaining autocratic rulers designed to afford the exercise of absolute power public legitimacy, or, in contemporary parlance, to give such a feudal system of governance 'an acceptable public face'. Of course, the Professor's findings on his Oman sojourn are now almost 20 years distant but even to this day Oman's now partially elected Consultative Assembly is still prohibited from discussing such vital aspects of the governance of the land as the country's oil and gas industry, foreign policy and defence expenditure. Two decades old they may be, but Profesor Eickelman's academic essays are brilliant in their setting of historical perspective and forensic in their analysis in identifying the pitfalls for the future of Arab Islamic good, peaceful and progressive government. Indeed, they have about as much resonance for the Arab Islamic world as they did when they were first written and as such have much to contribute to the peaceful evolution of a deeply troubled region of the world.

In Oman, there has been, of course, much progress, particularly in the rapid advancement of women in the professions, for which the Professor called. And singular credit and distinction must be given to Sultan Qaboos for such a comprehensive example of social advancement. But many of the structural imperfections and contradictions remain in the Sultanic system, one of which was starkly demonstrated just a few short years ago.

Muscat society, suitably attired, had gathered to welcome to Oman one of the world's last truly great explorer's, Wilfred Thesiger, author of arguably one of the greatest works on Arabia and its people, *Arabian Sands*, which, since its publication in 1959, has never been out of print. His presence in Oman was to celebrate its translation and publication in Arabic, thus making the work available to a whole new generation of readers. The reception was presided over by a Minister of the Omani Crown and a member of Sultan Qaboos's family. His Highness Sayyid Faisal bin Ali, the Heritage Minister, welcomed Thesiger, commenting that the publication of his work in Arabic was 'a great moment'. It had, incidentally, been on sale, in English, in Muscat bookshops for many a long year.

The very next morning, just before the Arabic edition was scheduled to go on sale, the book was banned and withdrawn from public display. There never was an official reason given for such a bizarre and counter-productive development, to the detriment of the government's reputation, but it was believed to have been due to a reference in the book to the Ibadhi sect of Islam, with its allegiance to an Islamic system of chosen leaders and, therefore, a nature of Islamic representative government.

Oman should cease to fear its past and face its future with a united confidence, and it is in such a belief, and in such a spirit, that the decision was taken to include Professor Dale Eickelman's essays in this book, essays which, while constituting observations from the past, have much, today, to contribute to the success of a land and people who so well deserve it.

FROM THEOCRACY TO MONARCHY: AUTHORITY AND LEGITIMACY IN INNER OMAN, 1935–1957

DALE F. EICKELMAN

The twentieth-century Ibadi imamate of "inner" Oman (1913–1955) constituted one of the world's last theocracies. In a demise unique for the mid-twentieth century, it became assimilated into one of the world's last absolute monarchies. The 1955 shift from theocratic to dynastic rule met initially with the support, or at least the acquiescence, of most of the tribesmen and notables of the interior. This acquiescence at first appears surprising because the fundamentalist Islamic religious and political principles for which the imamate stood continued to be properly supported. One of these principles for Ibadis was that the *imam*, the spiritual and temporal leader of the Islamic community, should be the most qualified of available candidates and chosen by a consensus of the community's religious men of learning and notables, a notion markedly at contrast with the ascriptive one of dynastic rule. Conflict between these two forms of rule is basic to much of Islamic political history and to that of pre-1970 Oman in particular.

The outbreak of a rebellion called the Jebel Akhdar war (1957–1959) in the interior a mere 18 months after the takeover of the region by Sultan Sa'id bin Taymur (r. 1932–1970) at first appears to contradict the notion that the shift to dynastic rule was unaccompanied by profound popular resentment. This essay suggests that the failure of the monarch to respond constructively to shifting popular expectations of what rulers should do, not resentment of the principle of dynastic rule in itself, contributed significantly to the deteriorating political situation of the period. A complementary theoretical goal is to suggest limitations and practical complements to Weber's frequently invoked typology of forms of domination, which at first would appear to be quite useful in analysing the replacement of authority based upon charismatic religious principles and consensus with that of ascriptive dynastic rule. Reliance upon Weber's typology to analyze the shift from theocracy to monarchy focuses attention upon ideal typical forms of rule at the expense of the central concern of this study, subtle yet cumulatively pervasive shifts in popular understandings of "just" rule.

A study of how twentieth-century imamate ideology was practically articulated, a necessary component of this essay, is in itself a topic of considerable interest. Prior accounts of Ibadi rule have been derived principally from an analysis of idealized theological treatises and the assumption that the local history of the interior and challenges to the imamate possess an "extraordinary atemporal quality." Although the description and analysis of the workings of the twentieth-century imamate cannot directly be applied to earlier historical periods, they suggest the comparative contexts and issues to consider in dealing with these earlier periods.

THE SETTING

Oman is unique in the Arab Gulf in possessing a sense of national identity which has been firmly established for well over a millennium and which is not tied to a specific dynasty. A major component of the country's sense of political distinctiveness derives from Ibadi Islam. Nonetheless, Oman is religiously, ethnically, and geographically one of the more complex nations of the Arab peninsula. Of its estimated population of 900,000 in 1980 (of which 17% were foreigners, a low proportion for the labor-hungry Gulf), roughly 55%–60% of its citizens were Ibadi, 30%–35% Sunni, and no more than 5% Shi'i. It is reasonable to assume that the proportional strength of these sectarian groups has remained roughly the same for the past half-century.

Ibadi Islam is the third, and numerically the smallest, of the three major doctrinal divisions in Islam, together with the Sunna and Shi'a. In addition to Oman, significant Ibadi communities are today found only in Libya and in Algeria's Mzab region. Ibadism originated in seventh-century C.E. disputes over succession to leadership of the Islamic community. Almost the sole significant doctrinal difference with most Sunni is that the Ibadi recognize only the Prophet Muhammad's first two caliphs, or successors in all claims to authority except prophecy, Abu Bakr and 'Umar. They also reject the notion that the caliphate or the imamate (spiritual leadership of the community) should be vested in any one descent group, even that of the prophet. The Ibadi are often called "the people of consultation" (*ahl al-shura*) because they select the most qualified member of their community as imam without regard to descent or tribal considerations. If no satisfactory incumbent can be found, the post in principle goes unfilled.

Since 730 C.E. there has usually been an elected Ibadi imam in Oman, but there have been major conflicts over succession and the country has been ruled at times by kinds who claimed temporal authority alone. This is the case for Oman's current dynasty, the Al Bu Sa'id, which has ruled the country since 1744. With the exception of the brief reign of 'Azzan bin Qays (1868–1871) of this dynasty, who briefly usurped power from another Al Bu Sa'id lineage, none of the dynasty's rulers has asserted the title of imam.

Until the present century the Al Bu Sa'id rulers were "essentially merchant princes whose interests and energies were directed primarily to enterprises outside Oman." For two centuries, from the mid-seventeenth century until Britain's ascendancy in the Gulf in the early nineteenth century, Oman was the principal maritime power of the Indian ocean; its domains once included Zanzibar and much of the East African coast. By the mid-nineteenth century it began an economic and political decline. By the late nineteenth century, reduced prices for dates and limes, Oman's principal agricultural exports, and British pressure to prohibit traffic in slaves and munitions accelerated the economic decline. In the first part of this century, remittances from tribesmen who had emigrated to East Africa and to Bahrain partially offset the precarious state of the local economy, especially in the interior. After World War II, Omanis emigrated in increasing numbers to Kuwait and Saudi Arabia, where for the most part they performed many of the unskilled, "coolie" tasks today performed by workers from the Indian subcontinent. The minimal wages for such work far surpassed anything available within Oman itself. Oman's economic stagnation was reversed only with the discovery of oil in 1964, its subsequent export in 1967, and the 1970 coup, after which oil revenues began to be applied substantially to the country's development.

Oman is composed geographically of four distinct major regions, which together are roughly the size of Arizona. First is the southern province of Dhofar (*Zufar*), a monsoon region in which the settled coastal population and cattle-herding tribes of the mountainous interior, some of whom speak South Arabian languages, are almost entirely Sunni Muslims. The Batina region of northern Oman is a coastal plain rarely more than 10 or 20 miles in width. Compared with the rest of Oman, the Batina and its port towns are polyglot and multiethnic, with Arab tribes (Sunni and Ibadi), Baluch (mostly Sunni), Persians (Sunni and Shi'i), and the Sindi- and Arabic-speaking Shi'i Liwatiya among the principal groups. "Inner" Oman, the region with which this essay is principally concerned, is a string of oasis towns and villages primarily situated on the inner (western) side of the imposing Hajar mountain range, with the addition of the town of Rustaq and smaller villages on the coastal side of the mountains. With the exception of a few passes, the Hajar mountain chain cuts access to the interior.

"Inner" Oman is almost exclusively Ibadi. In 1980 it held roughly 40% of the native population of northern Oman, or roughly 235,000 persons. In 1971 it held roughly 50%, or 225,000, of the country's estimated population of 450,000. The population of the villages and towns of these oases was almost exclusively tribal, the more important tribes including the Bani Hina, the Hirth, the Bani Riyam, and the 'Abriyin. These tribes were loosely allied through two main confederations of roughly equivalent strength, the Ghafiri and the Hinawi. The political relevance of these two confederations began to recede only in the mid-1950s. Until the advent of economic opportunities created by oil wealth in Oman and neighboring states, the majority of these tribesmen were settled cultivators dependent upon irrigation, although some tribesmen also owned substantial herds of sheep and goats. Dates and limes were the principal exports, together with emigrant labor. Small subsections of some tribes were primarily transhumant shepherds (*shawawi*); bedouin tribes such as the Duru', the Janaba, the Yal Wahayba, and the Harasis owned significant property rights in some oases. With the exception of the Yal Wahayba, these tribes are predominately Sunni, although some of them allied with the imamate in this century. They also inhabit Oman's fourth major region, the sands and gravel plains of the deserts located to the west and south of "inner" Oman.

THE IMAMATE: FORMAL DOCTRINE AND TRIBAL ELITE

The twentieth-century imamate came into existence in 1913 due to a convergence of factors. One was a religious resurgence among tribesmen and notables of the interior, inspired in part by a weakened Al Bu Sa'id, perceived as compromised by British domination. Another was the ability of the leaders of the two major tribal blocs of the interior, the Ghafiri and the Hinawi, to coordinate their efforts to restore imamate rule. The Al Bu Sa'id dynasty was saved from military defeat in Muscat only by the presence of British Indian Army troops. The scope of dynastic rule remained precarious until the conclusion of the Sib Agreement of September 26, 1920, prompted by British mediation, which implicitly granted internal autonomy to the region under imamate control and defined the terms of cooperation between the Sultanate and the tribes of the interior.

The imamate was the ideal Muslim state. The imam ordered his governors (*amils*) to "command that which is legal and forbid that which is not, to rule with justice, to take that which is due from oppressors and to give [it] to the oppressed, to protect the weak from violent and negligent uses of power and to give counsel . . . just as the prophet Muhammad gave counsel to his community (*umma*)." These admonitions and similar ones contained in other letters from the imam to men of learning deliberately replicate the caliph 'Umar's seventh-century instructions to his judges (*qadis*), a fact underscoring the value which the Ibadi imam placed upon legitimating his actions by precedents attributed to the prophet Muhammad and his first two successors as caliph.

Two key paradoxes emerge in considering how the imamate's principles of rule were implemented. As with other fundamentalist movements, imamate ideology stresses that the community of Muslims, not any ethnic, kin, or regional grouping, is the primary unit of identification. Although the leader of the community was "imam of the Muslims" and all formal discourse indicated no limits to the scope of the community other than adherence to Islam, the imamate in this century as in the past had fairly narrow territorial, ethnic, and tribal limitations.

Second, the men of learning and notables (*'ulama' wa-a'yan*) were supposed to select imams for the community on the basis of their moral qualities, knowledge of the Quran and Islamic tradition, and capacity for governing in terms of these principles. In practice, selection for leadership and control of the institutional apparatus of the Ibadi state were the nearly exclusive province of an oligarchic tribal elite, the key families of which managed to maintain their standing from generation to generation despite the apparent political turbulence of the region. For example, Imam Muhammad bin 'Abdallah al-Khalili (r. 1920–1954), a wealthy notable who sold his personal estates to sustain the imamate as its resources dwindled, was the twentieth of a long line of imams selected from his immediate tribal group.

Since the just society of the imamate was guided in practice by a tribal elite, it is important to delineate the bases of tribal leadership. With the exception of a few multitribe towns such as Nizwa, Bahla, Izki, and Rustaq, inner Oman was a region of one-shaykh towns and villages. Leading shaykhly families also tended to be major property-holders, and only these families possessed slaves (*khuddam*), who worked as agricultural laborers, domestic servants, and private militia. Major tribes also had client groups whose land and livelihood were protected in exchange for their subordination, military support, and, at times, stipulated payments in goods or services.

The 'Abriyin tribe provides a useful example of leadership patterns and their relation to control over persons and material resources, despite the fact that Omani tribes show a wide variation in specific patterns of internal leadership. Attempts have been made to invoke segmentary lineage theory to explain the tribal structure of inner Oman, yet the sustained inequality of control over persons and wealth in Oman, as in many other tribal settings in the Middle East, renders segmentary lineage theory inappropriate.

The 'Abriyin have a more visible process of "selection" (*intikhab*) or approval of shaykhs than is the case for other tribes. It should be noted that *intikhab* is a key term that some observers have misleadingly translated as "election", implying a greater sense of egalitarian participation in selection of leaders both for tribes and for the imamate than has actually been the case. For the 'Abriyin, the notables of various collectivities within the tribe assemble to nominate or confirm their shaykhs. A shaykh knew that he was replaced if in a formal gathering coffee was offered first to someone else, his successor. Since the eighteenth century 'Abriyin shaykhs have all been drawn from the same descent cluster, suggesting that they fit the widespread underlying pattern of oligarchic control over property and persons which appears to account for the continuity in leadership of most major tribes in the Omani interior.

Hamra, an oasis and provincial capital of 2,800 persons in 1982, is also the tribal "capital" of the 'Abriyin. Most of the 'Abriyin live in the region of Hamra, although there are major clusters of 'Abriyin elsewhere in the interior. The paramount shaykh of the 'Abriyin regularly visits these other regions, and tribesmen in one locale continue to rely upon those in others for support in pressing claims with the government. In the past such support extended to unified action in the face of intertribal hostilities.

Ownership of land and water resources, even for the outlying regions, is concentrated in the hands of a few members of the shaykhly lineage. Thus, over half the irrigated gardens of Hamra and roughly the same proportion of lands used for seasonal crops are owned by four or five households of the shaykhly lineage. In outlying regions, shaykhly interests are looked after by overseers who frequently double as local headmen (*rashids*). A similar pattern of ownership prevails in other tribes.

The remaining land and water rights are divided among the balance of the tribe, a significant number of whom own very little. For households without sufficient capital reserves, there has traditionally been a cycle of impoverishment which is caused by the difficult ecological conditions of the region and which still applies to households without adequate cash income for migrant labor. When water resources are low, individuals are compelled to purchase additional rights at high prices, which in practice only wealthy households can do. Others are compelled to go into debt and lose their lands and herds. Persons who lose their lands and herds are generally compelled to become agricultural workers or herders for one of the shaykhly families, or to emigrate in search of wage labor.

None of the tribes of inner Oman was economically or politically autonomous. In varying degrees, all depended upon outside trading relations and the support, or at least the indifference, of the imam and the Sultan. Many tribal leaders, especially those on the northern fringes of the interior, also accepted subsidies from the Saudis. In some periods, including the early 1950s, it was not unusual for leading shaykhs to accept gifts or subsidies serially or simultaneously from the imam, the Sultan, and the Saudis. Acceptance of such subsidies did not necessarily signify allegiance.

Of all the descent clusters of the 'Abriyin, the leaders of the shaykhly Awlad Zahran descent group possess the most elaborate genealogical knowledge, with significant parts of it written. They also carefully preserve the documents which give them title to their lands. Although the shaykhs do not participate directly in market transactions – their houses are located at the beginning of the oasis where water from a gravity-fed underground conduit (*falaj*) first enters the town, while the market is located at the other end where most of the ex-slaves live – they frequently provided the capital and protection for tribal clients to carry on such activities. The fortunes of most 'Abriyin were linked to those of their shaykhs in multiplex economic and political ways.

In addition to privately owned land (*milk*), there are pious endowment (*waqf*) holdings whose rent is devoted to various religious or community activities, such as the upkeep of mosques, Quranic schools, or, as is the case for one village near Hamra, the provision of coffee to every male villager in the guesthouse at mid-morning. Most pious endowment holdings originated as gifts by major shaykhly figures. Bestowal of such endowments and attention to the needs of tribesmen and clients were major means by which the control over persons and resources could be made to appear just. There are also large tracts of land called "treasury" (*bayt al-mal*) lands. In some regions, especially Nizwa and Bahla, revenues from the rental of these lands went to the imamate. In other regions, including those controlled by the 'Abriyin, "treasury" lands were (and remain today) under the control of the tribal shaykh. Its rental is used to meet what is considered to be the expense of his office, including hospitality on religious feast days and other occasions. In general, these lands are rented to tribesmen at modest sums, so that their allocation was another means by which a shaykh could secure tribesmen as clients.

Tribesmen were highly dependent upon their shaykhs for security of person and property. Anyone wishing to sell or to exchange property did so only after consulting with the tribal shaykh or with one of his agents, generally another member of the shaykhly lineage, acting as judge. Among the 'Abriyin, the Awlad Zahran lineage provided nearly all the persons reputed as having the education and standing sufficient to prepare a binding title. Intratribal disputes were invariably referred to the shaykh, as were intertribal conflicts over water and pasture rights.

The formal consensus among tribal notables implied by the notion of selection is an important component in establishing shaykhly legitimacy. Tribesmen distinguish between shaykhs who rule with the consent of the community or collectivity (*jama-a*) and those who do not. Shaykhs who make illegitimate exactions or who fail to settle issues according to justice as locally understood are considered tyrants (*jabbars*). The 'Abriyin consider their best shaykhs to have been those who possessed both reputations as men of learning (or a reputation for accepting the counsel of learned men) and effectiveness in practical tribal politics. The line between a strong, effective shaykh and a tyrant was often thin, and reputations were volatile. Older tribesmen recall that the most notable achievement of Imam Muhammad ibn 'Abdallah al-Khalili was to reduce intertribal violence and limit the possibility of some tribal shaykhs for arbitrary action.

The tribal shaykh and his immediate supporters recognize that unpopular decisions which cannot be justified in terms of Islamic tradition will be resisted. Although tribesmen emphasize the unity of the tribe to outsiders, rivalry for control of the tribe limits the arbitrary exercise of shaykhly authority. Other members of the shaykhly lineage can seek to gain support for themselves, or collectivities or tribesmen – I deliberately use the term "collectivities" because lineage identities are only one of several bases for political alliance – may take advantage of potential rivalries to limit the range of action of their shaykhs without formal challenge to his authority.

The concepts of jama'a and consultation (*shura*) are crucial to understanding popular Omani notions of authority. Jam'as vary in composition. They can be constituted by any cluster of individuals who usually consult with one another before making major decisions. In Hamra itself, to continue the example of the 'Abriyin, consultation over matters affecting the community occurs daily in the shaykh's guesthouse (*sabla*) and in the guesthouses of other nonshaykhly lineages. Depending upon context, such consultations involve anything from the 'Abriyin as a whole, individual settlements, or key members of the shaykhly lineage alone. The term is also used regularly in nontribal contexts to refer to any group of persons who habitually work or deliberate together, such as ministry officials. In general, a respected shaykh takes care to listen to all articulate opinion on a matter and to consult with tribal notables before making public his own decision.

IMAMATE RULE IN PRACTICE

An elderly ex-militiaman (*'askari*) for the imamate replied in 1980 to my question of whether the imamate was a government (*hukuma*) similar to the sultanate by vigorously affirming of the imamate that: "It killed; it taxed; it imprisoned." This minimalist definition of government clearly is at marked variance with the formal image of Islamic rule as elaborated by men of learning. Imamate ideology was undeniably important, but few ordinary tribesmen invoked the imamate's formal principles in discussions with me or among themselves. Several replied that such matters were for their shaykhs and men of learning to articulate, a deference to the received social order. The emphasis of ordinary tribesmen was more upon narratives revealing who was capable of imposing his will in specific circumstances. Nonetheless, most tribesmen showed a clear respect for the former imamate government, even when its effect upon their immediate tribal circumstances was not always strongly felt.

Nizwa was the seat of the twentieth-century imamate, where the imam, his key aides, a personal retinue of soldiers and slaves, and religious students lived in the seventeenth-century fortress complex which dominates the town. In the late 1940s the imam had fourteen governors located at principal settlements to represent his authority. All governors were men of learning. They were necessarily also men of action capable of activating tribal militias in the name of the imam. The imamate government, including militia, tax collectors, judges and governors, comprised fewer than five hundred persons and most of these were part-time. Salaries were generally low, for it was expected that most persons had complementary sources of income.

The claim of the imamate to rule exclusively by the laws and tradition of the early Islamic community in practice restricted the scope of government activities. Taxes were restricted to alms (*zakat*) and to an equally modest levy on certain market transactions. Since Quranic schools, mosques, and certain activities were in general financed by specific pious endowments, the only other imamate revenue came from public treasury lands. Even in times of major crisis, the level of taxes could not be raised, nor could pious endowment revenues legitimately be diverted from their initial purpose. A major dispute broke out between Imam Salim bin Rashid al-Kharusi (r. 1913–1920) and his advisers when he sought to expand the taxing power of the imamate and utilize endowment revenues for government purposes. He met stiff resistance from his advisers and was obliged to withdraw his proposal. Even basic written accounting of revenue and expenditures was not introduced until 1952–1953 1372.

Record-keeping and the adjudication of disputes were simple and direct. Land and water rights were bought and sold by written agreement, but copies of these agreements were retained only by the parties involved. There were no central registers or even records of tax assessments. In the absence of registries or archives, written instruments of sale were secure only when prepared and witnessed by literate notables. Disputes were settled by the imam's judges and governors bringing together the conflicting parties and issuing their decision. Appeals to the imam were rare. Serious cases, such as homicide, intertribal raiding or debts between persons from different towns, were resolved in the first instance by the imam.

The imam had no standing army, but had several resources available to achieve imamate objectives by force. One was to raise a militia against any tribal leader unwilling to accede to imamate requests. The other was for the imam and his counsellors secretly to designate certain persons (notorious bandits and at times certain tribal shaykhs) as "enemies of Islam" and thus "meriting death" (*mustahaqin bi-l-qatl*). Once a person was so designated, any deceit or stratagem could be employed to bring about his end. In general, however, since the imam constituted the embodiment of Islamic legitimacy and reached decisions only after consultation with his close advisers – men of learning drawn from the leading tribes – overt opposition to his decisions was infrequent.

The imamate elite was drawn principally from the leading shaykhly families of the interior. Given the small scale of imamate society, these leaders were well known to one another and there was limited opportunity for leadership to arise from outside this limited cadre. Since the actual course of political events was unpredictable and notables were aware that patterns of domination could suddenly shift, the leaders of major factions and tribal groupings were reluctant to take irrevocable positions. At the same time they affirmed their allegiance to the imamate and sought to justify in Islamic terms their pragmatic assessments of political realities. In the 1954 selection for the imam, many notables avoided making a clear commitment for either the imam or the Sultan because of the ambiguous political situation which prevailed prior to the Sultan's takeover of the interior in late 1955.

LEGITIMACY: IMAM AND SULTAN

Popular Omani assumptions concerning what is politically and religiously just become particularly apparent in analyzing the steps taken by Sultan Sa'id to achieve Oman's practical reunification. From the beginning of his reign in 1932, when he was 22 years old, the Sultan began to develop an amicable entente with Imam Muhammad. At first, this policy went little beyond the formal exchange of greetings on Muslim feast days and the occasional exchange of fugitives as mandated by the 1920 Sib Agreement. The Sultan in his letters was punctiliously respectful but never addressed his correspondent as *imam*. As Sultan Sa'id explicitly told his Minister of the Interior, the use of such a term would signify that he owed obedience to the imam. The imam, however, addressed Sa'id bin Taymur as *Sultan* in all communications dating at least from the early 1940s.

The Sultan took an important step in the mid-1930s by encouraging men of learning from inner Oman to serve as judges in his administration. Among the first qadis to leave the interior for service with the Sultan was Shaykh Ahmad Sa'id al-Kindi (d. 1963–1964 1383) of Nizwa. After serving as judge for nearly a decade (1928–1937) with the imam, he accepted appointments from the Sultan in varying locales until his death. In a pattern to be repeated by almost all officials from the interior who sought to work with the Sultan, Shaykh Ahmad first asked for the imam's permission. The imam answered Shaykh Ahmad by writing that he could serve Islam equally well by working for the Sultan. The Sultan's salaries were higher than those offered by the imam, and the imam placed no restrictions upon Sultanate officials returning regularly to the interior.

In 1939, Shaykh Ibrahim al-'Abri (d. 1975), a distinguished man of learning, tribal leader of the 'Abriyin, and counsellor of the imam, became one of the most influential imamate figures to make the shift. Shaykh Ibrahim soon developed a pattern of working as qadi for the Sultan in Muscat and returning summers to Hamra, where he continued to be the de facto shaykh of his tribe and the imam's appointed judge. Shaykh Ibrahim confirms that although the Sultan and imam initially viewed one another with suspicion, they soon developed a mutual respect. For his part, the imam recognized that the Sultan sought the well-being of the people of inner Oman (*qasdal-khayr li-ahl 'Uman*). The Sultan's predecessors had been popularly perceived as being aligned too closely to British interests, a factor which fuelled resistance to Sultanate rule earlier in the century. Sultan Sa'id himself had returned only in 1929 from education at a school for princes in India, Mayo College, and may have been at least initially handicapped by poor Arabic, but he quickly set about diminishing direct British influence in his administration. By insistently drawing upon the same source of popular legitimacy as the imamate – rule by Islamic law – and the same personnel, the Sultan took the first steps to facilitate Oman's practical unification. In essence he began to model the Sultanate upon respected elements of the imamate.

By the late 1930s, Sultan Sa'id had developed a limited, but in its context effective administrative apparatus. He corresponded with the imam over what tribesmen from the interior visiting the coast regarded as inequities in taxation. He also used some of his revenues, although not always successfully, to gain the allegiance of prominent shaykhs in the interior. The Sultan also became increasingly concerned with securing revenues from oil exploration. Without directly antagonizing the imam, who was adamantly opposed to allowing foreigners in the interior, the Sultan sought to facilitate the safe passage of oil exploration teams in the northern part of the interior not effectively under imamate control.

In the 1940s the augmented subsidies which the Sultan received in return for supporting the British war effort were judiciously used to strengthen his ties with the leading shaykhs of the interior. By 1945 the British consul in Muscat reported that the Sultan had secured for himself the role of arbitrator between the paramount shaykhs of the powerful Hinawi and Ghafiri confederations and had obtained their agreement not to take part in the selection of a new imam. The consul also reported that the imam had sent the Sultan a letter announcing the dispatch of an emissary "to discuss 'important questions.'" In 1946, the imam and Sultan collaborated in establishing joint administration in an area of long-standing tribal conflict, the Bilad Bani Bu Hasan in the southern Sharqiya.

The imam appointed the region's governor, but the Sultan paid for the cost of administration.

An indication of the Sultan's success in establishing his own claims to legitimacy in the interior came during a critical illness of the imam in 1948, when some tribal leaders reportedly suggested that the Sultan assume the additional title of imam. Sultan Sa'id was fully aware that he lacked some of the necessary qualifications and never personally entertained the idea. Despite the Sultan's cordial personal relations with the imam, which extended to providing a car and escort to take his sick niece to the American mission hospital in Muscat in 1949, he recognized that the imam's recovery effectively delayed a major opportunity to achieve the country's reunification.

Among the Sultan's reasons for vigorously pursuing Oman's reunification was the renewed postwar interest in oil exploration. In 1948 Richard Bird, a representative of the Iraq Petroleum Company (which then held an oil concession for Oman) entered Oman as far as 'Ibri. Along the way he made agreements with several tribal shaykhs to permit the safe passage of survey teams. Through the collaboration of Shaykh Sulayman bin Himyar, leader of the Ghafiri tribal confederation, Bird even hoped to proceed to Nizwa to speak with the imam. The imam, however, strongly rejected this initiative and forced Bird's immediate departure from 'Ibri. For his part, Sultan Sa'id was furious that Bird had entered Oman without his consent. The Sultan feared that the British might begin to regard Oman's interior as composed of congeries of independent shaykhs. Indeed, in late 1949 Sulayman bin Himyar informed a British explorer "that he wished to be recognized by the British Government as the independent ruler of the Jabal al Akhdar, with a status similar to that of the Trucial Sheikhs."

The Sultan wanted oil exploration, but at the same time lacked effective control over some of his domains and was under pressure from the imam to keep foreigners out of the country. When Bird visited Muscat to make amends to the Sultan in November 1948, the Sultan showed him a letter from the imam protesting oil exploration by foreigners and his reply, intended to allay the imam's fears. Bird obtained the Sultan's consent to reenter northern Oman with a survey team a few months later, provided he was accompanied by a representative of the Sultan. This time local tribesmen unceremoniously shot at the expedition and chased it away, saying that the Sultan's representative had no business in the area. The incident was eventually resolved in the Sultan's favor, but serves to indicate both the "thinness" of his effective control in some parts of the country and his early recognition that boundaries and effective rule were essential tests of sovereignty for international purposes.

The two major tests of practical rule in Oman came with the 1952 Buraymi crisis, in which the Saudis occupied one of the villages of this oasis and claimed it as their own, and with the death of Imam al-Khalili in 1954, after which Sultan Sa'id made his final moves to reunite Oman.

In the early 1950s the Saudis renewed dormant claims to Buraymi and to an adjacent region of northern Oman called the Dhahira (Zahira), which included the oasis of 'Ibri. Immediately after the Saudis occupied Buraymi in August 1952, they began a campaign to secure recognition of Saudi rule by tribal leaders in the interior. A message to the imam announced that the Saudi representative was appointed only after repeated requests by Saudi subjects in Oman. It also invited the imam to join with the Saudis in ridding Oman of "foreign" influence: the imam was subsequently offered a large cash gift, which was declined.

The Sultan's immediate response was to raise tribal levies to oust the Saudis by force, one of the most popular actions he ever undertook. He also informed the imam of developments by letter. Merchants in Muscat turned over their entire supplies of foodstuffs and ammunition for the expedition. Within the space of a month – a short time considering that all communications were by messenger (radio contact between the Sultan and his three military units was established only at the end of 1953) – an impressive force of 8,000 tribesmen from the Batina coast, most mounted on camels, was assembled at the northern coastal town of Suhar by October 7, 1952. Tribal response to the Sultan's request for support was unhesitating. When the expedition subsequently disbanded on October 18 because of British pressure and assurances that they would find a peaceful solution, the Sultan took care to have the British consul announce the fact to him in the presence of the assembled force, so that the British would be held publicly responsible for the expedition's failure.

When the imam had received the Saudi letter in Nizwa, he convened his key advisers. The imam's initial suggestion was to send a messenger with a letter directly to the Saudi monarch (and not through his representatives in Buraymi) saying that Oman at present had no quarrel with foreigners and that the Saudi presence should be withdrawn to avoid fighting between Muslims. One faction sought to advise the Sultan and the British consul of the letter, so that any reply could be taken in concert with them and would emphasize Oman's unity. Another wanted a delegation to be sent to the Saudi monarch for further discussions, without prior consultation with Muscat. Among those offering this advice were Talib and Ghalib bin 'Ali and Sulayman bin Himyar. These shaykhs appear consistently to have argued for an interior independent of the Sultan in order to augment their own political roles.

The imam finally decided to send two messengers to Sultan Sa'id. Shaykh Ahmad Muhammad al-Harthi, and Shaykh Talib bin 'Ali, with a letter offering his full cooperation. The Sultan informed one of the emissaries that the British consul was unnecessary, and sent the imam 100 camels, ammunition, rifles, and money to facilitate sending his own militia from the interior to Buraymi. The imam's force of 800 got as far as Dariz, near 'Ibri, before a message arrived from the Sultan announcing that the expedition had been called off. Nonetheless, the notion of Oman as an undivided entity continued to pervade the efforts of the imam and Sultan to prevent Oman's Dhahira region from falling under Saudi control. For a brief period in 1954 this cooperation went so far as the appointment of a governor supported by both the imam and the Sultan.

When Imam al-Khalili died, imamate notables gathered in Nizwa. Only a small faction of older men of learning held to the opinion that the imamate should be maintained just as it had been in the immediate past, with minimal contact with the outside world. Another faction, which included Ghalib bin 'Ali (soon to become imam), his brother Talib, Sulayman bin Himyar, and part of the powerful Hirth tribe, wanted to accept Saudi assistance. A third group, which deliberately did not participate in selection of the new imam, urged Oman's reunification under Sultan Sa'id. Among those supporting this course of action were 'Abdallah bin Zahir al-Hina'i, soon to become shaykh of the powerful Bani Hina tribe (which was Imam Ghalib's own), and Shaykh Ahmad bin Muhammad al-Harthi of the Hirth tribe, which was divided between support for the Sultan and the new imam. The notables who favored assimilation conveyed the Sultan's oath that he would take no action against shaykhs who supported Imam al-Khalili, provided that henceforth they submitted to him. Their hand was also strengthened by Imam Muhammad's withdrawal on his deathbed of his endorsement of Ghalib "after Ahmad bin Muhammad al-Harithi warned him that the succession of Ghalib would result in dissension among the Omanis."

Despite the Sultan's overtures, strong Saudi support enabled the faction favoring an imamate in the Saudi orbit to win over some notables of the interior. Others hesitated to declare open allegiance to the Sultan. From their point of view, the lack of a strong response to the Saudi takeover of Buraymi suggested that further Saudi expansion might also go unchecked.

By September 1955 the Sultan was compelled to alter his gradualist approach to the assimilation of the interior. An Egyptian intelligence major had arrived in Nizwa via Saudi Arabia and Buraymi to organize liaison with imamate forces. In late October 1955 the British-officered Trucial Oman Scouts, acting on behalf of Abu Dhabi and the Sultanate, expelled the Saudis from Buraymi. This action cut off the imamate's line of communication with Saudi Arabia and paved the way for Oman's reunification. From his southern palace in Salala, the Sultan drew up plans for the interior's occupation and subsequent administration. The Sultan's Batina Force, based in Suhar, occupied Rustaq and there drove out imamate supporters, led by the imam's brother, Shaykh Talib bin 'Ali. After four days' skirmishing, the town was captured on December 17.

In a separate action on December 15, the Muscat and Oman Field Force entered Nizwa and took over the imam's fortress without resistance. The imam was reported to have distributed arms and ammunition to his supporters the night before the arrival of the

Sultan's force, but the tribesmen immediately deserted and no tribal leaders committed themselves openly to his cause.

To culminate the takeover of the interior, the Sultan organized a motorized royal progress through his domains. It took him across the desert from Salala to the oil company installation in the desert at Fahud; went through the interior oases of Adam, Nizwa, 'Ibri and Buraymi; and then returned to Muscat by way of Suhar and the Batina coast.

The Sultan arrived on December 23 at an encampment not far from Nizwa. That evening he asked Shaykh Ahmad Muhammad al-Harthi to prepare for him the draft of a speech, to which he made revisions. With the Sultan present, it was read the following morning to the assembled notables of the interior in the long room in Nizwa fortress where the imam used to meet with his notables. An estimated 4,000 tribesmen from the interior were gathered outside. The Sultan stressed that he came to the interior to ensure Oman's unity and to avoid the shedding of blood between Muslims. No direct mention was made of the imamate, but the Sultan said that he was willing to grant an amnesty (*amana*) to all tribesmen and notables who accepted his rule: "The past will not be brought up again." In private meetings he assured those who had worked for the imam that he would continue to employ them. The move also ensured continuity in the region's admittedly minimalist administration.

A few days after the Sultan's return to Muscat by vehicle (he rode camelback from Buraymi to Suhar), a delegation of 500 tribesmen on camels arrived from the interior at the gates of Muscat and were given special permission to enter. The Sultan personally greeted each participant and thanked him for his show of loyalty. The incident deserves mention because, like the Sultan's royal progress to the interior, this direct contact with large numbers of his subjects was not to be repeated.

It was the support of notables, secured with the promise of continued authority and influence for the cooperative and retribution for others, that counted most to the Sultan. Few ordinary tribesmen in the interior at this time had a concrete vision of alternatives to a politics of notables. A senior official in Muscat, the son of a village headman and eighteen at the time of the Sultan's arrival in Nizwa, described his political perceptions of the mid-1950s as follows:

> Commoners like myself had no clear idea of what the "unity" of the country meant. Politics (*siyasa*) was the business of our shaykhs alone. We did not discuss it. Like most people in the Jebel Akhdar, I heard that the [Sultan's] army had come to [a village near Nizwa], but had no clear idea why. The region was held under iron control (*mughlaqat bi-saytara hadidiya*) by our shaykhs before and after the coming of the Sultan. There were very few radios, and most of us thought more of the bare necessities of daily life. This was a time when shaykhs could do as they wished. Everything came from the shaykhs and depended upon what they thought. For most of us, we did not even conceive that there was a choice between imam and Sultan.

Nonetheless, some notables and a few tribesmen of the interior were beginning to develop changing notions of what rulers should do. Some tribesmen had emigrated temporarily to Saudi Arabia and Kuwait in search of wage labor, and were aware of the changes that were beginning to occur outside their country because of oil wealth. Sulayman bin Himyar, Talib bin 'Ali, and, reportedly, a close relative of Imam al-Khalili made clear to the Saudis their personal interest in facilitating oil concessions. Many shaykhs in the interior initially welcomed Sultan Sa'id because they regarded him as modernist and forward-looking. They saw that their own roles would be enhanced if some of these benefits could be secured for their tribes. They recognized that Sultan Sa'id knew how to negotiate with outside powers over oil exploration rights. The economic situation in inner Oman had been deteriorating for years and was exacerbated by some opportunistic leaders close to Imam al-Khalili who took advantage of his inability effectively to manage imamate affairs during his final years. Even Sultan Sa'id, rarely attributed with active concern for the welfare of his subjects, was said to have remarked upon the poor health conditions apparent in the interior and to have mentioned his intent to set up a dispensary in Nizwa. It was never established, and in general the Sultan failed to facilitate the modest development programs urged upon him by the British.

In spite of the Sultan's indifference to "development," his assimilation of the interior made possible the construction of the first motor road into the region. It was intended primarily to bring supplies by road to the oil camp at Fahud, which until then had been supplied principally by air and a circuitous desert route. Once the road was established, however, it radically changed patterns of trade and brought a rapid end to camel caravan traffic. Clearly such a change entailed economic dislocations for many, but again it was principally the notables who had the capital to invest and the influence to secure the permits necessary to import vehicles – most of which had to be personally approved by the Sultan. Except for this significant change, little more occurred beyond the creation of a few military posts. As one tribal leader said retrospectively of this period: "Sultan Sa'id opened the door in 1955 and closed it again in 1957," referring to the beginning of the Jebel Akhdar uprising begun in June of that year, 18 months after the Sultan's arrival in Nizwa.

In 1955 the emigrant Omani community was still modest in size compared with what it was to become with the accelerated working-age male emigration beginning with the Jebel Akhdar war and continuing through the 1960s. Nonetheless there were significant communities of Omani manual laborers and shopkeepers in Kuwait, Bahrain, and eastern Saudi Arabia. A rumor widespread in these communities at the time and believed to this day among many non-Ibadis in Oman was that, when in Nizwa, the Sultan led the Friday prayers in a white turban, signifying that he had assumed the role of imam in addition to that of Sultan. Throughout his travel in the interior, the Sultan wore a multicolored (*sahrawi*) turban, as he did on the coast. For a brief period, a few notables of the interior addressed petitions to the *Sultan al-muslimin,* a title inspired by *imam al-muslimin*, but were immediately discouraged from doing so.

The "white turban" rumor is significant in several respects. To the extent that it was believed, it served to alienate Ibadi Omanis, who were aware of the Sultan's lack of necessary qualifications to assume the title of imam. Non-Ibadi Omanis saw a threat to their own position in any move by the Sultan to close ranks with tribesmen in the interior, given the threat these tribesmen posed to their own security earlier in the century. The rumor also indicates that as late as 1955, Omanis interpreted the Sultan's takeover of the interior principally in terms of the existing political categories of imamate and Sultanate rule. Only in later years did Omani emigrant communities begin to serve as major carriers of ideological orientations offering alternatives to monarchic and theocratic rule.

If through 1955 Sultan Sa'id's actions suggested a subtle perception of Oman's domestic politics and an effective manipulation of British officials concerned with Gulf affairs, the subsequent record of his actions suggests his disregard of slow, but significant and incremental transformations in how Omanis perceived their own society. Sultan Sa'id's "absolute" monarchy was a minimalist state in the sense that it exercised firm control over only a narrow spectrum of concerns. In the 1950s and 1960s the Sultan often repeated to his foreign advisers this observation: "If Oman's little rulers are all right, then so is Oman." The "little rulers" were the country's tribal shaykhs upon whom the Sultan depended to maintain order. Except for a small military presence and a small network of individuals personally commissioned by the Sultan to write confidential reports on local events, the scope of governmental activities remained what it was prior to 1955. Reliance upon tribal shaykhs provided an inexpensive means of governing the interior, but at the cost of maintaining an administrative system with neither the capacity nor the resources to undertake development projects of any sort or to assess local needs in any significant way.

CONCLUSION: THE CHANGING BASIS OF POPULAR LEGITIMACY
In his takeover of the interior Sultan Sa'id intended to maintain "the Oman that was." His actions guaranteed the interests and status of the existing oligarchy, provided that they supported his rule. The shift from theocracy to monarchy involved no significant shift in the existing pattern of domination. Imamate justice, like Sultan Sa'id's, guaranteed the peace and security of markets, upheld established

property rights, and lessened intertribal raiding. This narrow conception of justice offered no challenge to the existing social order.

In crucial respects, this attempt to maintain the status quo in itself engendered significant transformations. By the mid-twentieth century significant economic changes engendered by the emerging oil economy began to affect even the more isolated regions of the Arabian peninsula through labor emigration, remittances, and contact with Arab political movements elsewhere.

Notables were for the most part cut off from direct participation in remittance revenues, although exactions were frequently made upon emigrants to provide them with the necessary travel papers. In the heyday of the twentieth-century imamate, shaykhs received regular subsidies from the imam and often discreetly collected subsidies from neighboring rulers as well. Small quantities of arms were often provided in this way and facilitated the shaykhs' ability to affirm their positions. Outside subsidies, complemented by revenues derived from ownership or control of local lands, herds, and commercial opportunities, enabled notables to maintain a "pass through" system of benefits which provided a minimalist but in context effective level of security for tribesmen and clients. An inability to maintain this system threatened their status.

Since the imam had no standing army, there was a delicate reciprocity between the imam and tribal shaykhs, for the imam's military strength depended upon tribal levies. The same was true initially for Sultan Sa'id, whose last major use of tribal levies in northern Oman was in the 1952 Buraymi crisis. Some were used in the 1957–1959 Jebel Akhdar war, but they were by then decidedly peripheral to the Sultanate's full-time military units. The northern tribes of Bani Hawasina, Ruwaha and Bani 'Amir continued to provide levies for the southern region in the 1960s, but beginning in 1967 even these were largely replaced by Pakistani Baluch. The Sultan's reduced need for tribal levies may have been a major factor in the diminished subsidies provided to tribal leaders after 1955.

The significant difference between Oman in the mid-1950s and in earlier decades was an incipient awareness of practical political alternatives. Much of the initial acceptance of Sultan Sa'id was due to the perception of notables and at least some tribesmen that conditions in the interior would improve, that security would return to the region, and that the "pass through" system would work once again. Most notables and many tribesmen were aware of post-1955 military preparations being made by imamate supporters in Saudi Arabia. In the face of these preparations, several notables of the interior sought to encourage Sultan Sa'id to take a more direct interest in the region. On one occasion, a governor who was also a major tribal shaykh even courageously participated in a delegation of influential shaykhs who went to Salala on camel to see the Sultan. They were refused an interview.

Royal authority, like tribal leadership, is based in part upon popular expectations of just domination. Another component of authority is the ability to use force or the threat of force. A tribal leader or ruler might be considered to be unjust – a tyrant – but could still secure widespread acquiescence to his rule if the cost of resisting injustice outweighed that of resignation to it. Sultan Sa'id's growing reluctance to see notables of the interior on a regular basis cut him off from a reliable basis on which to judge the events of the region. Quranic-sanctioned consultation, after all, provides more than a means of communicating and demonstrating the legitimacy of the ruler's decisions. It also provides the intelligence necessary for effective rule and commits subordinates to the clear implementation of decisions. The Sultan may have intended to emphasize the firmness of his royal authority by becoming less accessible to his notables or, as some observers of the period have suggested, he may have lacked the resources necessary to entertain notables regularly and provide them with gifts appropriate to their status. Especially because the Sultan had begun to rely upon his standing army as opposed to tribal levies, he may have felt that less contact with all but a few shaykhs of the interior would have no major impact upon his rule.

The outbreak of the Jebel Akhdar war on June 14, 1957, demonstrated the Sultan's inability to assess the country's situation. As early as April 1957 he received reports of landings along the coast of insurgents, arms, and ammunition. On April 24, seven rebels were handed to the commander of the Sultan's Batina force at a northern frontier post. On May 5, 150 armed rebels were reported in the Sharqiya region, and on May 8 they raised the imam's white flag in a quickly aborted uprising at Ibra, the tribal capital of the region.

Among the many warnings passed along by loyalist tribal notables at the time was one from Shaykh 'Abdallah bin Zahir al-Hina'i, warning the Sultan of imminent rebel landings along the coastal region inhabited by the Yal Sa'd. The Sultan's brother, Sayyid Tariq, passed this message to the Sultan on May 17, and it was radioed the same day to the commander of the Batina Force at Suhar. He was ordered by the Sultan's military secretary, P.R.M. Waterfield, to take no preemptive action and to keep his regiment concentrated at Suhar. Shaykh Talib bin 'Ali and 150 heavily armed insurgents subsequently landed at precisely the locale specified in the May 17 message on the night of June 14. Despite nearly a month's warning, the Sultan discounted the possibility of a successful armed uprising.

Within a month Imam Ghalib's supporters had taken over the major towns of the interior, had routed the Sultan's Oman Regiment (which suffered such demoralization and heavy losses that it was subsequently disbanded), and had compelled the Sultan to obtain military support from a Britain reluctant to engage in new military commitments east of Suez. By August 1957 the Sultan's forces and British units with air support quickly recaptured the major towns of the interior with a minimum of casualties. The Jebel Akhdar itself was secured only after a combined Sultan's Armed Forces–British SAS commando assault in January 1959. Mining of roads and small-scale skirmishes continued sporadically until the summer of 1962.

After the initial success of imamate forces, the Sultan's advisers offered conflicting advice on the course of action to follow. The military were in favor of decisive armed action to eliminate rebel resistance. Some tribal supporters advocated a more moderate policy of amnesty for the principal insurgents, an approach initially disapproved by the Sultan. What followed instead was a policy of systematic reprisal. Beginning in July 1957, some loyalist tribes were ordered to destroy the houses, date-palms, and irrigation channels of dissident communities, extreme measures that many shaykhs avoided implementing because they recognized that permanent animosities would ensue. The regular army consequently was entrusted with some of these tasks. Some subordinates, notably the Sultan's brother, Sayyid Tariq bin Taymur, who temporarily served as deputy governor of the interior and liaison with the military, sought to combine firm rule with efforts at reconstruction. The Sultan did not encourage such efforts on the part of his brother, possibly because he saw them as giving popularity to a potential rival. After the submission of the Jebel Akhdar and the escape of rebel leaders in 1959, punitive restrictions were placed on the region's inhabitants. They were denied regular access to the markets of neighboring towns and forbidden to obtain passports to seek work outside Oman. Like many other Omanis, they nonetheless usually found alternative means of leaving the country. These restrictions were consequently effective only in increasing local resentment against the rule of Sultan Sa'id.

After 1957 the emigration of Omanis to neighboring countries to seek work, education, and political refuge accelerated. By the late 1960s, there were over 50,000 Omanis living in the neighboring Gulf states alone (excluding Saudi Arabia). Even when not directly involved in overt political actions, these sojourners became aware of political movements elsewhere in the Arab world and of the open attitude toward development of the rulers of some neighboring states. The large number of these emigrants, some of whom were able to return periodically to their villages in Oman, accelerated the transformation in popular conceptions of what a just ruler should do. Maintenance of Sultan Sa'id's regime increasingly depended upon the threat of intervention by a small standing army and reliance upon an older generation of governors and tribal shaykhs who, like the Sultan, were unresponsive to changing visions of social equity.

* * *

The familiar aphorism of Marx and Engels has it that "the ideas of the ruling class are in every epoch the ruling ideas, i.e. the class which is the ruling *material* force of society, is at the same time its ruling *intellectual* force." This dictum is elaborated with greater nuance in Weber's sociology of domination. Weber makes an important typological distinction between domination based upon interests and that based upon authority. For Weber, domination by interests is founded upon the possession or monopoly of essential skills or resources. Those subordinate to such domination remain "formally free and are motivated simply by the pursuit of their own interests." Domination by authority "rests upon alleged absolute duty to obey, regardless of personal motives or interests."

In setting out to analyze the social reproduction of the twentieth-century Ibadi theocratic state and its subsequent incorporation into the absolute monarchy of Sultan Sa'id, Weber's typological distinction appeared initially useful. The transition from theocracy to monarchy in inner Oman initially appears to involve no more than guaranteeing notables that their "interests" (a term notoriously difficult to define, especially in the context of traditional politics) would not be endangered.

The major difficulty with Weber's typological characterization, despite its improvement over that of Marx and Engels, is the near impossibility of conceiving of practical situations in which the line between the two forms of domination is not vague and shifting: neither appears in "pure" form, and components of both are always present. Moreover, the notion of "interests" is stretched particularly thin when used to analyze the situations described throughout this study in which a given rule is supported because the cost of resistance outweighs that of acquiescence, as is the case for the Omani political situation analyzed here. Weber's notion of "duty" similarly obscures situations in which there appear to have been genuine popular sentiment among notables and commoners in support of particular forms of rule, such as existed for the imamate until the early 1950s, for the Sultan in his initial moves to bring Islamic justice to that part of Oman under his effective control, and for his especially popular efforts to oust the Saudis from Buraymi.

This essay has sought to trace overall shifts in popular expectations of "just" rule. Concern with the loss of theocratic rule in the Oman interior was offset in large part by the initial expectation that Sultan Sa'id would preserve much of what was essentially Islamic in the political life of the interior (except for the nature of rule at the top), and would take steps to end the country's economic stagnation and desperate poverty. He failed to do so. His increasing aloofness and inability to anticipate and act upon the aspirations and expectations of notables and commoners alike contributed directly to the country's increasingly desperate situation, reversed only with the 1970 coup which brought his son to power.

KINGS AND PEOPLE: OMAN'S STATE CONSULTATIVE COUNCIL

DALE F. EICKELMAN

Have ruling monarchs become an endangered species? Most of the world's population was subject to royal authority until the 18th century; since then the number of ruling monarchs has steadily declined. Their replacements have for the most part claimed authority directly from "the people". The Middle East is the last major region of the world where ruling monarchs prevail. Aside from minor principalities such as those of pre-1967 south Arabia, the Middle East had 13 monarchies in 1952; seven remained in 1983.

In sharp contrast with past epochs, the subjects of contemporary Middle Eastern monarchs are profoundly aware of alternatives to dynastic rule. Even more so than in the past, royal authority in the late 20th century must be made to appear "natural" and "just". Even if some monarchs privately assert a divine mandate, publicly they stress their unique vocation to guide the nation's destiny. The late Shah went so far as to assert that Persian kingship was based upon the will of the people, and that Iran would never be devoid of a monarch because of his people's "customs, habits, history [and] religion". Other Gulf rulers continue to make analogous claims.

In such an absolutist view, the monarch *is* the state. By naming roads, ports, schools, hospitals, mosques and stadiums after himself, the ruler inscribes his presence upon the national geography. The monarch's untiring concern for his subjects is affirmed through the incessant repetition of his name, usually bracketed in honorifics, on radio and television, his photograph in every place of business and most homes, national days, commissioned poetry, popular music and occasional royal progresses through his domains.

A new and increasingly critical element in the contemporary assertion of royal authority is an explicit awareness on the part of both rulers and ruled of pressures for greater popular participation in decision-making and the exercise of authority. Slogans such as the late Shah's "Revolution of the Shah and the People," and Hassan II's "Revolution of the King and the People," may be considered banal by some subjects and hypocritical by others, but they formally acknowledge that popular legitimacy today necessarily implies the ruler's ability to self-transform and widen the base of participation in government. Ruling monarchs are in the paradoxical position of encouraging rapid transformation and self-renewal in all spheres of economic and social activity except that of selection for rule at the top.

THE CONCEPT OF CONSULTATIVE COUNCIL

Since the Ottoman reforms of the 1820s (the *Meçlis-i Mesveret*) and those of Iran beginning in the 1850s (the *majlis-e showra*), consultative councils have been the point of departure in making Islamic monarchies more responsive to changing historical situations. Although 19th century Islamic reformers consciously based their practical models upon Western institutions, the concept of consultation (*shura*) is firmly rooted in Islamic thought. "Consultation," a bland term in English, is as evocative in the Islamic context as is the idea of democracy in the West. Like democracy, the meaning of consultation is complex and shifting. The Quran refers to those "whose affairs are administered by mutual consultation" (*amruhum shura baynahum*), a passage invoked in the modern world to sanction everything from post-revolutionary workers' cooperatives in Iran to absolute monarchies.

The concept of consultation acquires a special poignancy in Oman, where Ibadi Muslims constitute just over half the country's citizens. Until recent decades there has been an almost constant historical tension between the principle of dynastic rule and the Ibädi tenet of selection for rule on the basis of consultation within the community, the basis for authority in the Ibadi imamate which prevailed until 1955 in the Omani interior. Ibadi notions of just rule continue to have a profound impact upon the popular attitudes toward government of all Omanis.

Oman's State Consultative Council [SCC] (*al-majlis al-istishari lil-dawla*), created in November 1981, provides a singular opportunity to discern how a late 20th century Islamic monarchy, one that has undergone especially rapid economic and social change since 1970, has sought to maintain popular legitimacy. After describing the context in which the SCC was formed, this essay analyzes the practical implications of the decrees establishing the SCC. A profile is then presented of its delegates, based upon interviews and discussions with 40 of its 44 members. An analysis of the decrees establishing the SCC and patterns in the selection of its initial members makes it possible to discern how the monarch and his key domestic advisers perceive the composition of Omani society today.

Once the SCC was established, its delegates developed practical, working notions of representation, internal procedure and relations with government ministries not fully anticipated by the monarch and his advisers. Popular Omani response to the SCC is discussed, together with what SCC delegates themselves see as their contribution to the process of consultation and decision-making in Oman and future directions the SCC might take. Finally, the monarch's public vision of the SCC is analyzed.

BEGINNINGS

The key formative event for Omanis now in their 30s or older was the coup of July 23, 1970, in which Sultan Qabus bin Sa'id replaced his father, Sa'id bin Taymur (r. 1932–1970). In his last decade of rule, the former Sultan received invidious distinction as the region's most reactionary and isolationist tyrant, progressively alienating his own people and most of his British advisers. Even after Oman began to receive oil revenues in 1967, the former Sultan willingly applied them only to military expenditures. When Sultan Sa'id left Muscat for his southern capital of Salalah in 1958, never again to return to northern Oman, he became almost invisible to his subjects. After a 1966 attempt on his life in Salalah by his own troops, he shut himself inside his palace for the last four years of his rule. Many Dhofaris and Omani exiles came to believe that Sultan Sa'id had died in the attempt on his life and that the British only claimed that he was alive as a convenience to themselves.

From the first days of his rule, Sultan Qabus bin Sa'id sought to establish a new image of the monarchy. Within a week of the coup he flew to Muscat and was enthusiastically welcomed. Shortly afterward, in the first radio broadcast by an Omani monarch to his people, Qabus declared an amnesty for all former rebels, changed the country's name from the Sultanate of Muscat and Oman to the Sultanate of Oman to emphasize its unity, lifted the numerous petty restrictions in force under his father, and toured the major towns of the Omani interior (accompanied by newly submitted Dhofari rebels) to meet tribal leaders and establish the fact of Oman's "new era."

Middle-range and senior officials today recall the Sultan's accessibility in the early 1970s and his willingness in private to entertain frank policy discussions. Minutes survive of one meeting from this period in which a group of self-described "young Omanis" raised directly with the Sultan topics including government corruption and extravagance, the personal appropriation by tribal shaykhs of subventions intended for the general welfare, the back of clear government organization, censorship and the lack of efficient information services.

By the mid-1970s, the Council of Ministers remained as the only forum outside the palace for the sustained general discussion of policy matters. Opportunities to make systematic suggestions concerning overall policy became confined principally to an elite inner circle. Various advisory councils were established from time to time, but most were short-lived and not intended to deal comprehensively with affairs of state. Foreign diplomats and journalists increasingly began to comment upon the lack of preparations for a parliament or other form of consultative body such as had by then come into existence in neighboring states.

The first modest effort to broaden consultation was the short-lived Council on Agriculture, Fisheries and Industry, which was established in April 1979. The express purpose of this appointed 12-member Council was to "discuss the economic future of the nation and to get citizens to participate" in the process of promoting growth. Meetings were held monthly. Former members of the Council, seven of whom were subsequently appointed to the SCC, recall with pride that they managed to draft the first policy recommendations to be made by an "outside" Omani consultative body. Their recommendations were limited in scope, unpublicized and often confined to highly specific projects. Former members of this Council regard their major accomplishment as having won the support or at least the neutrality of some senior officials for a more open process of consultation.

Preparations for the SCC itself date from November 1980. At the request of the Sultan, several ministers met to discuss how broader formal consultation might take place in Oman. According to participants, their wide-ranging discussions included such topics as what "democracy" might mean in the context of Oman, representation, a parliamentary versus a consultative body, and even the possibility of voting. It was obvious to participants that a major decision was being considered, but they were given no specific information beyond their initial mandate, and no feedback.

Muscat officialdom prides itself on its ability to learn of major developments prior to their official announcement, but in this case the veil of secrecy was remarkably effective. The decrees establishing the SCC and appointing its first members were published on October 18, 1981. Prior to that date, only the senior members of the royal family and government directly involved in drafting the SCC decrees and selecting its delegates had knowledge of the event.

DECREES

On November 3, 1981, Sultan Qabus opened the first session of the SCC, which he described as "a continuation of our policy aimed at achieving a greater scope for citizens to participate in the efforts of the government to implement its economic and social projects" through "the task of formulating opinion and advice" on the country's economic and social development. "Today we take another step toward . . . broadening the consultative base in conformity with the country's stages of development."

As its name implies, the SCC is strictly a consultative body, not a parliament or legislature. It is restricted to making recommendations to the Sultan, who approves or rejects them. Approved recommendations are passed in confidence to appropriate ministries. Issues on which the SCC has prepared recommendations include agricultural aid and local marketing, the prices of basic commodities, Tenders Board procedures, rural electrification, the granting of citizenship to non-Omanis, land distribution procedures, water resources, and health care outside the capital area.

As in other cases where consultative bodies have been introduced in absolute monarchies in the Middle East, a major concern has been to avoid any intimation that the SCC diminishes royal authority. Indeed, when the SCC was accused at a meeting of the Council of Ministers of aiming to limit royal authority, its defenders replied that the SCC goal was strictly to implement the explicit will of the Sultan, the same goal claimed by the SCC's ministerial critics. Both SCC critics and supporters were compelled to frame their arguments in terms which studiously avoided any implication of challenge to the monarch's absolute authority. The language of debate almost exactly parallels that used by defenders of consultative councils in earlier Middle Eastern monarchies.

The substance of the decrees establishing the SCC (81/84-86, dated October 18, 1981) suggest that their drafter is *plus royaliste que le roi*. Articles 3 and 51 of decree 82/86 guarantee SCC members freedom of speech *during* meetings (making, remarked one delegate, the SCC the only place in the Sultanate where this freedom is explicitly granted), provided that they adhere to the approved agenda, obey the laws of the land, and respect the state. Deliberations are secret. SCC recommendations (*tawsiyat*) are communicated by the President of the Assembly confidentially to the Sultan, who acts upon them as he sees fit. Several delegates suggest that the precaution of secrecy was to guarantee that the SCC would not cause embarrassment to high officials.

The SCC decrees also grant wide powers to the appointed President and seven-member Executive Bureau (*al-maktab al-tanfidhi*). All requests by delegates for information from government agencies or other outside organizations must be channelled through the President. Members may speak in general sessions only after recognition by the President (or the appointed Vice-President if the President is absent), and the President can interrupt delegates if he determines that they have raised issues not specified by the agenda. The President also automatically assumes the chair at any committee meeting he attends.

The Executive Bureau consists of seven delegates. The President and Vice-President are appointed members. The remaining five members were selected by the SCC itself. As specified in the founding decree, two members represent the government sector and three the public. The Executive Bureau approves all subjects for discussion in general sessions and committee meetings. In practice, the President and Executive Bureau have done everything possible to avoid the appearance of exercising arbitrary authority over the agenda and have approved the vast majority of issues proposed for discussion by SCC committees. Hence the main task of the Executive Bureau has shifted to deciding priorities of politically feasible issues and advising committees on how to shape their studies in politically acceptable ways.

SCC legislation indicates the difficulty of clearly defining notions such as representation (*tamthil*) and the "complementary" opposition of government and people in a context where no practical precedents exist. By decree, the SCC consists of 45 delegates, the named members of which are appointed for initial two-year terms. Seventeen delegates are designated as government representatives; 28 are representatives of the people.

Of the 17 "government" representatives, ten are undersecretaries appointed by reason of their official function. Thus, if a new undersecretary is appointed, he automatically assumes the SCC responsibilities of his predecessor. Although the decree designates ten undersecretaries, there have never been more than nine. One result of the secrecy with which the SCC decrees were prepared is minor errors of drafting. An undersecretary was appointed from a ministry (Posts, Telegraphs and Telephones) which has none.

Significantly, the Ministry of Petroleum and Minerals is not represented in the SCC, a fact which is not lost upon delegates. An estimated 95 per cent of government revenue was derived from oil in 1982. The consequent inability of the SCC to concern itself with mineral resources and the distribution of revenues derived from them constitutes a major limitation on its mandate to concern itself with "economic and social policy."

The remaining seven "government" delegates are appointed by name. They are the President, Khalfan Nasir al-Wahaybi, a former minister who continues to enjoy ministerial rank, two former ambassadors, two directors-general (one of whom was subsequently promoted to undersecretary in a minor government reshuffle in January 1983), an undersecretary and a provincial governor (*wali*).

The "people" are represented by 11 delegates from the private sector and 17 from "the regions" (*al-manatiq*). Ten of the private sector delegates are leading capital-area merchants; the other is a merchant from Salalah. One private sector delegate, Hajj Ali Sultan al-Fadil, is also appointed Vice-President and the former President of the Council on Agriculture, Fisheries and Industry.

The notion of "region" as used in the SCC decrees is a source of confusion for delegates. In interviews, regional delegates and several from the capital area clearly considered themselves appointed precisely because of their knowledge of specific regions and their standing in particular tribal and ethnic groups. Their subsequent problem was to discern what these representational units might be. In January 1982, the Executive Bureau decided that regional members represented "all" of Oman, not any special geographical region, province, ethnic or tribal group. The Sultan subsequently affirmed this interpretation. Many SCC members consider their mandate to represent "all" of Oman a temporary expedient which postpones to a later date the difficult issue of whom regional delegates represent.

A second ambiguity is the distinction between government and popular representatives. Eight regional representatives are also fulltime government employees, so that 24 out of 44 delegates (55 per cent) work for the government. Only undersecretaries designated by office have clearcut roles: they advocate official policy in issues concerning their ministries and serve as liaison between the SCC and their ministries. Other government representatives and employees were initially concerned that they might be expected to represent a "government" point of view. In a subsequent discussion between the SCC President and the Sultan, the distinction between government and people was effectively abrogated. Government delegates were informed that they were to deliberate upon all matters as Omani citizens, not as advocates of government policy.

THE DELEGATES

SCC delegates collectively represent what might be called the secondary elite – to use Mosca's phrase, "those who allow the rulers to rule." Eight delegates own or have a major family share in important Omani trading or contracting firms. None approach the much higher level of wealth enjoyed by a small number of key officials with mercantile interests, oil rights and access to commissions from major military and civilian contracts. Only two delegates are former ministers and none are members of the royal family.

To ascertain the extent to which the SCC brought new persons into the process of policy consultation, delegates were asked to indicate colleagues with whom they had prior personal, business or professional acquaintance. On the average, each delegate had prior acquaintance with 57 per cent of the others, not a surprising number given the small scale of Omani society. The most significant disparity was between members living in the capital area and those living outside. Capital-area delegates already knew 66 per cent of their colleagues. For the most part, they already possessed regular access to business and government leaders, most of whom reside in the capital, or were themselves such leaders. Regional members had prior acquaintance with an average of only 38 per cent of the other SCC delegates. The Dhofari delegates were the least known to members from elsewhere and had the lowest level of prior acquaintance with members from other regions (16 per cent).

Prior to the SCC, many regional notables felt isolated from the mainstream of Oman's political life, most of which centers upon the capital. Their low level of acquaintance with other delegates prior to the convening of the SCC lends support to their claim. A major achievement of the SCC has been to provide regional delegates with a structured forum through which they can develop working relationships with participating senior officials and delegates from other regions. Conversely, it provides officials participating in the SCC with regular access to the views from the periphery.

On the whole, the choice of delegates indicates careful attention to the nuances of Oman's domestic politics. The appointments from Musandam peninsula, long isolated from the mainstream of Omani affairs, are reasonably representative of the attention paid to local sensibilities. Both delegates are local officials, an unsurprising fact as there is virtually no other employment in Musandam. One delegate is the traditionally educated son of the qadi of Khasab, Musandam's main town, and from a lineage reputed for its religious learning and skill in mediating the region's fractious tribal rivalries. The other delegate is the regional Director of Education, a former schoolteacher and one of the first members of the locally dominant Shihuh tribe to acquire a modern education. He is locally respected both by the educated youth of the province and by older tribesmen.

Appointments from other regions include participants in the pre-1970 imamate-in-exile movement, one of the first tribal leaders to break with the shaykhly tradition of not engaging directly in commerce, and other notables who by one means or another acquired recognition extending beyond their own tribal group.

SCC appointments from the interior constitute what one Gulf intellectual has called a "shaykhocracy" (*shaykhuqratiya*). Of 18 delegates originally from the interior, 15 have fathers or paternal uncles who were tribal leaders. Three of these 15 are currently recognized by the Ministry of the Interior as official tribal shaykhs. Access to traditional education and positions of leadership in pre-1970 Oman were closely tied to shaykhly status, so it is almost inevitable that tribal leaders and their immediate relations should have an initial competitive edge in securing recognition as notables. The fact that only three delegates are official tribal leaders indicates a deliberate effort to avoid replicating the existing tribal elite and to select delegates who break the mold of an older generation of leadership.

TABLE 1
ORIGIN AND CURRENT PRINCIPAL RESIDENCE OF DELEGATES

Region (1980 population, excluding foreigners)	Origin	Current Principal Residence
Capital region (160,000)	12	30
Batina (coast) (200,000)	6	3
Interior (320,000)	12	5
Musandam (15,000)	2	2
Dhofar (55,000)	6	4
East Africa (n.a.)	6	–
TOTAL (750,000)	44	44

Source: Sultanate of Oman, Directorate-General of Statistics, unpublished population estimates, 1980.

ORIGINS AND CURRENT PRINCIPAL RESIDENCE

Given the structure of government and the economy, a large proportion of Oman's secondary elite has inevitably gravitated to the capital area. Four of the regional members have their principal residences in the capital. Nonetheless, SCC members residing in the capital but born elsewhere regularly visit their regions of origin. Most maintain second residences, agricultural holdings and small businesses there. Because of Oman's excellent road network, living in the capital rarely cuts delegates off from their regions of origin. Delegates have a constant stream of persons from their regions of origin seeking favors and advice, not because of their role in the SCC, but because of their previously existing roles in government or commerce.

SECTARIAN IDENTITY

The sectarian distribution within the SCC is: Ibādï, 54.5 per cent (N=24); Sunni, 29.5 per cent (N=13) and Shi'ï, 16 per cent (N=7).

Ibadi and Sunni representation parallels the estimated proportional strength of these two sects in Oman. Only the Shi'i representation is greater than their proportional strength in the population, an indication of their significant commercial role and tradition of service to the government. Prior to 1970, ethnic and sectarian identity was a significant determinant of residence, occupation, education, and marriage. With the advent of modern education and a proliferation of previously unavailable occupations and economic opportunities, the importance of ethnic and sectarian identities is becoming increasingly muted. Nonetheless, the composition of the SCC indicates that such identities have been taken into consideration.

TABLE 2
AGE DISTRIBUTION OF SCC MEMBERS

Age	Per cent	N
20–29	2	1
30–39	18	8
40–49	55	24
50–59	20	9
60+	5	2
TOTAL	100	44

AGE AND COHORT

The sociological notion of cohort or generation – that of shared significant events or experiences – is a more important concept for understanding the composition of the SCC than that of age. Moreover, since calendar age has been emphasized only in recent times, some SCC delegates can only estimate their age by referring to key events which they have personally experienced. As Table 2 indicates, most SCC delegates are in their 40s or older, so that almost all experienced as adults the economic stagnation and growing political disintegration that marked the repressive final years of the rule of Sultan Sa'id bin Taymur. In the late 1960s, 36 per cent (N=16) of SCC delegates remained in Oman (in prison in one instance), 21 per cent (9) described themselves as political exiles and 43 per cent (19) as "voluntary" exiles who left Oman for economic or educational reasons. Most members were subsequent active participants in the creative economic and organizational ferment of the early 1970s, which was also when Omanis of East African origin were finally allowed into the country.

EDUCATION

SCC delegates show a marked diversity in educational backgrounds, an unsurprising fact given Oman's near total lack of modern educational facilities prior to 1970. Table 3, based upon self-description, indicates studies at a given educational level and does not necessarily imply possession of a diploma. The categories "traditional basic" and "traditional advanced" require comment. Traditional Islamic education continued to thrive in many parts of Oman until a much later date than was the case elsewhere in the Middle East. Delegates possessing a "basic traditional" education usually possess a self-described ability to read and prepare short, descriptive administrative and commercial reports. "Advanced traditional" means skill in formal Arabic rhetoric. Only delegates with this skill, whether derived from traditional or modern education, are able to take a direct role in drafting reports and final recommendations.

TABLE 3
EDUCATIONAL LEVELS OF SCC MEMBERS

	Government employees	Nongovernment	Total
Traditional basic	32% (8)	48% (9)	39% (17)
Traditional advanced	4% (1)	21% (4)	11% (5)
Primary modern	8% (7)	21% (5)	13% (6)
Intermediate	20% (5)	5% (1)	13% (6)
Secondary	16% (4)	—	9% (4)
University	20% (5)	5% (1)	13% (6)
TOTAL	100% (25)	100% (19)	100% (44)

LANGUAGES

The ability to use languages other than Arabic, especially English, is an important skill in the SCC. The SCC is called upon to consider many technical matters, including studies of water resources, agricultural marketing, land registration procedures, low-income housing and employment policies. In some cases, vital information is readily available only in English, although essential documents are translated for the benefit of other members. In practice, active members' skills are often complementary, so that members with a facility in English may be unable to prepare a "polished" report in Arabic. Eleven SCC members (25 per cent) are fluent in English. They can read periodicals and technical reports with ease. Another 11 (25 per cent) possess an ability to conduct basic business or social conversations. Other major languages spoken by SCC members include Swahili (6), Baluchi (6), Sindi (4), Farsi (2), Urdu (2), Jebeliya, a language of the mountain regions of Dhofar (3), French (1) and Italian (1). With the exception of the Jebeliya speakers, all SCC members fluent in languages other than English are from the capital area and generally from households in which the second language is spoken in addition to Arabic.

There are two significant categories omitted in the selection of SCC delegates. There is no delegate from among the younger, university-educated Omanis who have completed the major part of their schooling since the beginning of the "new era" in 1970. The median age of delegates is 47, nearly three times the median age of the general population. As a category, younger graduates tend to be less tolerant than older cohorts of mismanagement and the use of government office for private gain. Due to the rapid expansion of Oman's civil service in the 1970s, graduates now entering government employ are resigned to slow promotions and years of minor responsibilities. In recent years the number of young Omanis holding university diplomas has rapidly increased. Although most graduates are presently consigned to minor bureaucratic sinecures, their growing importance would seem to warrant representation in the SCC. Finally, no women are represented although Oman justly prides itself upon allowing women to play a public role. Especially as the country is soon to open a university, the inclusion of women delegates should be given serious consideration.

CONSULTATION AS A LEARNING PROCESS

Once the SCC was established in early November 1981, its leadership was left to itself to prepare an agenda and decide how to proceed. With the next general assembly of the SCC only two months away, the President took the initiative in consulting the seven SCC members appointed to the earlier Council on Agriculture, Fisheries and Industry as to the procedures they followed and the issues they had under study at the time of its demise. Adoption of issues from their agenda and the continuity of some personnel enabled the SCC from the outset to undertake matters of substance. During this initial two-month period the President and the Executive Bureau also decided to create four internal working committees.

The important role rapidly assumed by SCC internal committees was unanticipated by the initial decrees. Committee work emerged as the major formative experience for SCC delegates. In the words of one delegate: "The committees are where our recommendations are 'cooked'. By the time issues are discussed in the full quarterly meetings, the major lines of recommendations have already been decided." Delegates learn in committee how to analyze policy issues and construct viable policy recommendations.

Decrees 81/86 specifically allows the SCC to form its own internal committees, but it specifies a schedule only for the general meetings. In principle, these are held during the first week of each quarter. The SCC established its own rigorous schedule of weekly meetings for the Executive Bureau and internal committees. These are: Legal Affairs, Economic Affairs, Services (dealing with education, health, welfare, labor, and information), and Utilities (*murafiq*) (concerned with water, electricity, roads, communications, the distribution of public lands, and municipal affairs). A fifth committee, Education and Training, was added in mid-1983. SCC participation requires a heavy time commitment from most members. Delegates whose attendance is slack are subject to informal pressure, usually successful, from more avid participants, indicating the seriousness with which many members assume their tasks.

Close informal coordination among committees is achieved through the deliberate overlapping of committee assignments, which were determined by the Executive Bureau. Twenty-eight delegates participate in one committee, seven participate in two, and two especially active delegates were given three committee assignments. Seven members have no committee assignments, and consequently have a reduced ability to shape recommendations. In addition, at least one member of the Executive Bureau participates in each committee.

In the early 1982 meetings, many delegates, especially those from outside the capital region, were hesitant to express opinions and waited for the Executive Bureau to take the initiative. This was especially the case for regional members and Dhofaris. As one regional member said: "We are used to having the government tell us what to do without explaining why." The participation of ministry undersecretaries at committee meetings initially intimidated delegates who had infrequent contacts with high officials.

To overcome this reticence, the more "advanced" SSC members – a term of self-description – informally sought to convey key skills to other delegates. All committee members were specifically asked to express an opinion on each issue raised at each session and were assigned specific tasks. Committee heads deliberately sought to involve a maximum of SCC members in committee work rather than allow a few of the more experienced and outgoing delegates to dominate the proceedings. As one delegate observed: "Our problem was learning to work together and speak our minds. This is not difficult for the Matrah merchants. We know how to talk. But delegates from the interior must learn to talk and discuss just like us." One index of the success of these informal but sustained efforts is the emergence of internal lobbies, appropriately called *lubi*-s. Although most delegates acknowledge that the capital area merchants tend to vote together on recommendations which if adopted would alter the commercial code, most deny the existence so far of clearly delineated factions (*kutlat*).

The record of the SCC in its short existence would probably compare favorably to that of state legislatures in the United States, such as Arizona, where part-time legislators have little or no staff support. In addition to evaluating studies often unavailable in Arabic, members had to learn how to make field visits (to rural hospitals and agricultural projects, for example) and to prepare written reports of their findings. Gradually, delegates have acquired the skills essential for SCC operations: understanding the complexities of governmental organization and framing policy recommendations within existing budgetary constraints and in a manner not construed as personal attacks upon the governing elite.

A major accomplishment of the SCC in its short existence has been gaining the confidence of some key officials. Said one delegate: "Even if most ministries have little to hide, they have developed a bureaucratic resistance to explaining policy to outsiders." Publicly explaining policies such as priorities in secondary road construction or land allocations has of course the added advantage of limiting the ability of officials to accede to private requests or to secure personal gain. The resulting recommendations are deliberately circumspect. As SCC delegates acknowledge, their major goal is to ensure the continued existence of the SCC. Hence they seek gradual improvements rather than confrontation.

Despite the tactful approach of SCC leadership, some ministers refused to cooperate. This reluctance was brought to the attention of the Sultan, who decided that ministers had to appear before the SCC when invited, but that they could be questioned only on general policy issues. Their undersecretaries, members of the SCC, were left responsible for detailed inquiries. By December 1982 the Sultan's support was obtained for televised SCC sessions in which delegates questioned ministers on policy matters, with the range of questions agreed upon in advance.

Internally, the SCC has succeeded in forging an effective, responsible advisory body. In his November 1982 National Day speech, the Sultan commended the SCC for the sound advice he has received from it so far. Through mid-December, the SCC President could claim that every recommendation sent to the Sultan had been forwarded by him to the concerned minister for action. Externally, the constraints upon the SCC are obvious. Each time that SCC procedures and responsibilities have been questioned by high officials and members of the royal family, the issue has had to be resolved by the Sultan, usually in bilateral discussions held with the SCC President several times a year. No member of the SCC except the President has regular access to the Sultan. This means of resolving disputes suggests that there has been no major alteration in patterns of high-level decision-making. This fact has not been lost upon knowledgeable Omanis.

PUBLIC REACTION

A consequence of the secrecy written into the SCC decrees is that the nature of SCC deliberations and recommendations remains poorly known outside of high government circles. SCC delegates, aware of this problem, point out that their current mandate is solely to provide advice *for* the state, although the Sultan declared in his opening speech to the SCC that it provides a new link between the government and the people. Delegates recognize that they have no delimited constituency other than "all" Oman and are barred from discussing their deliberations with outsiders. No delegate reported meeting with non-SCC members in any formal capacity to explain their work. As for representing the public sector, as specified by the SCC decrees, some SCC delegates explained that they knew the needs of Omanis so well that they did not have to ask.

The reputation of the SCC is so far inseparable from current attitudes toward the government. Despite the sustained efforts of the government to project a new image of itself, many Omanis alternate between seeing the government as a cornucopia of benefits and in its old light as a source of potential danger. The notion of government officials acting in a disinterested manner has also been slow to gain public credence. An SCC delegate observed: "Business in Oman is like a vast sea. There is enough for everyone, but some people in the government are trying to drink the sea by themselves. It cannot be done, and they will only burst their stomachs in trying."

The Al Bu Sa'id dynasty has not been known in the past for encouraging dialogue with its subjects, and this is a component of the "traditions" with which the present Sultan has to contend. A traditional senior member of the government characterized the tribes of the interior as "hypocrites, liars and deceivers" (*munafiqun, kadhdhabun wa-qhashshashun*). He claimed that the tribesmen and notables of the interior concealed their real concerns and intentions from Al Bu Sa'id, and that this dissimulation resulted in past conflict between rulers of the dynasty and the tribes of the interior. He acknowledged, however, that political prudence might also have impeded open expression.

Prudence continues to dominate popular comment on public policy. In a late 1982 discussion with soldiers from villages in the interior, I was told that no one would speak with me honestly about the SCC because "None of the high officials (*tal-kubbar*) want the people to know what they are doing." Beyond brief mentions of the SCC's existence on radio and television, they claimed that no attempt had been made to explain the SCC to the people and that in any case no one speaks critically of the government for fear of losing their jobs or worse. "You say you've been in Oman a long time. You know the corruption in high places. How can any Omani talk about that in public?" The remarks concerning the lack of attempts to explain the SCC are exaggerated, but the comment accurately reflects a growing expectation in the last few years that officials should be held accountable for their public actions and limit their use of office for personal benefit.

Since reliable means of eliciting public opinion are nonexistent in Oman, appraisals of "popular" reaction to the SCC must necessarily remain informal. Educated and politically aware Omanis know of the existence and general scope of the SCC; many uneducated villagers and townsmen have only a vague familiarity with the SCC or none at all. Villagers and tribesmen are often unaware that a notable with whom they have regular contact is also a SCC delegate. As of late 1982 even secondary school students, who constitute an educational elite in a country such as Oman, frequently could not explain what the SCC was, although many had heard of its existence.

Of persons aware of the existence of the SCC, a frequent comment was that the SCC is a council (*majlis*) in name only, because the government lacks real interest in soliciting Omani opinion or widening the base of decision-making. On one occasion a junior official asked a delegate in my presence to name just one way in which the region benefited from the SCC. The delegate replied quite correctly that SCC members could not influence government policy to benefit their regions alone. The questioner, himself on cordial terms with the delegate, responded that the SCC then must exist for the government's benefit alone, not that of the people. The observation was harshly put, but accurately construed the current SCC mandate as being to provide non-binding advice on designated issues. Delegates may see the SCC as a step toward participation in consultation, not decision-making, but ordinary citizens see no significant change as yet in their ability to influence national policy.

CONSULTATION IN TRANSITION?

Monarchs of the Arabian peninsula understandably feel uneasy at the invocation of the words of the late Shah, but in a remarkable series of recorded conversations held between 1949 through 1967, the latter expressed more thoroughly than other Middle Eastern rulers an awareness of the rapidly changing nature of 20th century monarchies. He said he intended, once the Iranian nation had a sufficient educational base, to "build a government that is based on democratic practice at the bottom, although perhaps a better term is 'cooperatively based'. I know that my people are very individualistic and find it difficult to work with each other, but I am certain this can be overcome." Comparing himself with his father, the Shah spoke of himself as "the revolutionary operating from the throne," whose objective was to broaden the base of decision-making in Iran "step by logical step" until the monarchy would "rest upon a foundation of self-government" adapted "to the nature of Iran." In the Shah's view, the Iranian's sense of history and tradition was that the national leader had to be a monarch, lifted above mundane life.

Recent statements by Sultan Qabus bin Sa'id place an equivalent stress on gradualist development or improvement (*tahsin*), with similar general appeals to history, religion and tradition as a reason to proceed slowly. The SCC, he has recently said, is a "political experiment." It is a "first step" with "no limits to what development may mean . . . But it must take its place in the proper time . . . It will be a very happy day for me when more people will take responsibilities from my shoulders. But we have to take into consideration the situation of our culture, our religious heritage and guidance, our traditions, and not to import a system that is already made and put in a package."

Most SCC delegates repeated His Majesty's emphasis upon the SCC as an institution in transition. This is evident from their personal interpretations of "Counsel." Nearly all referred to the Quranic passage cited earlier. One regional delegate cited an Omani proverb, which he claimed was also a saying of the Prophet: "A full man has an opinion and gives it in consultation; half a man has an opinion and doesn't give counsel; whoever neither holds an opinion nor speaks is not a man." Others referred to consultation as it occurs in the context of the family, tribe and the Islamic community.

One delegate, influenced by older notions of government in Oman, went so far as to gloss consultation in the following terms: "Shura? It is like relations between father and small children. The Sultan is our father and tells us what to do. That is consultation." An official referred to Oman as a unified house in which some household members are more knowledgeable or capable than others, and therefore placed in authority. Since all citizens work toward common goals, consultation takes place within the context of respect for religion and authority. Another poetically compared the Sultan to the brightest star in the sky, the moon when it was full. "Our work now is a secret between God, the Sultan and the members of the majlis, but the Sultan is bringing us more good things, one at a time." Another delegate, also from the interior, compared the SCC to a child just out of its womb, which soon will walk, speak, and eventually, with His Majesty's guidance, act on its own. Some members saw the SCC as the first step toward democracy (*al-dimuqratiya*) or some form of legislative body, although they are aware that the Sultan has never made such an allusion.

Significantly, no delegate referred specifically to the Ibadi conception of shura with its concomitant antimony to dynastic rule. The prevalence in Oman of this Ibadi interpretation may well explain why the Sultan makes only general invocations of religion and tradition when discussing political development.

SCC delegates, like other politically aware Omanis, often spoke openly regarding what they see as the major problems facing their country today: increasingly visible public corruption among some senior officials, bureaucratic inefficiency, a growing general awareness of major inequalities in the distribution of wealth and – a crucial issue for an absolute monarchy in which the monarch is without heir – the lack of any clear plans for succession.

SCC delegates who are also government officials are especially aware of the human and capital constraints upon what the government can do. One delegate commented: "Many Omanis say that the main problem with Sultan Sa'id was that he ruled too much; the problem with Qabus is that he doesn't rule enough." Another delegate, an undersecretary, observed that because the Sultan left a great deal of initiative to his ministers to carry out their tasks, abuses of office were inevitable but preferable to overly centralized control. He cited an Omani proverb to the effect that mankind wanted fast results from the day of creation (*khuliqa al-insan 'ajulan*). "Starting a new country isn't like building a house; in the affairs of nations, it takes time to draw up plans and even longer to achieve concrete results." He acknowledged the abuses of some officials. Giving an example from his own ministry, which has regulatory powers, he pointed out that the lack of an adequate technical cadre and trained investigators necessitated his ministry's carrying out its tasks largely through the voluntary cooperation of the persons being regulated. Despite the difficulties recently experienced by Oman in drafting effective conflict of interest decrees, he concluded that since 1981 the Sultan had made his wishes known to those involved and that the level of excessive commissions on government projects has begun to diminish.

No SCC delegates speculated on future developments of the SCC, emphasizing that the matter was entirely at His Majesty's will. Some delegates went so far as to say that the major question facing the SCC is whether it has a future at all. Appointative councils are not new to Oman, and others in the past have quietly fallen by the wayside. Such a bleak outcome seems unlikely, but at the same time there has been no communication between the palace and the SCC as to what form it may take in the future. As in Kafka's *The Castle*, communication with the top is episodic and decisions from the high seat (*al-maqam al-sami*) tend to be announced in an oracular and sudden manner, emphasizing the distance between the palace and the people.

A few indirect clues provide some reason for optimism. Plans are now underway for a separate building to house the SCC, parallel to the construction plans for Omani ministries. Architect's plans indicate that the main chamber will seat 120 delegates, so that future decisions concerning how representation will take place will be open as to number.

So long as the SCC is strictly an advisory body for the government, issues of representation can easily be sidestepped. Should the SCC be granted limited legislative powers and delegates given more ability to influence government policies affecting their particular regions, then the question of representation becomes more critical. One possibility is representation by provinces. There are currently 40 provinces in Oman. A difficulty is that representation solely on such grounds would be highly artificial. Oman's tribal structure is complex. Tribal boundaries are often discontinuous and rarely coincide with provincial ones or lines of effective political activity. Proportional representation is out of the question because no accurate population estimates are yet available.

Tied to the issue of representation is the selection of delegates. At present they are appointed, as is the case with members of Oman's quietly successful municipal councils. Elections, if conducted for at least some of the delegates, would serve as a direct measure of how Omanis feel about their political future and intend to shape it.

A bold possibility would be to allow delegates themselves to wrestle with the basic issues of representation, responsibility and the future shape the SCC might take, and perhaps even to open these issues to public discussion. So long as the future of the SCC is decided strictly from above and without systematic open consultation, Oman's domestic politics will be conducted in a form regarded as increasingly inappropriate.

The SCC may be a first step, but even SCC delegates are unclear what it is a first step toward. As a concerned official said, Oman is now at a crossroads. It can choose between increased internal security or more effective domestic consultation in wider spheres, and possibly even participation in decision-making. From the vantage of the late 20th century, the latter alternative might take more courage but also offers a more firm guarantee for long-term stability than a focus upon internal security alone.